GETTING TO KNOW WAIWAI

D0222926

Getting to Know Waiwai tells the story of Alan Campbell's encounter with the Wayapí people in a remote area of the Brazilian Amazon Forest, by looking back from a century into the future to consider the destruction of a way of life, and what will be left for these people as the devastation of the rainforests proceeds.

Dealing with ethnographic themes such as material culture and ecology, relationship terms and naming, political power and morality, myths and cosmology, shamanism, birth precautions, cultural change and ethnic survival, Alan Campbell examines the complexities of anthropological theory in a way which is accessible at the most introductory level, without losing any of its subtlety. He presents the cultural description of the Wayapí society in the context of the impact of the encroaching outside world. In doing so he addresses the complex questions of contrast between elegiac sadness for a lost culture and a romantic yearning for an imagined past, the nature of fieldwork as a personal relation, and the difficulties inherent in translating indigenous languages and interpreting other cultures.

Getting to Know WaiWai is a refreshing, beautifully written and original introduction to anthropology, and will be fascinating reading for anyone interested in indigenous peoples, the destruction of the Amazon forests, ethnicity and traditional cultures.

Alan Tormaid Campbell teaches Social Anthropology at Edinburgh University. He is the author of *To Square with Genesis: Causal Statements and Shamanic Ideas in Wayapí* (Polygon, 1990) and has been involved with the Wayapí Indians since 1974.

Waiwai

GETTING TO KNOW WAIWAI

An Amazonian Ethnography

Alan Tormaid Campbell

Imagine a forest
A real forest

(*William Sydney Graham*)

London and New York

First published 1995
by Routledge
11 New Fetter Lane, London EC4P 4EE

Simultaneously published in the USA and Canada
by Routledge
29 West 35th Street, New York, NY 10001

Typeset in Garamond by Florencetype Ltd, Stoodleigh, Devon

Printed in Great Britain by
Biddles Ltd, Guildford and King's Lynn

British Library Cataloguing in Publication Data
A catalogue record for this book is available from the British Library

Library of Congress Cataloguing in Publication Data
A catalogue record for this book has been requested

ISBN 0-415-12556-1 (hbk)
ISBN 0-415-12557-X (pbk)

This book is for all Wayapí inheritors in years to come.

With thanks to my three kindly helpers
C.F.   L.M.F.   H.M.

Parts of Chapter 8 were published in *Realizing Community: Multidisciplinary Perspectives*, edited by Leonard and Isobel Findlay (Saskatoon: Humanities Research Unit and Center for the Study of Co-operatives, 1995).

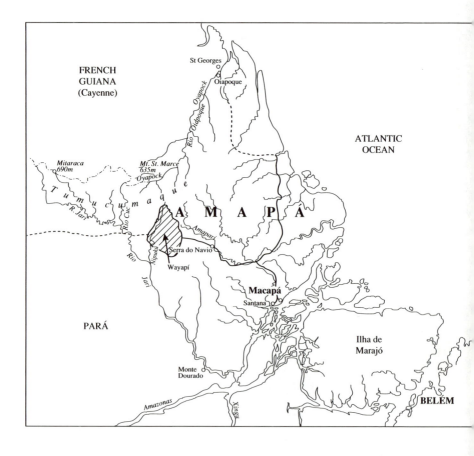

The mouths of the Amazon and the State of Amapá

CONTENTS

1

TELLING NAMES

Over a spell of two years I lived in a remote area of the Amazon Forest with a people called *Wayapí*. They had bows and arrows; they wore loincloths; they walked barefoot; they spoke a language of their own. For five centuries people like that have been called 'Indians', and for five centuries people like that have been on the run.

Going to live with them is a serious adventure. It's demanding in the long term and it can turn dangerous in a moment. The environment is a difficult one in some ways, insects and disease for example, but it's beautiful and baffling in its richness. And the job of learning about the people is like a journey without end. There never is a point where you can pack up and say 'That's it done'. All you can ask is: 'How far will I get in the time?' Even learning the language is like that, although to this day I hope that with some more time I could really get to a stage where I felt at ease hearing it and using it.

I found there was always an uncertainty about the venture. I don't mean surprises, insecurities, loss of nerve. I mean that in spite of an overwhelming conviction that this was the most fascinating enterprise that it was possible to undertake on this planet, who was going to pay any heed to anything I learned? Who would share the interest? Who would want to know?

The language effort reflected that uneasiness particularly well. When I first arrived there were 150 Wayapí left. I had then to plunge in to the desperate and painful struggle of learning an unwritten language from scratch in the sure and certain belief that, apart from 150 Indians, there would be no one else in the world that I'd ever be able to converse with in this tongue. But that simply didn't matter. Rather, it didn't matter then. It was only an uncertainty when I looked back over my shoulder.

There were other facets too. As I was drawn into their lives it became increasingly improbable to see the enterprise fitting in to a set of scientific or ethnographic expectations where, as if in botany or zoology, you take off into the woods and emerge again after your explorations with new discoveries that you can present to the world outside – reports of findings; *comptes rendus*. It was bizarre to think that I should eventually have to return home and deliver explanatory accounts of these people I knew so well, showing slides of them in seminar and lecture rooms. I would find myself addressing strangers about my friends as if I was addressing friends about strangers. How could I talk about them in that way – as patients etherized upon a table?

That was perhaps just a matter of interfering with a few conventions. I thought I'd sort that out when the time came. But whatever I tried I could never get rid of that uneasiness about just who was the *real* reader over my shoulder. I couldn't possibly write for the Wayapí themselves, at least not for these generations.

I got a shadowy sense one day of Wayapí survivors a hundred years on, looking back at these times and trying to make sense of them. It happened when I was in the Scottish hills looking down on the remains of what they still call the 'Old Caledonian forest', as if it never had been in a real time nor in a real country; a matter of myths and mysteries, maybe. So little of it was left there; just a defiant band of pine trees, gloomy and dark, straggling across the hillside, hunched against the wind, looking over their shoulders at the empty slopes all round them.

You can't get a real feel for a vanished forest like that. The loss is like a bereavement, like a yearning to know which will never be satisfied. I was sitting at some small ruins, a shieling most likely, from a time when Gaelic was spoken in these areas – a dialect of Gaelic that is now extinct. I'll never know that wood just as I'll never hear the words of those who have gone. All I can do is let my fantasy wander amongst whatever mythy fragments my memory might be able to make images out of.

Old Caledonia turned into Old Amazônia. One forest seemed to be the other. There are, today, destroyed areas of the Amazon forests that are left just like the remnants of the Scottish woods, sometimes just raggedy clumps, sometimes long slender islands of trees amongst vast spaces of weeds and prickly grass that cattle are supposed to graze on. Seeing these areas, once the dismay recedes a bit, I feel a defiant sense of relief. I've seen it; I've seen it before they did this. I know what it was like and they can't leave me suspended in ignorance. I was in it. I got lost in it (once or twice). And above all, I met *them*. I got to know these people, the ancestors of those shadowy presences.

During the closing years of the twentieth century that I'm living through, the destruction of the Amazon forests has become a dominant image of the anguish felt by millions of people in the industrialized world when they realize that the relationship between human beings and their natural surroundings has gone badly wrong. People who have never been near a tropical rain forest are profoundly dismayed by the pictures they see and by the reports they hear. School children with next to no awareness of the history and politics of the countries concerned know the names of the animals and birds that are threatened and can describe how the indigenous peoples traditionally carried on their lives. It's an accurate anguish; and to it has to be added the anger, the bewilderment, and the despair of the indigenous peoples themselves as they face the violence of invasion. It is their lands that are taken. It is they who are dislocated. When that has been done the forests are cleared for logging profit, burnt for cattle grazing, polluted by schemes for mineral extraction, flooded by the building of monstrous dams.

I knew the Wayapí during those decades of destruction. I thought, at one point in the 1970s, that they were doomed, that they would simply vanish, but they survived the major onslaught that took place then, and they can now dig in for a century of struggle as a tiny minority people within the colossal country of Brazil. It was in Old Caledonia that I got a sense of a small, intense group of them, a hundred years on, still calling themselves 'Wayapí', still aware of their past. How did the struggle go? How did it turn out?

I'll never know, and it's impossible to guess. But I think they will understand my thwarted curiosity about the future, just as I understand theirs about the past. I can get a sense of them, in their ruined Amazônia, looking back a century to our time, and I know how curious they will feel and how urgently they will want to grasp what's vanished. They do have certain advantages that I don't have since they can find so much themselves as they look back. If they've lost the language, not only will the grammar and vocabulary be in scholarly books, but they'll be able to see their people on film and hear on recordings the language, the songs, and the sound of the musical instruments. (They had tiny three-holed flutes made from the bone of a deer on which they played tunes like bird-song. They had another huge thing, 6 or 7 feet long, made out of a hollow palm, that made a noise like a tuba.)

Since that first glimmer, those presences a hundred years on fluctuate like weathery moods. Sometimes they make me get on to things like love, and wonder, and heartbreak, and at other times they get severe and I hear them say: 'Cut the cackle, and get the details down.' It's the particulars they need after all. What about names, to begin with? They'd want to know the names.

Names to start the spirits

Names are the weightiest nouns we know. Their meanings can swing unpredictably. I was looking at lists of their personal names and their place names, wondering what these would mean to the survivors next century. That made another place and time boundary slip and disengage. I remembered names from precisely a century ago, not from the empty areas of Scotland, nor from Amazônia, but from the North American plains. I had to hand at that time an account of the events at Wounded Knee in South Dakota on 29 December 1890, and part of it went like this:

> Suddenly Yellow Bird stooped down and threw a handful of dust into the air, when, as if this were the signal, a young Indian, said to have been Black Fox from Cheyenne river, drew a rifle from under his blanket and fired at the soldiers, who instantly replied with a volley directly into the crowd of warriors. . . . At the first volley the Hotchkiss guns trained on the camp opened fire and sent a storm of shells and bullets among the women and children, who had gathered in front of the tipis to watch the unusual spectacle of military display. The guns poured in 2-pound explosive shells at the rate of nearly fifty per minute, mowing down everything alive. The terrible effect may be judged from the fact that one woman survivor, Blue Whirlwind, with whom the author conversed, received fourteen wounds, while each of her two little boys was also wounded by her side. In a few minutes 200 Indian men, women, and children, with

60 soldiers, were lying dead and wounded on the ground, the tipis had been torn down by the shells and some of them were burning above the helpless wounded . . .

The incident was called 'the battle' of Wounded Knee as if it was just another in the list of those violent struggles between opposed ambitions, like Agincourt, or like The Somme. But the names declare that it was not a 'battle' like that at all. Listen to the names. You can hear in them both the echoes of something being finally destroyed, something disappearing from the earth forever, and also the power that's doing it.

Colonel Forsyth was the officer in command, along with Major Whitside; and those Hotchkiss guns were under Captain Capron and Lieutenant Hawthorne. Present amongst the other officers of the Seventh Cavalry were Lieutenants Robinson, Nicholson, McCormick, Tompkins, and Gresham. A list like that is so reassuringly familiar to the people of the English-speaking world that they can all just about hear the twang of the men's accents. The soldiers did battle against Yellow Bird, Black Fox, Blue Whirlwind, and chief Big Foot, ill with pneumonia. It is a mark of how comprehensively the world of Forsyth and Whitside took over Dakota and all the many thousands of miles around it that two baby girls found alive on the battlefield were adopted by army officers and christened (not just named) 'Marguerite' and 'Jennie'. Yellow Bird's infant son survived. He remembered having seen his father shot through the head and the blood coming out of his mouth. The boy was adopted by a teacher and called 'Herbert'.

Well, they are all dead now; Forsyth, and Blue Whirlwind's sons, and Jennie and Marguerite, and Herbert Zitkalazi. (The teacher had known the boy's father and left him the Sioux form of his father's name 'Yellow Bird' as a surname.) All the sorry circumstances that led to Wounded Knee lingered on for many years, but 1890 was the end of a way of life for the Indians on the North American Plains. And I think now of those Wayapí survivors, looking back at our times, only for them it's not the North American Plains but the South American Forests, not the Missouri but the Amazon. And the names of the peoples who lived there seem more outlandish to the dominant culture: not the Sioux, the Cheyenne, the Apache, made familiar to my world by cowboy movies and adventure yarns for small boys, but more mysterious forest names: Yanomami, Txukahamae, Uru Eu Wau Wau, and the name that means so much to me and to the survivors I think of: Wayapí. The survivors may well look back to the 1990s as marking a significant end for the Tropical Forest peoples, not in the sense of final extinction, but in the sense of a watershed in the possibilities of their existence.

In 1990 that northern extremity of Brazil where they'll still be living was called Amapá. It hadn't even been a full state of the federal union until that time; still a Territory, as if it had not been properly taken over. Brazilians in the big cities away to the south thought of Amapá as one of those impossibly remote places in 'Amazonas' which, in general, they associated with a kind of threatening backwardness.

But the eastern side of the Territory was not typical of Amazonian Brazil. There was a huge manganese mine there called Serra do Navio, sitting on the banks of the Rio Amaparí. The mine had been developed since the 1940s by the vigour of United States capital, and for thirty years or so was owned by Bethlehem Steel Inc.. They had built a railway from the mine down to the port at Santana on the mouth of the River Amazon and administered pretty well everything in between. As you rode up the railway towards the mine you looked over expanses of undulating country, stripped of the original forest, and replanted with geometrically perfect lines of dende palm, grown for the oil that the tree produces. Later massive acreages went under quick-growing pine. But beyond the mine, to the west and to the north, the rivers went on up to their headwaters through miles and miles of the old woods. And away up, where the main courses of the rivers broke into smaller streams, that's where the Wayapí lived when I got to know them.

A hundred years of devastation. What on earth will be left? I try to imagine the immediate surroundings of the future as I see those hundreds of little prosperous towns all over the Dakotas and the Midwest in the USA – peaceful, trim, and affluent, with lawns, flowering trees, and tarmacked roads, except that people on the equator won't have the cold winters to put up with. Those pretty clapboard houses of the United States are so much nicer than the flimsy brick and cement things they throw up in Brazil at present.

The forest is bound to go, just as the Great Plains were put under cultivation and concrete. But I can't imagine a credible pattern of towns and roads at all. I can't envisage the maps of the future, even though the rivers will still be there. Perhaps the Brazilians will keep an Indian name or two as they move in. Perhaps there will be towns called Aramirán and Mariry. The Brazilians won't like the sound of 'Nipukú' if they've settled it and made a town there. When they were first building the road into Wayapí lands in the 1970s the surveyors had the name marked on their maps, and although they never saw the place, they enjoyed turning the word into a smutty pun: '*limpo cu*', 'clean bum'. Not the nicest name for My Home Town. I'm glad their damned road never got as far as Nipukú in my day.

Nipukú or *ini-poko* means 'long hammock'. When the Wayapí lived in the woods they were good at making hammocks. They gathered cotton from their garden clearings. The women would card it and spin the thread by twirling small hand spindles for days on end until they wound up a large ball of white thread. Then they'd thump two posts into the earth floor of a hut, about a couple of yards apart, and wind the thread back and forth between them. In the old days they made two kinds of hammocks: a net one, and a closely woven one called an *ini*. But an ini used up so much thread and took so long to do, that they stopped making them when they were able to get the more brightly coloured factory-made equivalents from the Brazilians. Wounded Knee and Long Hammock. They're good names, aren't they?

Will the survivors keep their Wayapí names? Or will the Brazilians give them names like 'Maria' and 'Helena'? That's not really fair. Brazilians have always shown a carefree imagination in their naming habits, not just in their nicknaming but in their proper naming too, and they easily accept Indian names into the repertoire in a much more generous way than the staid habits of white English-speakers would ever allow. So perhaps the survivors can still call their children Kuyuri and Apeyawar and Waimisí without it counting as an eccentricity or a stigma.

I never really got the hang of how they used their names. There were a number of different little games going on simultaneously. And even when people were playing the same game they might play it with different intensities. To some it mattered. To others not. And of course more and more contact with Brazilians was always changing the stakes. The basic rule was that proper names were private – never to be used in public when you were addressing someone. You had to use the correct relationship term for that: 'Hello Mother's Brother', 'Hello Sister's Daughter' sort of thing. But of course since *children's* names were not hidden like this, by the time you grew up and by the time your name had become private, all your contemporaries knew it anyway.

'The Grandfather-People didn't use names,' they'd explain. 'To call someone by their name gives that person *shame*.' I might be going through genealogies and, on stating a name, get a really excited question: 'Who told you that name?', or I might ask the name of a person from another settlement that I'd visited and be asked: 'Didn't he tell you when you were there? What did *he* say his name was?'

There were three common ways of getting round the naming difficulty. It was easy to use a child's name when addressing its close relative, for example, a child called Koropi might allow you to say 'Hello, Koropi's big sister' to the appropriate grown-up woman. Second, among close friends, they might use nicknames for one another: 'just being playful'. People would be more comfortable using nicknames when talking with me of others. Finally, Portuguese names, given by the Brazilians, solved the problem. These were freely admitted; and I suppose I could reveal a long-term secret right now: 'Waiwai', Our Big One, the 'chief' at the Nipukú, is not Waiwai's real name. I think I know what his real name is, but shouldn't say. I hope the survivors have other ways of finding out.

These three solutions, then, children's names ('teknonyms' as they are known in the anthropology trade), nicknames, and Brazilian names were really just useful stop-gaps when there were outsiders around. Amongst themselves name privacy was just taken for granted. Although they said that naming in public caused 'shame', it was never used as a deliberate technique for shaming, say during a violent quarrel. Waiwai might get furious with his daughters' husbands and say: 'They are not *real* daughters' husbands any more. They're no good. I'm going to stop calling them "daughter's husband"!' He'd shame them by changing the relationship term, but however angry people got they wouldn't start naming one another. Perhaps it would so obviously defeat the purpose since the person who did it could so easily be shamed in return. Names were just private.

It was a privacy that then found itself flagrantly invaded by the arrival of Brazilian frontiersmen who were inordinately garrulous in their use of names, constantly naming each other in open conversation, even shouting out names to attract one another's attention. Imagine what the Indians had to put up with in these initial boisterous encounters with the Brazilians: loud aggressive greetings, and a habit which they found so odd of being expected to stick out your hand and have it roughly grasped and waggled by the intruder. (I found handshakes odd in those early days when I too thought it was an appropriate gesture, and I'd find myself trying to tighten my grip on the limp hand of a fierce looking man.)

So imagine if you were an Indian in one of those encounters. You have your hand waggled, then the guy grabs your shoulder at the same time and shakes you, and all the time he's shouting in your face as if he was drunk: 'Hey, *amigo, tudo bem*, everything fine, OK, WHAT'S YOUR NAME? EH? WHAT'S YOUR NAME? My name's PAULO. And this is my pal ALGIMIRO. SO WHAT'S YOUR NAME?' And while he's doing this all *your* folk are standing around giggling. Everybody's face is broken open in great smiles, although nobody's feeling at all at ease. So what do you do? Do you tell your name out loud, there and then, to these rough looking creatures with bristles all over their faces, or do you make up a name on the spot? And whether you do it one way or the other, your relatives will snigger about it later on and make fun of you across the hammocks in the dark.

1974: The arrival *topos*

This is how I first met them, in June 1974. The government department responsible for Indian affairs (known by its acronym FUNAI, 'National Indian Foundation') had arranged for me to get to the Indian Post that they had set up in Wayapí lands. I was to travel with a medical team: a doctor, a dentist, a lab technician, and a nurse, who were visiting the post as part of an immunization programme. It was a jolly group; everyone kindly and straightforward. From the moment we got off the plane in Amapá we were in the hands of the people from Bethlehem Steel's manganese mine, known by *its* acronym ICOMI. (Bureaucratic Brazil pours forth acronyms. People would never say 'Eff Bee Eye' or 'See Eye Ay'. They'd make a word out of it.) ICOMI vans took us to ICOMI quarters then on to the personnel carriage attached to a long train of empty wagons on their way up the line to the mining town at Serra do Navio. There we were again put up in neat, efficient quarters, we ate in an excellent canteen staffed by waiters in white shirts and black bow ties, and we whiled away the evening with drinks in wicker armchairs looking down on the swimming pool and tennis courts – frontier Brazil, Bethlehem Steel style.

We met up with the young man in charge of the Indian Post. He must have been about 20 years old. Tall, blond, and confident, he could have been an American marine. He was with his motorista, the outboard motor man, about the same age but small and scrawny. It was turning into quite an expedition. That was seven of us, with all the gear and supplies. In the early morning, still chilly with mists rising in the trees, ICOMI vans took us down to the landing stage and left us there. The river, running fast and full, was the colour of milky coffee. On the far bank was a line of small wooden houses on stilts, some brightly painted, others faded grey. These were the modest homes of local people who were not company employees. It was a glimpse of rural Brazil hardly seen while travelling through Amapá, sealed within the prosperous world of Bethlehem Steel Inc.. And yet that little line of houses marked the end of 'our civilization'. Upstream it was just the river and the trees for miles and miles until Wayapí lands.

Off we went in two canoes, long thin ones each with its Yamaha outboard motor. The motorista drove one, the Head of the Post the other. The rest of us sat crouched up wherever we could amongst the tarpaulins. It was a wonderful journey. The first part was uneventful as we cruised up the wide river. But in the afternoon we turned off the Amaparí into the Rio Felício, a much smaller river, and almost at once came to the first set of rapids. It was fun pulling the canoes up through the rocks. There was a lot of boisterous showing-off, and some recklessness too. By the time we came to the last set of rapids it was night-time, with a brilliant moon lighting the way. Our young leader, at the helm in our canoe, decided there was to be no portage on this one, and we revved up, straight into it. We lurched into the flume and got about half way up. There was a bang as the propeller hit a rock. The motor cut out. The bow swerved round and we were about to be sent sidelong down the rapids, but with great skill and strength our helmsman, who had grabbed a paddle, managed to straighten up and get us shooting through stern first and out into the large still pool that we'd charged out of a few moments before.

We'd all had a bit of a fright, but I was angry, unashamedly and selfishly so, since I felt that all *their* stuff was replaceable (the sacks of beans and rice, even the medical supplies) whereas had all my things gone to the bottom (tape-recorder, cameras, trade goods, the whole lot, and of course the beads, don't forget the beads) then I would have had to turn around, go back to Belém, and start all over again. And all because of a silly piece of machismo. We were close to the bank, but still slipping downstream. 'Grab that branch,' someone said. I did, and held the canoe – but only for a few seconds. I found myself being bitten on my scalp, face, and shoulders. I had shaken a branch-load of fire ants down on top of me. Over the side and into the cold black water it had to be. Everyone else, of course, thought this was hilarious. It knocked out my anger too. Our final bit of dragging and pushing, in the moonlight, up that last set of rapids was the noisiest of the journey, everyone in high spirits.

Still three or four hours to go. During that last part we all became subdued; weary certainly, and no doubt everyone was unsure and expectant. Somewhere back there we had crossed a shadow-line. The pull of our world had dwindled away and the pull of their world, those we were going to meet, had become strong. We'd managed the little tricks and traps that the passage required, like the trials of a rite, and now the game was over. The banks were squeezing in. The river went into long meanders, and the moon would disappear then emerge again in an unexpected part of the sky – impossible to keep a sense of direction. Finally there were murmurs that we were arriving. We slowed up and turned into the mouth of a small creek, the Onça. Going slower and slower, we went round one tight bend, then another, and came out to a clearing on a high bank. It was just on midnight. The moon was still high. Silhouetted against the sky was a line of about ten people. The motor cut out, we glided in, and I heard their voices for the first time.

29 June, FUNAI post, third day

Oh my god, it looks like a disaster. It's such a stealthy process of degradation. It's all done with smiles and boasts, blandishments and teasing, soft promises and mild threats. Why do these people have to be undermined like this? This is the start of it – the long, long decline. All it takes is a team of six Brazilians and their 'Attraction Front', as it is officially called when a newly contacted people has to be brought under control. And they joke about it too. 'Listen, chum. It's so easy here. This is a *Distraction Front*. Ha ha ha! This lot here are really tame. Just like a bunch of women.'

11

The idea is to concentrate the people. It's the old technique that the Jesuits used in the 1600s away to the south in Paraguay and Southern Brazil. 'Reductions' they called their settlements in those days, where they pulled the Indians in so that they could have them under control. It was the British during the Boer War that used the word 'concentration' for a similar sordid business. And here it is again. 'Get these people in. Get them where *we* want them; where we can control them.'

And it looks as if FUNAI *is* pulling them in. Two more families arrived yesterday. I'm told: 'They'll all come. Even Waiwai is coming. He's coming with all his people from the Nipukú. He's been sent for.' Nipukú. The name is my heart's desire. According to the Brazilians, they are looking at three settlements: Capoeira and Aroã on the near side of the area, and Nipukú away out to the north-west. The two on the near side have borne the brunt of the contact so far. It's the distant one I want to get to.

Waiting, 'waiting for Waiwai'. There's a place further up the Felício that they call 'the Sabão'. Waiwai has been due there for days now. He's supposed to send someone on and the FUNAI people are supposed to go up to meet them all there and give them their injections. The medical team has gone back. They had a look at everyone who happened to be on the post, gave injections, pulled a few teeth, did some blood and stool samples, and that was that.

Those Wayapí men who are visiting have been ordered to get going with clearing the surrounding forest for gardens. All morning the trees have been crashing down. They are cutting in three areas: beside the landing place, along the north edge, and on the far side of the creek. To the north, they've pushed out as far as one of those massive trees, a sumaúma I think, where the lowest part of the bole pushes out in huge buttresses. They've built a platform about 10 feet high, getting above the root ridges to where the trunk becomes circular, and two of them are up there hacking away. Another is sitting on a felled tree well back keeping an eye on the crown for the first sign of it moving. When it begins to go, he'll yell, and the cutters will scurry down and get away. The big trees take a great swathe of surrounding forest down with them when they go. After the crash, if you're close enough, you'll hear the cloud of broken leaves susurrating down; the forest shedding its tears.

Three women come to the cookhouse shack to ask for things

in their bits of Portuguese. They give their names easily, used to being asked. Tzapo'í, Takorapó, Patauka. Tzapo'í leans her breasts on the table where I'm writing. She smells of wood smoke. All the young women seem to have gingivitis and all have lost a lot of teeth. Why so? Chewing their own sugar cane can't do that, can it? Surely they can't have had that much refined sugar from the Brazilians *yet*. Maybe Senhor Jawbones in the medical team just yanked out anything that caught his eye, in the good old Tiradentes tradition.

A number of the young men have been employed by FUNAI to do 'service' (as it's put in Portuguese) on the post. They wear shorts and shirts. One of them even has a plastic hard hat, the emblem of frontier Brazil. This is the sort of thing that so offends me. When they wear their red loincloths they look superb. ('Loincloths, breechcloths, laps' – awkward words in English. Portuguese says *tanga*. Wayapí says *kamisa*.) Women wrap it round like a miniskirt. The men put it between their legs and loop it over a cotton string round their waists letting it hang fore and aft. They so appreciate manufactured cloth. The colour is fast and the material is lighter. Their own cotton cloth was coarse and stained an orangey colour with *urucu*, that red dye that comes from the seeds of a bush.

A hundred years of loss

So there you are. I saw Kumai in his shorts, T-shirt, and sneakers and I thought he looked pathetic. I saw Pirirí stride past in his tanga, bare-footed, long straight black hair away down his back, and I thought I was looking at one of those Plains Indian braves in the sepia photographs of the nineteenth century – images of those dignified people who were to be massacred by the Hotchkiss guns. My emotional responses revealed, didn't they, that I was in the grip of a romantic illusion, wanting to maintain indigenous cultures as if the people were creatures in a zoo. Apparently I had not properly appreciated that these people, like people everywhere, had a history and should continue to have a history, that they had changed and adapted to the circumstances that had come their way in the past, and that they will change and adapt to the circum- stances that come their way in the future. I was just like one of those old-fashioned anthropologists that takes part in a conspiracy to present cultures in a spurious picture of synchronic integrity. I was being naïve, blind, and self-indulgent. That, at any rate, is what's said these days about such responses. And that, as the survivors would recognize, is itself unforgivably short-sighted.

Yes, I was alarmed when I heard how much Portuguese was being spoken. And yes, my alarm was misjudged. They had only been officially in contact for a year, according to government records that is. But they'd had years of 'unofficial' contact before that, with gold-prospectors and hunters. Of course they were going to pick up a smattering of Portuguese to get along with, especially the men; and of course they were very good at doing so. There was nothing particularly alarming about that. And if the Brazilian frontier was going to continue to encroach on their lands and into their lives then it was essential for them to wise up and be able to deal with what was coming at them. But there was nothing naïve or romantic in my responses of distaste and alarm when I saw the first signs of disintegration. In a hundred years' time the language *will* have gone. That's part of their predicament. The mysteries of an extinct language make the mysteries of a lost past so much more poignant.

I doubt that there will be many left to feel that particular loss. The forest is coming down, now, in my time, and uncounted species of plant and animal life are being destroyed in the flames. Most people living a century on will understand the horror of what is being done and will never forgive. But so few will understand the loss of a language. Sure, languages change. Sure, languages develop. Sure, dialects get flattened out and lose their local charm. That's just the way of the world. Certainly, there's no such thing as a unique, integral language. They're all related. They form great family chunks. Wayapí is just one of the Tupi-Guaraní family, after all, and there are plenty of them, or at any rate there were.

Those kinds of argument just miss the point. The extinction of a language, like the extinction of a natural species, is an appalling tragedy. People can't just go making them up again. It's no romantic illusion to feel such regret. It is, on the other hand, just swaggering ignorance to be indifferent to such destruction. The point is that the Wayapí had their own language until Brazilians began to invade their territory. From that point on all the most powerful material forces required negotiation in Portuguese speech. From that point on Wayapí language was doomed. That's why the survivors won't speak it. And that's why I was afraid when I heard those bits and pieces of Portuguese being spoken.

14

The same goes for all the other romantic illusions. There's nothing romantic or illusory about them. They are a way of appreciating a certain condition of material and cultural integrity that these people had – something that was destroyed rapidly and irrevocably. Certainly the Wayapí had all sorts of relationships with other forest peoples over those centuries that we know of. They migrated, thousands of them, in the 1700s from an area on the Rio Xingú, moving northwards, crossing the Amazon and entering the Guianas. Certainly they traded and fought with others. They met Brazilians on the Rio Jarí and French on the Oyapoque River in Cayenne. Certainly they had a history and certainly they 'adapted and changed'. They were hit by the fearsome smallpox epidemics that swept that area during the 1800s. (Is that enough 'change' for the sociologos? Is that enough 'adaptation'?) The point is that in those days, however many died, there was always somewhere to go.

Yes, there was a time before their lands were invaded by bands of gold prospectors; before the Brazilian government set up its 'Attraction Front'; before they were told they had to do this and had to do that; before they were ordered to move here and move there; before shotguns were introduced; before Portuguese became a necessary medium of negotiation; before T-shirts and mosquito nets; before a road was forced through their territory; before missionaries arrived with their obsessional bletherings about a fantasy god; and before they had nowhere else to go.

There are three strands in a tangle here. The first looks like this. In 1916 Bronislaw Malinowski went to the Trobriand Islands off Papua New Guinea, when the tradition of fieldwork in anthropology was just beginning. There were traders, missionaries, and government officials there at the time, but he felt that *as a matter of proper scientific procedure* he had to ignore these outside influences in order to get at the essential ethnographic facts of Trobriand life. The outside influences were irrelevant accretions that were obscuring the reality, and therefore had to be cast aside and ignored. So the picture of Trobriand life presented in the three great ethnographies, *Argonauts of the Western Pacific*, *The Sexual Life of Savages*, and *Coral Gardens and their Magic* barely mentions the subjugation of these people by Europeans. That's an illusion on Malinowski's part; but it's not a romantic illusion. It's a scientisticky illusion inherited from nineteenth-century positivism regarding what counts as 'real' and 'objective', and what does not.

Tangled up with that is a second strand: the long, long elegiac yearning of human beings everywhere for better times that have passed away. In our relentlessly urban times that sense of longing and loss so often looks to pastoral images to find expression; rural images that suggest comforting alternatives of simplicity and peace. Raymond Williams in *The Country and the City* discloses that these Arcadian longings have been around since the Greek and Roman bucolic poets. No surprise, then, especially for those of us immured 'in the corrupt heart of the city' that we should find ourselves drawn to idealize rural communities and isolated peoples and see them as survivors of some remote, changeless tradition that we have been banished from. What is surprising is the dogged persistence over the centuries where generation after generation of dreamers have always assumed that the Genuine Tradition has *just* vanished. It's *just* back there over the last hill. That's romantic, and Raymond Williams goes a long way to straighten up those illusions.

These two strands are simple assessments, illusory assessments, of what is seen to be there. The third strand is different. It is indeed informed by the first two. It does indeed see 'their culture' as having some sort of integrity. And it does indeed ask with a sigh: 'Mais où sont les neiges d'antan?' But it's different because it's looking straight at a relationship, not just at an essence. It's not so much an attempt to describe something as an attempt to assess a relationship. It's assessing the nature and the extent of the way the outside society interferes with 'their culture'. The image of their integrity is not an illusion dangling in the void. It's a way of appreciating the nature of 'their culture' when officials can't get in, when missionaries can't get in, where there are no roads and no land invasions. The less intense the conditions of interference, the more the integrity can be appreciated. Similarly, it's noticing, with broken-hearted regret, that it doesn't *have* to be like this; that there was a time not so long ago, indeed just back over the last hill – the invasion of gold-prospectors in 1972 and the arrival of the 'Attraction Front' in 1973 – when it wasn't like this for Wayapí people.

They could always deal with desperados, gangsters, jaguar-trappers, anthropologists. They could always deal with lone arrivals. They could manage a clutch of explorers passing through. They could get what they wanted from a team of surveyors arriving with their weird instruments and their weird interests in stones and earth. All these visitors came and went with little inclination to start ordering people about, telling people what to do, moving people, interfering with their beliefs. All the loners might have wanted was food, shelter, company, and conversation. Let's give them the benefit of the doubt anyway.

But Wayapí culture couldn't deal so easily with a camp of seventy gold-prospectors on their doorstep ('doorstep'? – I mean the creek that they drink from); seventy or more men who brought, along with their other goods to exchange, influenza, measles, gonorrhea, syphilis. (Brazilian doctors are taught as elementary clinical practice to 'think syphilitic' and to reflect on the clinical pun: Brazilian Syphilization.) They couldn't deal with a few hundred colonizers who took countless hectares of forest and declared ownership of them. Nor with mining operations that cut airstrips and that, in the by-going, poisoned the water with chemicals. Nor with logging operations and ranching operations that wiped out all existence in the pursuit of lots and lots of quick bucks.

Nor could they even easily manage a handful of government officials, nor even a family of missionaries; because the handful arrives to rule their movements, and the family arrives to rule their minds. The first destroys their Marxist integrity. The second their Weberian. Bang goes the integrity of the mode of production, and bang goes the integrity of thought.

August 1974: the second journey

Nipukú. We got there, the whole lot of us. All Waiwai's people. Well, more or less. There were fifty human souls in Waiwai's group and we lost two kiddies in the fiasco – two beautiful children. Just think of the logic of this. FUNAI, the government agency, decided to vaccinate them. A couple of runners were sent with instructions that the whole settlement was to get themselves, kitchen sink and all, through 80 miles of empty forest and present themselves for immunization jabs. Compliant as usual they did so. 'They said they'd give us manioc. They gave us hunger and influenza.'

I'd got fed up waiting on the post. It seemed that Waiwai wasn't going to appear. I'd waited a week. The FUNAI people were not keen that I leave, but I got them to agree that they let me go. I was to be guided by three Wayapí youngsters. One of them had been hanging around the post for too long anyway and they wanted rid of him. The other two were 'in service'. We were offered a lift in the canoe as far as the Sabão, the series of big rapids up the

Felício, which was the the highest point on the river the big motorized canoes could get to.

We were a few hours out, buzzing and droning up the river, when we heard a gunshot. Great excitement. One of the boys let off a shot in reply and we slowed down. Round a few corners there were two Wayapí men waiting on the bank. They were in their tangas. Each had a shotgun and a small carrying basket made from palm leaves. These were the runners who had been sent with the summons. They would have got to the post that evening. As they climbed in, one of them got teased by the FUNAI man for having had his eyebrows plucked out while he'd been away. 'Hey, buddy, you look just like a spider monkey.'

The news was that there were already some people waiting at the Sabão, but that Waiwai hadn't come. There was illness at the Nipukú. On we went and finally pulled in to a tiny clearing just beside where the rapids started. Twelve people were waiting there – three men, three women, two adolescents, and four children. The boys and I were dumped, and with a tremendous commotion all twelve who had been waiting and all their carrying baskets somehow got into the canoe, and in a few moments they were off. A bizarre meeting – I was supposed to be getting to know these people, and instead we were off in opposite directions: 'Ships that pass in the night, and speak each other in passing.'

There was a single shelter there. I was to get to know the style of these very well. They could put them up so quickly, in less than an hour. Four posts, four cross poles, a roof ridge, and finished off with the long fronds of whatever species of palm there might be to hand, even moro-moro, that awful spiky one, if there was nothing else. They'd last a few months, and it was handy when travelling to come across one recently built. Within a year the thatch would wither away and termites would have got into the posts. It would gradually disintegrate and finally vanish.

Here at the Sabão they'd run three or four shelters into one long one, so there was plenty of room for hammocks. We got settled in because there had been thunder and the rain was going to come. One of the boys 'in service' produced a tanga and stuffed his shorts away in his belongings. The boy from the village was already tanga-ed. I got mine on for the first time (the FUNAI people would not have approved) and I'd another length of red cloth already cut which I gave to the other 'servant'. That was us all dressed up for the part.

18

We were to start walking the next day. Meanwhile we'd açaí fruit juice and manioc flour to eat. The boys sat at one end of the shelter talking in low voices. They were not comfortable with me, and attempts at conversation didn't go well. The rain came and blotted out the sound of the rapids. It wasn't the cheeriest of evenings.

The following two days were awful. I wasn't fit or prepared for this kind of jaunt. I also thought I should try to do the decent thing and see to it that I was carrying more of my stuff than any of them were. I had no idea of distance, of how far we had to go, or what sort of terrain it was. I got so tired and so sore. Towards the end of the first day, staggering along on my own well behind the others, I thought the trees were thinning out. I thought I could see the outline of a house. And I heard the most exquisite sound which I took to be a Wayapí bone flute. Perhaps we're arriving, thought I, not knowing that there were some 40 or 50 miles to go. There was no clearing. The shape was a collapsed shelter. The sound was the uirapuru – an Amazonian wren that whistles the most eerie and beautiful tunes in the world.

Within the first half hour of my first walk in the forest we had come across a jararaca ('pit viper' they say in English) which I could hardly see even when pointed out. At the end of the second day's walk, while I sulked at one end of the shelter, and while the rain teemed down, one of the boys raised his voice to say that my rucksack was getting wet. It was a delicate lesson in manners that I didn't quite appreciate at the time. He was squatting right beside the rucksack, but after all it was my responsibility. Why should he bother? I asked him to pull it in. He put out his hand to grasp the frame and was hit on the finger by a scorpion.

A jararaca two days before and a scorpion that day. It looked just like a matter of time before I came into real pain. I gave the youngster two codeine phosphate. The rest of the afternoon he giggled away, explaining that his arm was throbbing, that his back was sore, and that it hurt under his armpit. The medical book said something about scorpion poison going for the lymph system. That would explain the pain under his arm. Apparently the poison goes from there to the testicles as well.

So there they were; the three of them, Nonato giggling with the pain of his scorpion sting, Toro who had been in trouble all day with the weight of what he was carrying but who had plodded on without a word of complaint, and De Antonio who had a big cut on the sole of his foot, but went off to hunt as soon as we had arrived at the shelter. Meanwhile I'd jump or shout at the slightest prick or surprise. I'd have to learn about putting up with pain. Another grey morning, the thatch dripping, the woods looking bedraggled. Off we went again for the third time. We'd hardly started out when we heard someone up ahead slapping a tree with a machete. It was a young man, all loaded up. He'd heard us coming and this was his warning. The whole lot from the Nipukú were on their way, just behind him. He was out front looking for game. My three hoofed it very smartly back to the shelter to get their hammocks up so that we wouldn't have to build a new one. I went back too and waited.

The place was called Yiro-yiwa (River-meanders). In they came, one small family group after another. I stood by the path, shaking hands with as many people as I could, an idiot smile on my face, feeling like someone on a receiving line. It seemed to be something like eight families with various adolescents attached. One man had three red macaws on a stick. Another was leading on the end of a liana a full-grown peccary (a fierce little wild pig). There were a number of tame jacami trotting about (long-legged fowls that are called 'trumpeters' in English). Everyone was carrying heavy baskets, except the man who came in last, Yanuari, who was to become such a good friend, hobbling along with two sticks, both his legs withered away after an accident years before when he broke his back. Fancy making this man walk 80 miles. I was asked almost immediately to examine his legs. Below the knee they had shrivelled to the bone, and felt cold. He'd lost his toenails and one big toe looked black.

That was the end of walking for the day. They got up a long shelter, very quickly, and got fires going. I was given food and fumbled away trying to do exchanges for everything, thinking I had to reciprocate with cigarettes every time I was given a banana. So stupid. It just wasn't necessary, but how was I to know? Marcel Mauss, the French sociologist whose ideas are part of the loam of anthropology, had said that the basis of primitive life was 'the obligation to give, the obligation to receive, and the obligation to repay'. All very well to put it like that. I hadn't a clue how to go about doing it. For instance, that night, I was given a huge red banana (of a variety unknown to me), a piece of curassow (a big black game bird, about the size of a turkey), a large white fish steak, and a bit of monkey; each offering coming with a helping of crunchy manioc flour. Having scoffed all this, I thought I had to reciprocate, so I made as big a pot as I could of packet soup, thick with monosodium glutamate, and handed that around. For forty people, no more than a sip each.

The men sat close around me that day and the rest of the evening. One, his name sounded like 'Paurandōe', was really good at the language teaching game. It was strange that he should just take to me like that at the very first meeting. He was to become my closest friend. I made up names for them all that I could use in my notebook. I called him 'Parahandy'. As for the 'Paurandōe' that I thought had such an authentic ring, it was his rendering to my ears of 'Paulo Antônio', the name given to him by the gold-prospectors.

Back to the Sabão then. Three days just ambling back the way the four of us had come. I'd walk behind Waiwai and in front of crippled Yanuari. The first few hours was an intensive botany lesson. Waiwai would cut leaf after leaf and give it to me, shouting its name. I'd try to write as we walked along and try to think up some way of remembering what the leaf looked like. This was his way of teaching me the language: learn the words for all the leaves. Well, why not? *Ka'i-kroá* (long pointed leaf), *namo-ka'a* (waterproof leaf), *kori-mako* (sweet-smelling, dark green), *pa-ku-ku* (small herring-bone leaf). And trees too, identifying them by their trunks, since it was hardly possible to get a view of their habit: *pe-ry-ry, para-kuta, waro-si, moro-moro*. As a botanical lesson it was hopeless for me, but it was as good a way into the language as any, getting a feel for the phonemes and the word structure.

We'd walk till about midday. Up would go the shelters and that would be that. Off down to the Felício to bathe, where I found that even when it's just the men together they were surprisingly prudish about their private parts. A man is supposed to keep them cupped in one hand if he's naked and above water. And if he needs two hands to scrub himself, he sticks his penis between his legs and crosses his thighs.

The tiny group of men that sat around me presented such a sweep of personalities. Parahandy was open, happy, and reassuring. Waiwai was very fierce and chiefly. Desperate Dan looked like a pathological murderer (but turned out to be a genius). Jimmy Peerie and his brother, each the spitting likeness of the other, had long doleful faces that never smiled. If Jimmy P. was any distance away and saw me reaching for cigarettes, he'd bound over with indecent

21

haste. An older hairy hippie character that I called Mike Maguire had a manic, mystic aspect about him (which I came to recognize later as excruciating shyness). Parahandy and he were sitting with me. I asked Mike M. his wife's name. (Isn't it just the ticket that one of the first questions I'd learned to ask in Wayapí was 'What's your name?' It must have been like someone approaching you at a party and asking in a firm voice, thick with a strange accent: 'Please tell me how much you earn?') Mike M. looked uncomfortable and grunted a laugh or two then turned and shouted to her: 'Hey, what's your name?' No reply. The question was reformulated in various apparently distinct grammatical forms, until back came a shrill crisp answer, from wife to husband, which sent both Mike M. and Parahandy into giggles. Parahandy translated in his best Portuguese: 'Não tem nome disse': 'Said doesn't have name'.

We got to the Sabão and settled in. Parahandy built me my own shelter. Some got into the long one already there. The rest built new ones, and we ended up in a small circle under the trees. My three youngsters immediately left for the post. The rest of us pottered about for three days. The main activity was in a grove of açaí palms nearby. The fruit was ripe and red macaws came in every day to feed. When the men had finished taking down as many bunches of fruit as they wanted, they built hides high up in the adjoining trees from which to shoot the macaws. We ate them, but their main value was the feathers that were used for making crowns.

It's worth noting that the three macaws and the jacamins and the fierce little peccary back at the camp were certainly not seen as a food resource for hard times. They were clearly 'pets'. Months later, at the Nipukú, when it was decided that the peccary had grown too dangerous, Jimmy Peerie and his brother, who owned it, agreed that it should be killed, but they would have nothing to do with the slaughter nor the distribution of the meat. And Yanuari once explained that when they were first given chickens by the Brazilians they found it difficult to understand that they were supposed to kill them and eat them from time to time. When they got round to it, they decided that the only way to kill them was with a bow and arrow, as if they were game.

These were three idyllic days, as if everyone was on a camping holiday. Once I got over worrying about the food, the beauty of the whole thing surged in, gathering at night round the camp-fires with the rapids roaring in the background, or watching the dawn light grow through the dripping trees.

Someone with a quick ear heard the buzz of the FUNAI motor at about mid-morning. The sound grew steadier for the following half hour or so. Those who had left the camp to hunt had hurried back. All present for the encounter. All present for a lethal fiasco. Three FUNAI men (medical attendant, motorista, and odd-job man) arrived with injections packed in a cooling box. I think they were supposed to be doing a BCG immunization programme to prevent the spread of tuberculosis. The qualified medical people had long gone back, and had left a box or two of doses for any-one who arrived. They were to be administered by the attendant whose knowledge of medicine was firmly bush-quality. The motorista had to write down the names he was given. He did so in groups of one to nine, then back to one again. He'd estimate their ages by an exaggerated critical glance and a shrug. It was soon clear there were not enough doses. About fifteen souls were bundled into the canoe to be taken down to the post, injected there, and, men, women, children, and babies, sent back walking – one and a half to two days' plod.

They were taken down on the Wednesday. On the Friday they walked back into the camp (having spent Thursday night in the woods) with the news that there was flu on the post – four men, two women, three children ill there. Six in this party already complaining. I started on the temperatures: Kasiripin 38°, Nazaré 38.5°, Payari 37.8°. . . . What a disaster. Why on earth take them there *knowing* there was flu? Saturday; ten people ill: Peryry 38.1°, Payari up to 39°, Mariki, sweating, got it really badly, 39.2°. . . . Meanwhile Waiwai and Teyo and their families took off, back to the Nipukú. I tried to keep the temperatures down with the supply of analgesics I had been given by FUNAI, but I didn't have enough. I arranged to go to the post with Siro, who was still fit, leaving at dawn and getting there about 4 o'clock. Two roadmen were still there. It was a group of them coming up river to visit the post that had brought the flu in. Siro and I got back to the Sabão the next day carrying as much as we could take from the pharmacy. The fires were very low that night.

Tuesday: people were beginning to get up and about, and there was word that we would start off the next day. Will we go, won't we go? Thursday: Jimmy Peerie came along: Why don't all the men go to the post, then on to Capoeira, and get bananas and manioc flour? Well, said I, going to the post would mean more illness. Ten minutes later Jimmy P. came back to say no one was going to the post; that we were all going to the Nipukú. The same day Yanuari, the crippled man, left with his family. Friday: we were all finally off.

Five nights we spent on the walk through. We had no shelters to build since they had stopped at so many places on the way. Beyond Yiro-yiwa it was new country for me. We got to the head-waters of the Felício, where it broke into five small streams. There we caught up with Yanuari and his people – at Warikoro-Ry – a lovely spot on a mound where the trees were like a beech grove above the river, now very shallow. A hard day that. When they got going, they really shifted. I was *in extremis* at the last bit. On and on the next day. Over the hills, and into Nipukú waters, where I felt it had got warmer once we had crossed the watershed. Down to Aima.

'Aima' – that beautiful name. A beautiful place too. I don't know how to explain the sense that different parts of the great woods have their own feel to them. If you flew over the canopy in a helicopter or a light plane you could never tell that, but down amongst the trees the land changes mood constantly. You came down off the hills to Aima and felt that you were in a big flat forest, and the river was like one of those pretty ones in the tame English countryside. And flowing *south* at last, towards the Amazon, not east to the Atlantic. At last we were getting there.

They walked so well. Their feet were so wise. Farming people and manual workers at home have wise hands. But none of us, since poor people have been shod, are used to clever feet. In the Musée d'Orsay in Paris there's a large fantasy painting by Cormon called *Cain*, inspired by a Victor Hugo poem, depicting Cain and his family of about a dozen fleeing before Jehovah, like Yanuari and his family fleeing from the flu. The catalogue notes say that Cormon painted each figure from life and that he showed 'a profound concern for archaeological realism in his rendering of primitive existence'. Well, perhaps the archaeology of feet let him down. Their feet would never have been like that. He must have copied from models whose feet had lifetimes in shoes or sabots. These aren't wise feet. Wise feet have bulbous big toes that stick out the way, and a great space between the big toe and the next one. Someone with wise feet can pick up a dropped utensil and lift it towards the descending hand. Wise feet also keep you in such immediate contact with the world. You can just swing out of a hammock and walk, no fumbling for sandals. And you must have bare, wise feet for balancing along a tree-trunk bridge. In the forest, we outsiders have to learn a new way of walking. It's not like thumping along rocky paths in our wildernesses. You have to learn to place each foot carefully, and above all, to lift your feet much higher – altogether a more delicate gait. I don't think I'll ever learn how to run barefoot with the abandon they showed when in hot pursuit of fleeing game. They went belting through pathless woods with no apparent concern about sharp sticks hidden under the leaf litter, about thorns, or about snakes. To do that, you'd have to see so much, seeing both the tiny details at your feet while also keeping an eye on what was round about. There was a heavy price for mistakes or inattention. They did, sometimes, come back with awful foot wounds. The sole of the foot is such a tender part of our anatomy, and I found treating wounded feet, holding them, washing them, binding them, a surprisingly intimate act in a culture where formal touching, like a handshake, was absent.

Some kinds of practical knowledge are so elusive that it's difficult to know whether or not I inhabited a different physical world from theirs. I could easily have developed wise hands. I think I could have got round to wise feet too, had I been there long enough. But what about physical orientation? I can do the Scottish hills quite well, but there you're always looking at far horizons. The real test in the Scottish hills is when the mist comes down and everything comes in close and turns eerie. Orientation in the big woods is like being in a perpetual mist – no horizons, no views, *ever*. How did they get about? How did they know?

When Kuyuri and I were hunting near the Sabão, an area at the edge of the land they know, we put up a tapir and tried to follow it. We caught up with it a couple of times, but eventually Kuyuri gestured in the direction it had gone and said it had gone off into *ka'a wasu* – 'vast forest' – as if we were on the edge of a shore line looking out at the expanse of an ocean where we could not go. What baffled me at that moment was how we were to get back to the camp. To me it was 'vast forest' whichever way we looked.

Henry David Thoreau quotes an Indian he met in the Maine woods who yarned away saying:

'Some years ago I met an old white hunter at Millinocket; very good hunter. He said he could go anywhere in the woods. He wanted to hunt with me that day so we start. We chase

25

a moose all the forenoon, round and round, till middle of afternoon when we kill him. Then I said to him, now you go straight to camp. Don't go round and round where we've been, but go straight. He said, I can't do that, I don't know where I am. Where you think camp? I asked. He pointed so. Then I laugh at him. I take the lead and go right off the other way, cross our tracks many times, straight camp.'

'How do you do that?' I asked.

'Oh, I can't tell *you*,' he replied. 'Great difference between me and white man.'

Thoreau goes on to comment:

It appeared as if the sources of information were so various that he did not give a distinct, conscious attention to any one, and so could not readily refer to any when questioned about it; but he found his way very much as an animal does. Perhaps what is commonly called instinct in the animal, in this case is merely a sharpened and educated sense.

Well of course it's a 'sharpened and educated sense'. The point is whether or not any of us can sharpen ourselves and educate that sense enough to get proficient at it. Or are we doomed to incompetence? I still find it shocking to sit with people in a room here and ask them to point to where the sun rises. The responses are so hesitant. And when, as frequently happens, they point in entirely the wrong direction, it's equally baffling to me as to how they go about making up any mental maps at all. Maybe many of my compatriots live in a sort of undifferentiated spatial gunge, without any mental maps, and get about by sticking to a few well tried itineraries.

I don't know how the Indians do it in the forest. They'll know every trickle of water and every slope and every distinctive stand of trees, even though flat forest on an overcast day must be tricky. It will be a knowledge laid down in sediments that go back to infancy. And it's not that 'they can't refer to any of the details when questioned about them', as Thoreau muses, but that they've never been asked before, and are unpractised in the idiom of explanation, like asking someone to explain the grammar of a sentence they've just produced. They learn and teach by imitation and example, not by refining abstract rules and principles.

After Aima, another night, another little circle of shelters. So glad to get rested, hammock-sagging as the night comes down.

Sleep was often disturbed, though. Usually it was Parahandy's children who started wailing; the two infants who were to die. Everyone would then stir and the coughing would start up. They couldn't get rid of these coughs and when they all got going together the noise was appalling, each person in turn ending their fit with a loud hawking and spitting routine.

Off again for the last day. Getting closer we began to pass through areas of what's called *capoeira* in Portuguese, the dense, matted growth, a few years old, full of thorns and razor grass, that appears where gardens have been abandoned and the forest is returning. Then through the gardens themselves. I suppose 'gardens' is the word I have to use, but they were neither like Kubla Khan's, 'bright with sinuous rills where blossomed many an incense bearing tree', nor were they neat little dibbled rows of cabbages and carrots with box hedges by the paths. They were a chaotic sight of whitened tree trunks lying all higgledy-piggledy, like a scene from a First World War painting. Finally we came out on the bank of the Nipukú river and crossed in a dug-out to the village on the west bank. We'd made it.

We'd been in the woods for nearly a month. It was exhilarating to see the open sky and the sun, and to feel the heat of the village clearing. The roofs were baked to a straw colour and everything else looked beige. For them, it was a relief to be home. It would be easier here to nurse the coughs and fevers. Yes, they were home, but the illness still had a long time to run. Parahandy's toddler, that he had carried throughout the journey, had five more days to live, and the baby, slung permanently to the young mother, another three weeks.

2

AT LONG HAMMOCK

The 'arrival *topos*' makes some people uneasy. A *topos* is a standard theme, a stock topic that's trotted out on order, and there's a current line of thought suggesting that anthropological authors write about the journey and the arrival both for the purposes of self-aggrandizement ('Look at me; I cut a brave figure'), and to establish the writer's authority ('See! I was there; you, reader, were not; so pay attention').

It's an unsettling reversal of values, but it's appropriate for my times. In the past, from Aristotle to the Romantics, *topoi* were what you were *supposed* to write about. There were only certain possible themes, and the skill was to be able to write originally within them. You could write about 'crabbèd age and youth cannot together live', or 'modesty', or 'the promised land', or you could try one of the small repertoire of accepted 'tragic plots'. It was the equivalent of writing a poem within a strict form, like a sonnet or a villanelle.

The old *topoi*, like the great symbols – the labyrinth, the rose, the flood, the great fire – are endless sources of inspiration. So are actual journeys, strange places, unknown languages, and other cultures. The modern commentators should overcome their reservations. The journey and the arrival are episodes of intense awareness and intense emotion; episodes of confusion, of apprehension, of wonder.

'Look! We have come through!'

We'd got to the Nipukú. It was the end of the path. Once settled in, I'd think back over that journey, trying to remember each stretch and each turn and each detour. It was like a piece of string, seven, eight, nine days long, winding back to the east, with knots in it every so often marking those spots where the shelters were. I had to remember every nuance, as if it was an arcane test to see if I could find my way out of the labyrinth having got to the innermost point. Also, I felt it was important that I should be able to do the return journey alone.

At that time I had no idea that I was the first outsider to see this particular settlement. A year before, the FUNAI people had arrived by helicopter, but then the village was on the east side, the nearer side of the river. The visit resulted in an epidemic. Six people died and were buried in the earth under their houses. The place was abandoned and a new clearing made on the far side of the river. I'd come to the new settlement.

You couldn't see the ghost village. It was back from the bank of the river and well away from the main path. I first became aware of it when the babies began to die, and they'd take the bodies across the river, wrapped up in miniature hammocks, to bury under the abandoned houses alongside the graves already there. A detour off the main path would take you in a few minutes to a complete deserted village. The roof thatches were getting thin, but had not collapsed. The outline of what would have been the village space was clear enough, although the weeds were pushing up everywhere, a green covering over the grey earth. Not much of a 'Sweet Auburn'; it was an eerie place:

> Thy glades forlorn confess the tyrant's power . . .
> Amidst thy tangling walks and ruined grounds.

When I first approached Eerie Auburn, this secret, abandoned place, hiding just next door, it was to a secretive sound. Three or four teenage girls had gone ahead and were digging a grave for the baby with axes. The thud was deceptive. It tricked your senses of sound and space. You were closer to it than you thought. It seemed to come from further on, and suddenly this death procedure was just beside you. A prominent journalist talked of a similar *dérèglement des sens* at the funeral of an American president – on hearing the sound of muffled drums. The grip of fear that takes you at that moment is an analogue of the arrival of our own death. Our senses tell us that it shouldn't be quite upon us yet; and then there it is, that little extra bit closer than we thought it was. They always dug graves with axes, and I was to hear that sound again.

For the next year and a half there were only two occasions when the village was visited by outsiders – the FUNAI people came through once, and a Wayapí family arrived from one of the eastern settlements to arrange a wife for their son. Every now and again one of the Nipukú families would pack up and go east to the FUNAI post or to the other villages. They would reappear a few weeks later. On two or three occasions the travellers brought back coughs and flu-like fevers which immediately took hold of everyone and led to a miserable fortnight or so. But none of these outbreaks was anything like as serious as that first one I'd seen at the Sabão. Apart from the bouts of illness, there were no further alarms, no further deaths, and only one serious accident – a case of snakebite which the victim survived. It was a peaceful time *à huis clos*, behind closed doors.

That spell realized the best of their self-sufficiency, a time without daily fear, a time without tragic drama, a time of material contentment; not enough to block out the Great Fear, but a time to lessen its urgency. There were seventy souls living there, with hundreds of miles of empty forest all around them, and a single path connecting them to the rest of their people and to that outside world which was building up its pressure of encroachment. It was as well that they were not counting the hours, nor measuring the advance of the road, nor checking the progress of the surveyors' plans. It was as well that their time was allowed to hold its breath for a year and a bit, while the road moved closer.

The settlement was tucked into the north end of a huge opened area, open to the sun and the sky. It was an oblong shape running down the west bank of the river. Most of the opened space was a garden area prepared by two particular households. It was unusual to have such a view from a village, seeing a far horizon. It was also unusual to be at the edge of a fair-sized river rather than a headwater creek. Wayapí settlements were usually by trickles of water. Like many other Amazonian refugees who wanted to get away from strangers, outsiders, and invaders, they had withdrawn to the most remote headwater areas. You wouldn't have wanted to call them a 'river people'. But here they were by the Nipukú where canoes were a necessary part of everyday life. An unusual combination: big sky and big water.

All but one of the houses were built on stilts, with a raised floor of slats from the açaí palm. The exception was one in the old-fashioned style: four main posts, an earth floor, the thatch curving round at one end and cut straight off in an inverted V at the other. There was no plan to the layout of the houses, but the pattern

The old-style house at Nipukú

remains in my memory as if tattooed there. I close my eyes and it comes back.

I loved the peaceful rhythms of the place. It took an effort to remember that those few seasons, from sun to rain and back again, and that village space that I got to know so well, were a respite from a shocking history of fleeing, running, hiding. The six deaths of the previous year, and the consequent move from one side of the river to the other, was a relatively minor trauma. What had happened in the years before that was appalling. In low voices they would go over the names of the places they had all come from; names from the Aroã, from the Igarapé Massiwa, from Kumakary, and from Aima. They would tell of entire villages being destroyed by terrifying surges of disease, and explain how each household at the Nipukú represented the last survivors: Siro from Kani-Kani, Teyo from a place near Kumakary, Yanuari and Waiwai himself from the old settlements along the Aima.

What seemed to me an arrangement of such permanence and peace was no more than a resting place for them. 'All is flux, nothing is stationary' (παντα ρει, ουδεν μενει) is supposed to be one of the best-known sayings of Heraclitus, the Ionian philosopher of the sixth century BC. If he did indeed say that, he's the best philosopher for Amazônia. Seventy souls gathered in the one clearing like this was an unusual Wayapí arrangement. So many people living together was a consequence of the turmoil of those times. Not that it was planned like that. There was no overt discussion, no communal decision of how things should be done, or of when movements should be made. The Nipukú settlement was an *ad hoc* adjustment to the pressures coming on to them from the east. After a few years, as the pressures changed, the settlement would crack, crumble, and vanish.

Where you built your house was up to you. Where you cut down the forest for your garden was up to you. Looking at this from afar, we should try to learn from the idyll. It is not a romantic fantasy. It's there for us to see, and we should be ready to recognize it, and to accept the fundamental lessons from these peaceful rhythms. There's so much to learn:

> The first man who, having enclosed a piece of land, thought of saying 'This is mine' and found people simple enough to believe him, was the true founder of civil society. How many crimes, wars, murders; how much misery and horror the

human race would have been spared if someone had pulled up the stakes and filled in the ditch and cried out to his fellow men: 'Beware of listening to this impostor. You are lost if you forget that the fruits of the earth belong to everyone and that the earth itself belongs to no one!'[3]

That's one of Jean-Jacques Rousseau's best-known speculations on the nature of primitive life. As so often, his accuracy was uncanny. During those decades when Wayapí people were still able to run for it, and make their settlements where they thought they would be safe, there were many other indigenous peoples all over Amazônia who were finding out what it meant to have roads pushed through the woods that they knew, areas demarcated and fenced off, lands suddenly becoming 'owned' and which could then be bought and sold. Eventually too, in the future beyond me, Wayapí people are also going to find their woods removed from them. They were all born in free land, but everywhere the chains are closing in.

Night and day

Because of the big clearing, the huge night skies during the dry season were stupendous. Since we were just to the north of the Equator by a degree or so we could see everything in its turn from the Southern Cross to the Great Bear, and during a season the entire zodiac swung round in an ellipse overhead. The rhythm of equatorial days and nights, twelve hours of day and twelve hours of night, always has the full moon appear at its best. There's also a particularly strange light in the dawns just following a full moon. The shrinking moon, still big but not quite fallen in the west, bathes the place in its light from that direction while the eastern sky is brightening with the real dawn.

At times I'd waken at that uncertain hour, in the dark before the first of the dawn. I found my thoughts and feelings unusually still then, without relation or association. Memories were calm; no projective fantasies; no anxieties of cause and effect. With those turmoils quiet, my appreciation of immediate senses was more acute.

If you looked out in the dark before dawn, about 5-ish, you could see whole new heavens, perhaps Orion high in the eastern sky, Taurus higher, and the Pleiades overhead. You'd be catching a preview; constellations that were not due in familiar evening skies for months. When you hear of Indians reckoning times of the year by the appearance of certain constellations, it's their first appearance just before dawn that counts. Siro was the person who paid most attention to the stars and was often awake at that time, playing his tiny flute made from a deer bone.

As the sky turned grey the village began to stir. At that place the river ran due north–south, so the sun came up from behind the curtain of trees on the other bank of the river and went down behind the distant edge of the gardens. Mornings, especially during the dry season, were chilly. One of Waiwai's usual points during his chiefly harangues was that women should get down to the river to bathe first thing, since that would show that they were not lazy.

Men going hunting would often leave at crack of dawn, but usually there was no hurry to get the day going. Fan up the fires and eat something, either a nibble from leftovers or a bowl of peppery manioc soup. During the spells of good health when I wasn't doing the rounds of those who were sick, I'd be looking for an opportunity to get sitting or hammock-sagging with someone. In the early days I knew I could get a genealogy in half an hour, a set of relationship terms in five minutes, or a new verb in three.

Parley

As the months went on the struggle with the language gradually grew, from initial, carefree bouts into daily skirmishes, and from that into a full-scale campaign. It was 'foot – slog – slog – slog – sloggin' over Africa' all right. No discharge in that war. All I had to start with was a missionary's list of twenty words or so collected in French Guiana, and another made by a nineteenth-century explorer in the same area and written in pre-phonetic script French. No dictionaries, no grammars; and no training in how to go about this most mysterious of all learning procedures. I had no idea what I was up against, what to look for, whether it would even be possible to 'learn the language' at all. Could there be such a thing in the world as a language that was impossible to penetrate?

No, there isn't. The bafflement of Babel is accompanied by the miracle of translation. Wherever languages find each other, time and again the astonishing processes of translation begin to grow. It didn't come easily for me though. The start was fine. It felt like leaps and bounds each day. But that initial sense of speed quickly vanished and for months I felt trapped in a painful effort that seemed to be getting nowhere. A particularly depressing stage was when I began to record myth telling, and I'd have a few half-hour tapes that meant next to nothing to me. I'd play them over and over again, baffled.

The limits of my language became prison bars. On a day in midsummer I tried to hurl myself against them, grasping them and shaking them in a mixture of anger, frustration, and despair. Would the effort make them bend any quicker? Would my world expand if I howled and beat myself against its limits? Would that break the frozen stream of language and make it flow? That day I took two or three sentences and sat with Parahandy going over them and over them till I thought I saw what was going on, and till he was fed up. By the end I felt I'd struggled to the top of a small hill only to realize that Yanuari's myth on the 30-minute tape still reared up in front of me like a huge mountain. Would I ever scale that?

It's a commitment for years, not months. And yes, the sense of freedom does eventually come. To this day I return to note-books, grammars, vocabularies to enjoy new discoveries and to keep familiar with the paths and clearings of the language that I've already come to know. It isn't just like 'knowing another language'. I've got to know a number of European languages. One or two I'm quite good at. Others I've got a smattering. The thought of having a look at one or two more doesn't dismay me. I know I *could* pick up modern Greek, Romanian, maybe even a Slavonic language. But the thought of starting on another unwritten language, while it would be a marvellous undertaking, daunts me.

When going well, it was satisfying to get talking and to start getting used to their peculiar conversational ways. I might start talking to a particular person within the hearing of others. My interlocutor would often be helped out and told what to say by the others, in lowered voices. Part of the game was that even though I heard the others perfectly well, I hadn't to answer them. I had to wait until the answer was repeated by the person I'd initially begun talking to. Sometimes it was a help, when, for example, my interlocutor didn't understand me and the bystander did. Often, though, it was a nuisance if the bystander was a busybody, determined to intervene.

I'd often be asked questions by someone who knew the answers perfectly well. Indeed, if I was having difficulty remembering the proper words, I'd have the answer supplied for me by the questioner. These performance aspects of conversation waxed and waned depending on the context. On fine evenings all the men would sit in line near a fire. I'd talk to everyone. But some men, although living together in an intimate village like that, maintained a social distance of silence. They were relationally remote and regarded each other as formal strangers. They wouldn't ordinarily talk. If they did it would be a rehearsed conversation, all the questions being familiar and all the answers heard before.

Waiwai's harangues were the most formal. He'd often start up at night, from his hammock, having engaged Yanuari, in his hammock across the village, as his partner in the performance. Waiwai's speech would be delivered in a loud singing monotone. When he paused he would be answered by expletives and assents on the same frequency. Now and again I'd be sitting with Yanuari when he'd have to take part in a harangue, and he'd carry on a hurried, whispered conversation with me on one subject, breaking off at the required moment to cry out the responses on the artificial pitch.

Siro, independent and happily self-sufficient, was perhaps the man on the most formal terms with Waiwai. They found themselves one night at the communal fire with no one else there. They sat on their stools, their backs to one another. Waiwai went off on a harangue. His main theme on that occasion was to go over and over the deaths, making the point again and again that there were so many Brazilians (*karai-ko*, as they call them) and so few Wayapí. Back came Siro's responses on the same pitch.

Like the songs, these formal harangues seemed to be tied to an anchor note, like the A of the oboe as the orchestra tunes up. I like to think it's possible that they shared a sort of perfect pitch and a chosen tonic in which their songs and formal speech were rooted, but my musical ear is not accurate enough to say.

The woods, the wind, and the weather

The surrounding forest was always green. There was no autumn and winter when the leaves fell. Leaves were always falling and new tendrils were always pushing out like sinuous snakes. Always green, green, green. 'Green-dense and dim-delicious, bred o' the sun', as Caliban said of the warm sea. It's curious how the imaging of forests as holy *buildings* endures. John Evelyn (the diarist) in *Sylva* 1679 says: 'Paradise itself was but a kind of nemorous temple, a sacred grove planted by God himself.' Baudelaire's *Correspondances* goes:

> La Nature est un temple où de vivants piliers
> Laissent parfois sortir de confuses paroles;
> L'homme y passe à travers des forêts de symboles
> Qui l'observent avec des regards familiers.

Nature is a temple, in which living pillars sometimes utter a babel of words; mankind traverses it through forests of symbols that watch him with knowing eyes.

And a rock star, with a commitment to saving the Amazon forest, talked recently of its 'cathedral-like beauty'. The trouble with these pictures is that the direction of the metaphor is the wrong way. It's diminishing to think of forests in terms of buildings, however grand and however numinous the constructions may be.

In the forest, so much was to hand – leaves, lianas, palm fronds, wood of all sizes from sticks to poles. With a sharp knife you could slice off a leaf at the side of a stream to make a cup. Palm fronds were everywhere, for making baskets or shelter roofs. There was a thick, soft, pliant bark that was stripped off for the carrying straps that were tied to baskets. Ubim, a broad flat leaf of a dwarf palm that grew to the height of a fern, was for house thatch, but you had to know where to find it in quantity. Bark from the *tawari* tree came off like brown paper and was used for rolling tobacco into long cheroots. A thick woody vine was beaten and processed to make the famous fish-poison *timbó*. And so many items were made from leaves and stems cut into strips, woven and plaited and tied: fire-fans, sieves, squeezers, baskets.

There was an unexpected blandness about the elements in the forest. The contrasts swung gently to and fro – sun and rain, warm and chill, earth and mud, blue and grey – although arriving as I did just at the end of the rains I started off with nearly half a year of perpetual summer. That was a superb beginning. Weather in the forest was genial; no extremes of temperature. It was even steadier in the woods than in the settlement clearing where the nights could be nippy during the dry season and the days a touch on the hot side. Even the wind was soft; nothing of that bite it gives you where I come from, where the cold toughens your skin with numbness. In the woods the wind softens you up, not just your skin but deep into your flesh and muscle.

For months on end during the dry time the clouds drifted in from the east and north-east, but down on the ground the puffs of breeze had no preferred direction. The wind rarely turned wild, and then only for a few minutes, when it went berserk. You would hear it coming a long way off, first like the sound of a distant waterfall, then a sudden crescendo, that made your senses spring up. It would then arrive like an express train and burst over you like a breaker. The forest would heave and creak and roar, then with a big sigh it would all subside. As the turbulence began to fade you'd notice that at the back of it was the steady hish of rain, a sullen coda to the previous flourish, and a coda that was to go on and on.

These wild outbursts arrived as dry season turned to wet. Since they were brief and infrequent, the fragile village culture didn't anticipate them. So, when they came in, everyone started scurrying around, catching whatever was blowing away. They did that silently. No one shouted. (It was people shouting near water that caused such outbursts in the first place, so they said.) An event like that was most dramatic at night when the fires flared up and streamers of sparks and glowing cinders scattered everywhere.

These wind bursts made me remember the wildness of the weather at home, its fierce unpredictability, its constant changes, and the implacable bite of the wind. At moments like that I'd feel pangs of homesickness. I'd remember Stevenson's 'hills of sheep, and the howes of the silent vanished races, and winds, austere and pure'. Thinking of the poem as an unforgiving mutability canto, the emotion would turn to concern for the Wayapí. It was all going to go. It was all to be destroyed. Here too, I thought, were Wayapí people poised on their last seasons of integrity.

Summer stretched on. Every day the river sank by a few more centimetres. It was one of those rare years when the acapu trees had blossomed, and the yellow flowers were falling in the woods. (These trees come into blossom every three or four years.) As the season of the sun came to an end we went into a lean time as far as the hunting and fishing went. Very little game came in; a spider monkey one day, a cayman's tail a few days later, a sloth the day after that, and only the odd trahira-fish now and again. There had been a full-scale fish-poisoning expedition, where timbó poison was prepared by squeezing and beating that vine. The stuff was then released up-river. The active ingredient of timbó is called 'rotenone' in English. The fish caught in this way, floating as if dead, are apparently just stunned, and would recover if left. The chemical substance is toxic to cold-blooded creatures, but does little harm to mammals. Unlike our chemical poisons, theirs has a brief effect and vanishes without destroying the ecosystem of the river. Once again, they get it right.

They said there would be a lot of fish when the water got low during the dry season. It got low – no fish. They said the otters had eaten them all. Everyone began to complain about hunger, but I enjoyed the vegetarian diet. The great pot bellies which develop, especially after a beer spree, disappear as quickly as they come. You can certainly get a big belly on an Indian diet but it seems difficult to get fat. My belly went in and out like a bellows by the day.

Men hunting

It's difficult to talk easily about hunting in the world I live in, where so many people are noticing that the way humans treat animals is appalling, and where destroying animals and birds for fun is more and more being recognized as an unacceptable activity. Scotland has a particularly acute problem in that most of the Highlands is owned by rich 'toffs', as they're referred to locally:

> Red-faced, merely physical people
> Whose only thought looking over
> These incomparable landscapes
> Is what sport they will yield
> – How many deer and grouse.

And when these specimens, the merely physical people, claim that their urges to destroy animals are 'natural', it is *they* who invoke Man the Hunter; as if *they* were the guardians of a noble tradition that has been carried down through the ages since the Palaeolithic; as if *their* paragon of stately manhood is barefooted, in a loincloth, and carrying a bow and arrow; as if it's *they* more than anyone who recognize their intimate kinship with Amazonian men, and who would spring to the defence of the Indians were that particular hunting way of life to be challenged. The puerile fantasy is resolved, as we know, because really the only good Tarzan is a . . . Lord Greystoke in disguise.

The red-faced, merely physical people are a monstrous deformity of Man the Hunter. They haven't the slightest appreciation of the relationship between humans and the natural world within which Amazonian Indians do their hunting. It's a point I'll come back to again thinking about the myths, and thinking about shamanism, the key being always how human beings regard themselves within their natural surroundings. The killing goes on both in our world and in the Amazon forests. Both we and they destroy animals and birds and fish. The key is that our civilization *takes* from nature because it thinks it owns the place and can do what it likes. Wayapí people *accepted* from nature because they thought they were being offered a gift. What follows is grisly, but it has its place as hunting for food, in a way that our hunting of animals does not.

Going hunting alone was out of the question for me since I couldn't navigate properly. Although I was always with skilled hunters I found myself doing a lot of killing. On some occasions when really quick reactions were required, if for example a deer or a collared peccary (a small, long-legged pig) got up, one of my companions would get it. But mostly birds and monkeys were left to me. It saved their ammunition, and the hunter I was out with could claim anything I killed. Here's one sequence of murderous episodes. They are all consecutive; one rhythm of killing.

Destroying animals

20 September: Mariry. Out for the day with Matam from 7.45 in the morning until 4.30 in the afternoon in a long arc to the north-west through the woods up the Kani-Kani way. We tried a trumpeter-bird, a macaco-prego monkey, and a spider monkey, but failed on all three. On the swing towards home Matam got a brocket deer. To carry the animal home the small miracle of making the carrying basket took place: two lengths of palm frond woven together and two strips of bark tied on to make the straps. That was our only stop.

23 September: At Wirau-Ry (Stream of the Harpy Eagle) – six of us there in shelters. People were awake at 6 o'clock in the grey light, and sat around for an hour before setting off in two lots of three – Pau, Joaquim, and I went south. Not long out we found honey, so that was a long break. (They had to climb, and hack it out. It was eaten immediately.) At about 11 in the morning we heard howler monkeys coming towards us. These are the heavy red ones with the magnificent call. We stopped and waited, unable to see them. Crashing, rustling, and grunting, they came in, and then they too stopped and went quiet, invisible somewhere up in the canopy. We moved closer, and suddenly there was the big male. I got him, and he came thudding down – that hellish heavy thump. The rest of the family moved off at speed. They emerged at an unusually large space in the canopy and began to jump across it. First I got a little one, another male, just after he jumped; then the mother when she appeared. She didn't fall all the way, and Joaquim made a dangerous climb to get her down from the branch where she'd been caught. By 12.30 it was all over and we were back at the shelters skinning this family group. The adult male was a particularly wonderful creature – a deep red, like the colour of red squirrels, with a thick mane round his head and throat, where you could feel the bony cavity in his gullet, about the size of a ping-pong ball, that allows him to make the surreal grunting roar that ebbs and flows through the woods at twilight.

Back at the shelters the other party came in. Piko'i had killed a female spider monkey with a young one on her back. The young one was still alive, but badly wounded by the lead-shot. It was thrown to the edge of the shelters and left to die, no one willing to kill it. Hard to call it 'cruelty'. It was a kind of indifference.

28 September. At Mariry, not long after dawn, Pau appeared wanting me to go hunting with him. Off we went, south-south-east into steep hills. It was easy hunting with Pau. He wandered. He didn't go like the clappers as Matam did. We wandered off after some howler monkeys but didn't get near them. Tried some jacu birds, but missed them. At about midday Pau suddenly got a shot at a collared peccary. It took off down a slope. Running down in pursuit I lost it for some moments then suddenly found myself in front of the creature. It was badly wounded but still moving. I killed it and and got down to gutting it while Pau made the carrying basket. I carried the thing home, starting off at 1.20 with a 4 o'clock arrival. You need a tough skin on your back and shoulders to carry these baskets comfortably.

4 October. At Waráporo-Ty Reápyry. Now there's a name. 'Waráporo' refers to the cacao trees found there. (Chocolate is made from cacao.) 'Ty' means numerous. So it's 'Headwaters of the Many-Cacao-Trees Stream'. It was a smashing place – a lovely little stream, one of the headwaters of the Felício, in an area where the surrounding hills were steep. These the watershed hills dividing Amaparí waters which flowed east to the Atlantic and Jarí waters which flowed south to the Amazon – lovely, but murderously steep for hunting through.

We were a small group: five men, one woman, and a small child. We'd arrived about midday and camped. When the shelters were up, Piko'i and I went hunting. Nothing doing. Empty woods. On the way back we heard a spider monkey – these are large, black haired ones, with long gangling limbs. Off we went running. We were on the side of a steep slope when I finally saw it. I got two shots into it, that's with a .22 (you can hear the thuds). That stopped it, but it stayed hidden in the canopy. Ten blasted shots wasted trying to get it down. It finally emerged, dangling from one arm and obviously done for, swung slowly, then dropped; a long silent plummeting fall; then a violent thud on to the ground away down the slope. It was still groaning when we got there. 'It's no good,' said Piko'i in an offhand way. 'It's a male. Grandfather-people said "Don't eat male spider monkey".' Male howler monkeys are fine. It's only male spider monkeys that are supposed to be too smelly to eat on account of the musk gland on their chests. The poor creature was supposed to be inedible, but Piko'i took out his knife and removed the two hind legs. Legs? or arms? what are we to call them in the case of these beautiful limbs with feet like hands? God, it was still alive when he did that. He cut off one arm too. The second was broken by a shot. He tied up these three limbs with a liana and gave the bundle to me. We left the mutilated corpse lying on its back, and off I went with that gruesome little cargo of three long hairy black arms, each with its long perfect black hand, palmar wrinkles just like ours, and blue finger nails. What a waste of life. You can't get involved in that kind of chasing, and killing, and butchering without compunction. Violence like that is never entirely innocent.

9 October: Out of a camp at Aima, we were at it again. Three of us were out. Spider monkeys were coming towards us. This time Joaquim told us to wait until we were sure it was the female we fired at. DOWN she came. Not long after, in the same place, toucans came in to feed on some fruit-bearing trees. I got one on a long shot and winged another which fell, but disappeared. Beautiful toucan – white, white breast, the patch of bright red feathers above, amongst the sleeky black, and that marvellous heavy beak. It's a morsel to eat and the feathers would be kept for head-dresses. Another murder.

The sloth captured at Aima

11 October. In shelters. The purpose of this camp was to prepare a garden. While felling a tree, Joaquim got a sloth. He didn't have to kill it; he humped the thing back to camp and tied it to a tree – the equivalent of refrigeration. For three days before being killed and eaten it sat there mute and motionless. Occasionally it would stretch a limb. All the other animals, the monkeys, the big cats, the pigs, and so on, move so fast that our encounters with them force us to speed up and get our glands pumping. But watching a sloth's movements slows you down. It's hypnotic. You gaze at this creature as if you were looking into a different dimension of time.

12 October. Off south from the camp, down the Aima, three of us again. I missed a shot at a macaco-prego monkey, missed a *cara-cará* falcon (the flesh is used to bait the lines for fishing), and saw an ocelot – rather I saw a dappled smudge disappear in a flash. Minutes later we found that spider monkeys were behind us. We stopped and hooted to attract them. In they came. I got one. It was a male. Then the female came in – got her too. Thump, thump – down they came. This time the male was left untouched, just lying there. We didn't even take the legs. A bullet had gone through the female's belly, and as she lay there, face up, a live tape worm began to wriggle in spasms out of the bullet-hole.

14 October. Out from the camp on a half-day walk and took home one curassow (that big black bird), a macaw, and a female spider monkey.

15 October. Another half day, and not a good one. We found some trumpeter-birds. Joaquim imitated their cry and called them towards us. I shot too soon, missed, and sent them all away. Later I missed a toucan. We came across some spider monkeys and I got a small female. It fell still alive. Joaquim whacked it with a machete, but it didn't die. He cut a length of liana and hung it by its neck from a tree to strangle it while he made the carrying basket. I missed another spider monkey on the way back.

25 October. Back at Mariry. Up at 6 o'clock and off at 6.20 with Siro. He was a joy to be with. He took such care and such plea-sure in everything. He pointed out three hanging japu nests and explained how these birds live. When we came to a wide open dip he bounded down one side and up the other simply out of *joie de vivre*. We climbed the biggest hill I ever came across in that area.

He had taken me there because he wanted to show me a view. He knew where a fallen tree had cleared an area near the summit. It was the first and last time I saw a view. It was dazzling, stunning, entrancing, looking over the undulations of forest to distant blue hills on the horizon. Such a pleasurable day, but all we got was one jacu bird and a coati – an animal like a raccoon which some Wayapí won't eat, but which Siro thinks is fine.

30 October: Joaquim arrived late, about 9 o'clock, on a damp grey morning and asked if I'd go hunting. Again we went south into forest I didn't know. I got a jacu bird. In a tiny stream Joaquim nearly stepped on a large cayman hidden under a fallen tree. We killed that too. It's the tails of these alligator-like creatures that are eaten, but I remember we lugged the whole thing home. Later we got a female spider monkey. We were home at about 5 o'clock.

19 November: On the Capoeira path with young Arema. We spotted a small monkey which I shot down. When we got to it, I recognized it as a type of marmoset. It was black, but with extraordinary bright red paws. Arema had never seen one before, and said it wasn't 'food'. We left it there. Later that day we got to Seremeté's place, and when we described it to him he identified it (*kusiri-piyon* was the word) and said that of course it was 'food' and that we were stupid to have left it. Now, years later, I find that what I destroyed, according to our scientific classifications, was a midas tamarin – a rare thing of beauty in those parts.

And so it went on. There was a particularly dramatic form of night hunting that they'd learned from the Brazilians using battery torches: *lanternando* the technique is called. We'd go out at night on the Nipukú river. I'd have a torch tied to my head, attached by lianas to the plastic lining of a construction helmet the FUNAI people had given them. I was placed in the prow of a canoe with a rifle at the ready while my companion paddled silently from the stern. My job was to scan the banks and rocks. The torch beam would pick out the eyes of caymans – deep ruby red – and my steersman would edge us towards them until I judged it was near enough for a shot.

When various stands of trees came into fruit, men would go out and build hides, little platforms and screens, away up near the level of the fruits. These skills were beyond me. They'd cut a liana and make a heavy hank out of it. They'd stick both ankles through this and use it as a gripping device as they shinned up thin trees, grasping the trunk with their arms, pulling up their feet, pushing up their bodies, grasping again, and so on. Perched on a branch they'd haul up short poles, more lianas for tying the poles, and palm fronds to make the hides. When prepared they'd crouch in the hides for most of the day waiting for toucans, macaws, and other brightly coloured birds to come in. The birds were shot silently with specially designed arrows. The main purpose of the complicated and risky operation was to get coloured feathers for the marvellous head-dresses they make.

Tree-climbing and hide-building were superb skills, as were many everyday activities. It was brawn, together with delicate hands and artistry. Making canoes was another example of that. It was a difficult job. They had to use axes with the precision of planes, day after day, hollowing out the log. Then, in a short, feverish burst, the narrow hollow half tube had to be forced apart over a fire into a more oval shape by rushing up and down its length, amongst the smoke and flames, jamming in lengths of stick at the appropriate places. Too thin a hull, too much forcing, and the sides might have cracked and weeks of work might have been ruined in a moment. It's so easy to give bland descriptions: 'They made canoes', 'They made tree hides', 'They practised slash-and-burn agriculture', leaving out the skill and patience required, and the effort and pain that has to be endured.

'They hunted.' That too leaves out the skills; the speed of reflexes, the co-ordination of hand and eye (that fearful symmetry that kills the animal), and the hard bursts when you had to run like hell after fleeing game and risk getting torn on spikey bits or tripping and having a bad fall. (And when you were on a run like that you just put the matter of snakes *out* of your mind.) But all in all hunting was enormously exciting and as long as you were fit enough for a day's walk, and as long as you could manage the short bursts of pursuit, it wasn't a particularly demanding physical activity.

Modes of destruction

They related to their natural surroundings in a different way from the way we do; different in scale and in quality; different in conception and in feeling. Our relationship with nature is catastrophically destructive. Theirs was healthy. That said, I'm going to risk the view that it was strictly the differences in material constraints that maintained that difference. It's not their knowledge, beliefs, or sensibilities that maintained the benign state of affairs they found themselves in. It was the physical constraints of the mode of production.

We share a common humanity, ourselves and Amazonian Indians, all the way back to the Neanderthalers:

> There must have been laughter amidst the apes when the Neanderthaler first appeared on the earth. The highly civilized apes swung gracefully from bough to bough; the Neanderthaler was uncouth and bound to the earth. The apes, saturated and peaceful, lived in sophisticated playfulness, or caught fleas in philosophical contemplation; the Neanderthaler trampled gloomily through the world, banging around with clubs. The apes looked down on him amusedly from their tree tops and threw nuts at him. Sometimes horror seized them: they ate fruits and tender plants with delicate refinement; the Neanderthaler devoured raw meat, he slaughtered animals and his fellows. He cut down trees which had always stood, moved rocks from their time-hallowed place. . . . He was uncouth, cruel, without animal dignity – from the point of view of the highly cultivated apes, a barbaric relapse of history.

We're all implicated in that barbaric relapse. It's a *homo sapiens* problem. Give a Wayapí a chainsaw and he would take down forest as profligately as any Brazilian frontiersman. Wayapí people did indeed have a rich cosmology that made sense of their relationship with the woods and waters around them; images and beliefs about tree-masters, animal-masters, and the all-powerful Anaconda, the master of water. These images reflected their sense of a shared existence in a shared environment with other living things; an intimate and immediate relationship. But the images didn't hold back the tide of technological elaboration.

During the first contact phase in the middle 1970s I used to argue with the authorities that introducing steel axe heads was fine, but that the liberal distribution of shotguns was a serious blow to their self-sufficiency. If they gave up bows and arrows, forgot both the skills of making them and the skills of using them, they would forever be dependent on the outside world for brass cartridges, percussion caps, powder, and lead-shot. I was guessing, having only just stepped into the woods. I was only beginning to come to terms with the spectacle of an isolated group entering an intense period of contact. My major worry was seeing them getting into habits that made them dependent on the outside world. I wasn't aware that there was any immediate threat to the fauna.

There was no doubt about it; they *wanted* shotguns. They could kill so much more. The day out would be much easier and much more successful. You could easily prepare ten brass cartridges in a morning. Bow and arrow making involved a small culture of its own. Bow wood came from a certain tree, found only in the Capoeira headwater area. I never saw it done, but apparently you had to cut through the decaying trunk of the fallen tree to get at the heart which was particularly hard wood; a deep dark red wood. The bow length, more than 6 feet long, was roughly shaped with an axe or machete, then carefully scraped down with the jaw bone of a white-lipped peccary, using the edges of the incisor teeth as a plane. Nothing else would do. No knives, no machetes for the last fine stage. Pigs' teeth it had to be. (I suppose we'd call that 'magic'.) The bowstring was made of cotton cord strengthened with resin. The arrows were bamboo with expertly bound flights of feathers tied at the nock end and with various points, some for big game, some for birds or fish.

I took part in the last hunt from the Nipukú that was entirely with bows and arrows. (It was Siro, so skilful as usual, and it was white-lipped peccaries he got too.) I also remember the moment when the last set of bow and arrows from the Nipukú was traded in for a shotgun. It was part of FUNAI's 'attraction' policy to swap a bow and arrow set for a shotgun – satisfy the Indian, establish the dependence, and take the artifact back to the city where it could be sold in the Indian Craft Shop to recoup the outlay.

A decade later, two of the best hunters, two Nimrods if ever there were any, blamed the matter of the disappearing game on their own changes in technology. Joaquim had seen that the change to firearms had shot out the game in the area and he explicitly blamed FUNAI for removing their ecologically friendly bows and arrows and substituting the destructive technology of guns. Siro pointed to his 8-year-old son and explained that the boy had never in his life seen a white-lipped peccary. The great herds of these pigs, the most prized game after the occasional tapir, had vanished from their lives. Everyone knew that the incursion of the road and the arrival of Brazilians had something to do with the disappearance of the white-lipped peccary herds, but these two mighty hunters were willing to incorporate their own new-fangled habits of guns into the equation and accept that their own mode of destruction had become too profligate.

As the Brazilians came upon them, they could see a dramatic contrast between their mode of destruction and that of the invaders. They were aware of how enormously greater the destructive power of the Brazilians was. As a result they feared for their surroundings as much as they feared for their autonomy. In those days Waiwai had a fierce harangue that he returned to again and again, a formulaic declamation, as if in iambic pentameter, describing how 'the Brazilians spoil the earth; they spoil the waters. The Brazilians empty our great woods of game.' Their appreciation of what was happening made them conservationists *avant la lettre*.

Women and manioc

The word 'manioc' is a Tupian borrowing. It refers to a fat, oblong tuber, like a large potato. Wayapí say *mani'o*, with a glottal stop. 'Cassava', the other word by which the plant is known today throughout the world, comes originally from Taino, a now extinct language that was spoken in the Caribbean islands when the European invaders first arrived. *Manihot esculenta*, 'eatable manioc', is one label our scientists use. Another is *Manihot utilissima*, and extremely useful it is too. It is the basic foodstuff found right across the Amazon Tropical Forest.

It is a profoundly important plant. In the cultures where it takes centre stage it's accompanied by an elaborate technology of its own; its own special set of scrapers, sieves, squeezers, and pans. It is also dramatically dangerous. The Brazilian Portuguese term *mandioca brava* gives the clue; *brava* you could translate here as 'wild' or 'fierce'. All the commonly used varieties contain hydrocyanic acid, sometimes called prussic acid (since it was found in the pigment 'Prussian blue' discovered in Berlin in 1704). When this substance reaches our stomachs it can release cyanide and kill us stone dead. Prussic acid is found in laurel leaves, in peach and cherry kernels, and in bitter almonds. Before the Second World War it was manufactured commercially in Germany as a pesticide under the tradename Zyklon-B, produced in the form of crystals that turned to gas when released into air. On 3 September 1941 in a cellar at Auschwitz Main Camp the gas was first tried out in the murder of 600 Soviet prisoners-of-war and 300 Jews. The experiment was judged a success, and for more than three years after that an infernal technology of prussic acid was refined at that place, its name now an icon of evil. The substance that did it all is what makes manioc so dangerous.

How on earth did these Tropical Forest cultures discover and develop a plant like manioc, learning how to transform a deadly tuber into a staple crop? That question remains mysterious. *Why* these peoples continued to rely on it as a staple when they might have taken to simpler crops like yams, potatoes, or maize, does have a few answers. First, there are straightforward functional reasons: manioc is easy to plant, produces good yields, and the tubers keep well if left in the ground. Second, the process of preparing manioc results in a remarkable range of products and by-products. In that sense it's an extraordinarily rich plant. Third, and more speculatively, you could argue that there's a cultural value in the elaborate preparation processes. Wayapí, like everybody else, were delighted by technological advance and labour-saving techniques. Machetes and steel axes made life in the forest enormously more comfortable. Switching from bows and arrows to shotguns made hunting a lot easier. But if some kind of futuristic manioc-processing machine had been introduced and accepted, all sorts of aspects and nuances of art, ceremony, technological knowledge, role activity, and daily rhythms would have vanished.

Fourth, if you appreciate the cultural value of the procedures (call it the symbolic or ritual aspect of manioc preparation if you like) then you could go on to suggest that the complicated arrangements for the processing of manioc reinforced a status quo where any imbalance of gender status is weighted in favour of men. Certainly men did the work to prepare the gardens. They felled the trees, cleared the area, and burned it. Both men and women did planting. Both men and women weeded and cared for the garden. But just as you wouldn't see a woman arriving back in the village carrying a basket of game, so you wouldn't see a man come into the village lugging a heavy basket of manioc tubers. When the morning's work in the garden was over the women got loaded up to carry the produce back. Similarly, the array of scrapers, sieves, and squeezers was made by men, and it was indeed wonderful art work, especially the tipití squeezer. But the drudgery of using the things was work for women.

New gardens were prepared at the height of the dry season, by our reckoning we'd say about September or October. Frequently a man with no appropriate male relatives to call on would do the work on his own. The undergrowth in the chosen area would be cut first then a start would be made on the trees. There was some planning to the extent that a few trees in the same area would be only half-cut, then a larger one cut so that it would fall in a direction that would take the half-cut ones down with it. But apart from a minor design like that, the trees crashed down in all directions. The original choice of the area would try to avoid gigantic trees, but if that was not possible they would just be left.

The felling took a few weeks to dry out. November was usually the month for burning. It was a tremendous display of *son et lumière* when the fire got going. The noise was a gamut of sizzles, crackles, bangs, and explosions. During the day the sun ran through and through, lighting up the smoke palls in different ways, sometimes fog-white pillars, sometimes huge domes of sulphur-coloured fumes. At night the flames came into their own, and you could gaze at the spectacle for hours.

Planting had to be done before the rains came and work started as soon as possible after the burning. Although the garden looked as if it was the result of a bombing raid, a successful burning did clear a surprising amount of space amongst the confusion of criss-crossed fallen trunks. Leaving out the manioc, I noted a list of what I spotted in the various gardens at the Nipukú: six varieties of bananas (and they mentioned a few more they knew), yams, sweet potato, maize, ground nuts, pineapple, gourds, urucu dye, cotton, papaya, sugar cane, pepper, pumpkin, tobacco, cashew (valued for the delicious fruit rather than the nut), and a bush with small berries said to be a remedy for snakebite. You could do a thesis on each one of these.

Also, to add to that, were some wild fruits gathered at the appropriate times of year. The açaí and bacaba palms, found in large stands in swampy bits of the forest, produced their bunches of fruit as the rains abated and the dry season came on. Both I found disappointing as 'fruit' – a category I associate with soft, fleshy, sweet food. Açaí and bacaba fruit are rock-hard marbles that have to be soaked to get off a thin rind which is then made into a liquid flavouring. Açaí ends up an impressive deep purple, but is pretty tasteless.

What else? Brazil nut trees were rare in that area. These were large trees found in tight groups. The big brown capsules containing the nuts lay scattered on the ground. These were carried home in dumb-bells, two at a time forced on to the end of a sharp stick. The hard spheres were cracked open with a machete to get at the closely packed triangular nuts inside. The kernels of these were grated into a flour. Finally, pupunha ('peach-palm' in English) was delicious; big bunches of orange-coloured fruit the size of small eggs that were fatty and savoury when prepared. Pupunha palms you could say were semi-cultivated. People knew where they were, usually near old abandoned gardens, and even talked about them as belonging to particular individuals.

But manioc was foremost. It was very easy to plant. Sections of the twiggy, knobbly stem were cut into sticks and these were stuck into a little mound of earth that had been scraped up. That's all there was to it. They would be ready the following year. There was no harvest since the tubers didn't keep for long once they had been dug up. They were left in the ground and at each visit only a few days' supply was taken. The women carried the load home. Sitting one day with two young women who had just arrived with their loads of tubers, sorting through them, and asking about the different kinds, they produced words for fifteen distinct varieties.

The tubers were cleaned, peeled, and grated. These days everyone had sheets of tin made into graters by punching rough holes into the sheet with nails. Grating was strenuous and looked like the way old fashioned washboards were used here before the days of the washing machine. The result was a large pile of mushy pulp. This was kneaded through a basketwork sieve, the liquid pressed out being collected for later use. The drier pulp was then fed into the tipití, a long thin cylindrical basket with loops at both ends, the bottom end closed and the top end folding out into an opening as if it were organic and sensual. The tipití was filled up, and a gourd or piece of wood stuffed into the top. It was then hung by the top loop usually on to a jutting-out house pole. Another pole was put through the lower loop and wedged under something to act as a lever. Each woman knew a spot where there were suitable poles both for hanging the tipití and for wedging the lever. The woman would then sit on the end of the lever – a restful part of the process – pulling the basket tight and squeezing out more liquid which was again collected in a pot set below the tipití.

When the tipití was taken down the pulp could be extracted by taking the tension off the basket, pushing the ends together as you

Squeezing the tipití [A flute dance in the background]

would a concertina. The pulp came out in fairly dry cylindrical lumps that looked like white artillery shells. These were piled up one on top of the other and could be left like that for some time before they were broken up into flour on a basketwork sifter. The flour was spread out in a thick, even film on a large circular pan, like a griddle, heating over a fire. The heat took off the last of the volatile prussic acid. The flour became glutinous and the bread formed. When lightly browned on one side the large circular loaf was flipped over and browned on the other. The finished bread was tossed up on to the sloping roofs of the houses to dry off in the sun.

The juice, that was previously squeezed out and collected, separated into a clear liquid on top (called *tucúpi* in Wayapí) and a chalky white sediment on the bottom. This sediment was *tapioca*. The tapioca could be separated, squeezed, and made into a second kind of bread, either in thick white glutinous slabs like the ordinary manioc bread, or in thin white wafers of the consistency of Melba toast. Two kinds of tapioca bread, then, to add to the standard manioc bread.

The *tucúpi* liquid, the clear liquid on top, was boiled up (which evaporated off what was left of the prussic acid). It was now ready to make *mingáo*. Dollops of chalky-white tapioca were mixed with water and boiled. It turned into a grey, viscous liquid. Into this went a little *tucúpi* liquid mixed with hot red pepper. It was gently stirred so that the *tucúpi* goes through the grey tapioca and was suspended in brownish tracks. Although the most honest metaphor I can think of for the appearance of *mingáo* is grey runny catarrh, it was the most perfect breakfast. It was served in a calabash, about a pint of it; a great pint of snot in a bowl, and hot in both senses of the word, both heated up and peppery. Incidentally, in Amazonian Portuguese the word *tucupí*, with the stress moved to the end, refers to Wayapí *mingáo*. *Mingao* in Brazilian Portuguese has come to be a general word for porridge of various sorts. Semantic drift like that, when a vocabulary lurches over from one language to another, can be particularly wayward when it concerns food words.

Going back to the flour that is sifted from the cylindrical lumps that come out of the tipití, there was one other important product made: *kwaky*, or, as it's put in Portuguese, *farinha de mandioca*. Instead of baking the flour into bread, it was thrown into a large pan with high sides and while it was on the fire it was agitated to and fro with a wooden hoe. It didn't coagulate into bread but remained grainy and ended up like oatmeal. Kwaky was a basic subsistence food, always prepared before a journey, and loaded into large heavy sacks. You could eat it in handfuls when you were peckish, mix it with water into gruel, mix it with açaí juice, eat it with fish or game, and it seemed to last forever without going off.

Manioc bread, two kinds of tapioca bread, minga'o made from tucúpi, and kwaky were the main products of the tuber. There were further names for all sorts of other concoctions made by mixing things to the bread (for example Brazil nut flour or banana flavouring). And of course it was from manioc bread that beer, caxiri, was fermented. You can see why, in basic functionalist terms, the manioc tuber was a cornucopian source of food.

But it *is* the case that manioc preparation was bad news for women. While it wasn't a daily grind, a woman seldom got more than a couple of days off the carrying, cleaning, scraping, grating, stuffing, squeezing, baking, boiling, mixing, fermenting, and distributing. You could never argue that the division of labour evened up; that the men did the strenuous exertions of hunting, leaving home sometimes at dawn, facing the dangers of the woods, having to run, shoot, and carry, and that that was balanced over against the tertian or quartan carrying and grinding and squeezing and everything else that women had to do in manioc preparation. That's nonsense. The drudgery for women was much more relentless, and they were frequently having to get on with it while carrying a baby in a sling at their side. It was the familiar scene – as well as the manioc preparation, there was the child care, and the cooking, and the serving, and the whole damn lot.

That part of the procedure when the tipití squeezer had been set up and the woman sat on the levering stick appeared like a welcome spell of rest. A similar restful period came her way when she was menstruating. She would stay in her hammock, or at least within the house, and would not do any cooking. She would, though, spend her time spinning cotton. The lumps of cotton seed would have been taken home in a previous trip to the garden. They were emptied on to a mat and beaten with a stick to fluff them up, rolled out into strings, and attached to a spindle, a stick looking like a slender top with a notch at one end and a disk near the other. Spinning that again and again produced a remarkably strong thread with a variety of uses: tying feathers in

55

headdress-making, tying on arrow points and flight feathers, waist-belts, and so on. Huge balls were used up in hammock weaving.

When Waiwai would do one of his chiefly harangues in the morning, complaining about everything, one of his favourite themes was that the women should get up early and bathe in the cold river so that they wouldn't be *lazy*. The concern that women should be industrious was the explicit reason given for subjecting girls to an ordeal when they first begin to menstruate. We'd call it an initiation ritual or a rite of passage. Because there were no similar trials for boys to go through to mark any change in their status, it leaves the Wayapí way of doing things seeming particularly unpleasant in its treatment of women.

When she began to menstruate the girl had her head shaved and was strictly secluded. She was kept off the ground, and if, for instance, she had to go to relieve herself, she had to make her way to a suitable spot along tree trunks or by walking on something. Before her seclusion ended one of her male relatives wove a small belt out of a palm leaf, which, like the tipití squeezer, could be slightly expanded and contracted, tightening and loosening the weave. He then went off to the forest to collect tapicium ants; monstrous shiny black things that were about an inch or 3 centimetres long. They had a poisonous sting in their abdomens. The ants were stuck into the belt, perhaps ten to fifteen of them, and were held there wriggling. Then, while the girl was held firmly by her mother, various male relatives applied the belt to her arms, legs, abdomen, back, and brow. The excruciatingly painful procedure would, it was said, see to it that she would not be lazy and would get on with all the work women were supposed to do. When I first saw it being done, older girls and women were happy to confirm the ideology, explaining that it had been done to them and hence they weren't lazy.

This is the sort of example that raises controversial questions about the relative status of women in such societies. Between Wayapí men and women the imbalance was obvious, reflected in the division of labour, a painful initiation ritual, and manners of speaking that made laziness a particularly female vice. That condition was established with particular firmness through the details of manioc production. Since manioc was the staple food, and since the form of preparation was so elaborate, the processing worked both functionally and expressively to fix the gender relations between Wayapí women and Wayapí men: doing the endless manioc-work as well as most of the child care made a woman's role relatively servile.

But an oppressive blear and smear of toil? That would be an exaggeration. Women had a great deal more to do than men, and had more put upon them by men. But both men and women enjoyed that ease of existence so characteristic of primitive life; 'the original affluent society' as it was once described. As a Marxian mode of production it was one of the best that has ever existed in the world, one of the best there's ever been, in any example to be found from sociology, ethnology, or archaeology.

Accepting that, the imbalance between the sexes remains a dilemma inviting ethical judgements. Could it have been otherwise? Are there better alternatives? Suppose material life had been based on something less elaborate than manioc preparation, would that have ameliorated the women's role? Some examples of what are called 'hunting and gathering' societies (societies where agriculture is at a minimum), do indeed suggest that the simpler the technology the less likely it is that such an imbalance between roles will emerge. Generalizations like that are tempting. Materialist explanations like that are attractive in their grounded finality. But alas, they hardly ever survive a check against the complexities and varieties of cross-cultural comparisons. Cultural possibilities are unending.

3

OTHER VOICES

'What was it like?' People ask that with such genial curiosity. I enjoy the unintended nuances of the question. What did the forest look like? What did it sound like, smell like, feel like? What were the people like? What was it like to live like that? At first the words sound awkward. It wasn't *like* anything at all. It was so *unlike* anything else. But there are imaginative surprises in the question. Perhaps it's asking for a metaphor in its most exciting form: 'We haven't been there. Throw us an image to carry us across. The metaphor will take us there.' Or perhaps they are resigned to the practicalities of metaphor in its humdrum mode: 'Don't tell us what it *is*, since that is away beyond us, so instead tell us what it's *like*. The metaphor will bring it home to us.' Both movements of metaphor are implied in the innocent question.

Early on I found an easy response. When asked, I'd start telling yarns about exotica; about animals, or food, or initiation rites. Tell about the sound of howler monkeys at dawn, about eating grubs, about what's done to a girl when she first starts to menstruate. Recount a few adventures: the 'hunting wild pigs' story; the 'shooting the anaconda' story; the 'cayman's eyes in the torchlight' story; the 'getting lost in the forest' story. One or two like that and, like magic, the questioners are entranced.

I've never been comfortable telling these stories. As the audience turns away, animated and pleased, I'd want to say: 'Hang on a bit. You don't think *that's* what it was like, do you? There was so much more to it than that.' But it's too late. You had the experience but missed the meaning. The yarns can be interesting in themselves, but they're really only worthwhile if they're a way to get further in; make people see more connections; make them think and change.

If the 'What was it like?' question, put to me today,
satisfied with a few anecdotes, when put from a hundred years
it becomes much more demanding. Those who ask it will want
something more than entertainment as they strive to grasp the
vivacity of being there. They will have the advantage (which we
don't when we look back a century) of tape-recordings and disks,
photographs and films in unprecedented quantities. With that they
could get pretty close. Making the supreme effort of learning the
language would get them even nearer. But it will always be just
out of reach. No matter how much can be learned in those ways,
no matter how many facts or images are available, people will still
ask: 'What was it like?' They will always need commentary.

So far, all that is available for them are commentaries from the
outside, like mine. There are none yet from Wayapí themselves.
Here, as alternatives to mine, I'm going to offer a few hints of
what it might have been like from three other very different points
of view. When I went back to see the Wayapí after a space of some
years, there were three new arrivals there, three men, each making
his own kind of impact on the lives of the Wayapí. A missionary
had managed to get in; that was Tobias. A new FUNAI official
had been appointed, Lusitano by name. And a Wayapí youth who
had been removed from his home as a child and brought up in a
Brazilian city had finally been sent back to his people. The first
two said quite a lot. The third, Namiro, kept his mouth shut, but
every gesture and movement of his body was loud with confusion
and pain. Three voices, then: the holy, the bureaucratic, and the
exiled.

Missionaries

I know that the word 'missionary' covers a multitude of sins. But
no matter what they dedicate themselves to in terms of other good
works (medical care, social comfort, political intervention), it's a
reprehensible activity whenever it involves proselytizing. The
Christian sects of monotheism (rather than the Islamic and Judaic
ones) are especially prone to produce people gripped by a drive to
draw into their obsessions as many other mortal souls as possible.
Their efforts become particularly unpleasant when they target the
most vulnerable societies left on God's Earth, and think it's some
kind of achievement to gain control of their minds, hearts, and
spirits, and their souls too. The Summer Institute of Linguistics is

a worldwide missionary organization dedicated to this kind of wickedness:

> A Summer Institute of Linguistics worker once said that the most important thing that he'd done was to convince the people who thought that humanity was fundamentally good, that in fact it was fundamentally bad.

If I was ever to feel forgiving, I'd be easier on the bluff businessmen, the stern entrepreneurs, and the scrawny frontiersmen. They see the Indians as an irritation that has in some way or another to be got rid of. Theirs is an ignorance that has a tinge of honesty about it. They live in a technological world and have nothing to learn from what they see as backwardness. But missionaries don't have technological pretexts for their interference. Certainly they declare that they want to keep their subjects alive, that they want to protect their health, that they want to look after their well-being. Of course they do. They can then get on with enthralling their subjects into their theologies of damnation, destroying *en route* delicate ways of thinking, ways of being, ways of acting, ways that are quite beyond their comprehension and compassion, all the time saying that they are doing good. How can that kind of hypocrisy be forgiven?

Let's blame the crime and forgive the criminal. On the day I met him I became very fond of Tobias. He was charming and gentle, welcoming and warm. He had established himself, with his wife and two women helpers, in a large concentrated settlement on the Igarapé Onça, a few hours' walk upstream from the FUNAI post. I'd been visiting a few scattered, isolated settlements further into the woods, and was coming down the Onça, heading for the post. It was nearly the end of my time in Wayapí lands.

There were really only three more days, but they were such uncertain days that I longed for them to be over. I didn't know the big settlement on the Onça and was worried about what I'd find – anxious about meeting so many people I hadn't seen for so many years, and anxious about seeing what the missionary had done. Since leaving the village I knew best, the one at Mariry, I'd been trying to see every single person before I had to go home, and although I was fit for the walking, it had tired me out. But worst of all was the strain of being constantly asked for these things I didn't have.

You arrive at an isolated hut where there's a family you haven't seen for years. 'Now, *tairo*, now,' you say as you walk in. 'Yes, now,' comes the reply. 'Is your day well, *tairo*?' 'Yes, yes, it's well.' And a few moments later you get asked: 'What have you brought?' Oh no, not that again. I'd long exhausted my gifts and had nothing to give away in these scattered dwellings. I'm sure they didn't mind that much, but I could never brush the question aside. It always made me feel tense, especially since I depended on them for food. The best I could do to ameliorate my anxiety was to accept promissory shopping lists of things I'd bring back in some hazy future. And here I was off to the last village – a big one, where all the problems would be magnified.

Off that morning, then, on the second last walk – from Matapí's place to the big settlement on the Onça – guided, as I'd been for the previous few days by young Arema and his child wife. A strange little group, the three of us. The girl hadn't said a word or made a sound; never looked in my direction; always rested some distance away from us. Was she shy, unhappy, terrified? Her shell of silence was daunting, and I didn't dare try to break it.

We'd had our adventures along the way. We'd come across a puma. That was the trip where I shot the small black marmoset with bright orange feet, which turned out to be a red-handed tamarin, the 'midas tamarin'. On that remote path we also came across a burnt down angelim tree with bananas planted along the swathe the falling tree had cleared. 'Yasito did this.' It was an ancient grandfather-people practice, making little oases of food along the paths. Angelim trees are huge. They have bark like a redwood, and you can burn down living trees by setting a small fire at the base of the trunk. The fire takes, and in a few days burns out the base of the tree.

A short day's walking that time. Soon we were at the abandoned airstrip cleared for FUNAI some years before. The remains of the unfinished post were sticking out of the secondary growth, white, like Greek ruins. 'Here's where they killed Sarapó. They did it with clubs. Nothing left of his face and head.' This was also where the 'buffaloes' had been abandoned – another one of FUNAI's crack-brained schemes. I'd heard of them but somehow got it into my head that this talk of 'buffaloes' was just a slang way of saying 'cattle', but not a bit of it. Before we got to the end of the airstrip there they were: four massive black buffaloes, one of them a bull with an enormous spread of horns, crashing about at the edge of the strip. The bull began to charge, stopped, turned and went off bellowing and snorting into the bush. What a frightening legacy to leave behind. Matapí's and Toka's people were terrified of them but had no idea what to do about the problem and were resigned to running the gauntlet every time they used this path.

Just on three hours and we were there; huge garden clearings with the village set down by the waterside. We appeared without warning, arriving from the hinterland rather than coming in, expected and announced, on the main path from the direction of the post. What excitement and what a welcome. Smiles everywhere, boisterous greetings, and children crowding around. I was unused to so many people. Tzako, Yapakani, Yurara, Mikotó, four men I knew best from before, showed me where to hang my hammock and came to sit nearby. Lots of joking; good jokes too.

There was a lull and a silence as I began to unstrap my rucksack to get my hammock out, so I said *sotto voce*: 'I've nothing left to give.' 'Oh, it's all right that you haven't brought anything. We can just be friends,' they said. And finally, Tzako, lowering his voice too, said: 'It's all right. The *karai-ko* [Brazilians] bring things.' Then he gave a little smile. What a relief that arrival was.

Through the crowd came Tobias – crisp white shirt and dark trousers, quiet and confident. He took my hand: 'A great pleasure. You are much talked about. You will eat with us later.' As he turned to go I realized I was being invited into a Brazilian's home to meet his wife, family, and two young women. But I'd only Wayapí garb – I'd be going to his house half-naked. 'There is no difficulty. To that we are well accustomed.'

The schoolroom was on one side of the village, walls of wattle and daub, and a door. Inside were planks for seats and desks. Four o'clock that afternoon was men's time. (Women's time and children's time was earlier.) My friends left and wandered to their houses. They ambled out again with stout plastic bags in their hands. These were for their pencils and writing books. They drifted around a bit, then filed into school. There was a gentle reluctance in their movements, as if unsure of this new rule of time and space where all the men had to do the same thing in the same place at a certain appointed hour. The door was closed. For an hour or so the mournful chanting of letters rose and fell.

The dinner that evening at Tobias's was wonderful, especially the coffee that finished it. I knew exactly what I was doing with the prim etiquette and the dainty table manners, knives and forks, side plates, and so on, and I also knew the rules by which I could accept that gift of hospitality. (The anxiety that accompanies

In the mission schoolroom

accepting from the Indians is a result of your never being absolutely sure what the rules are.) The meal over, the dishes cleared, the rest of the family disappeared to another part of the shack. Tobias and I were left chatting. I rudely changed the tone and burst into an interview, but his pace never hesitated even a syllable. It was as if he'd been waiting for it.

Yes, he was under the umbrella organization of the Summer Institute of Linguistics. Baptists and Methodists were all involved in the SIL, although his particular church was founded in Brazil by a Scottish Presbyterian last century. So what *was* Tobias's role here? 'It's to give general support, to give medical assistance, to teach them how to write, and to leave them the Bible.' What about the autonomy of Indian life, their self-sufficiency? Shouldn't we respect that and not interfere with their ways of living? 'Well, yes of course, but you must remember that this country needs development; it needs change. Indians can't be left in isolation. It is their aspiration to be integrated into the national society. You can see that. It's obvious in the way that these Wayapí are becoming more sedentary.' How do you know they're becoming more sedentary? 'You can tell by the way they count their gardens over the years. It's their aspiration to become more sedentary. We don't interfere. We don't judge. We show the direction and leave it to them.' But what about their beliefs, their myths for example? 'Well, once they're integrated, their culture can be conserved. They can then transmit their myths better themselves.'

But you always mention the Bible; you always quote the Bible; what has the Bible to do with their culture? 'The Bible carries the message of life into *every* culture. It satisfies *every* culture. This matter does not concern relations between cultures. It is a message about man and his creator.' Well, why not just teach them Portuguese so that they would have access to a Portuguese Bible? 'We missionaries live in the present. I am blessèd that the Bible was translated into Portuguese for me. We translate the Bible into their language for them. We don't force anything. We make options for them. They are free to choose.' Are you going to translate the *entire* Bible? 'The Bible is an integral book. Yes, we have to translate it in its entirety.' And how long will that take? 'It doesn't matter. We live in the present.'

The argument was relentless but at the same time amiably relaxed; the result of utter conviction and, no doubt, many rehearsals. It was punctuated by numerous biblical references, chapter and verse, and accurate quotation. These mild, compelling cadences – 'We are volunteers', 'We live in the present', 'We don't force anything' – they were like a balm. How many hours did I spend with Tobias? I haven't the slightest idea. I know I was at peace with myself, all anxieties over. And perhaps it was because of feeling so at ease that I drifted into an understanding of that point of view – the consistency, the confidence, the certainty; resigned and blind.

> Here was perfect purity, perfect intrepidity, perfect abnegation; yet there was also narrowness, isolation, an absence of perspective, let it be boldly admitted, an absence of humanity. And there was a curious mixture of humbleness and arrogance; entire resignation to the will of God and not less entire disdain of the judgement and opinion of man.

> I have surely the right to protest against the untruth . . . that evangelical religion, or any religion in a violent form, is a wholesome or valuable or desirable adjunct to human life. It divides heart from heart. It sets up a vain, chimerical ideal, in the barren pursuit of which all the tender, indulgent affections, all the genial play of life, all the exquisite pleasures and soft resignations of the body, all that enlarges and calms the soul are exchanged for what is harsh and void and negative. It encourages a stern and ignorant spirit of condemnation; it throws altogether out of gear the healthy movement of the conscience; it invents virtues which are sterile and cruel; it invents sins which are no sins at all, but which darken the heaven of innocent joy with futile clouds of remorse. There is something horrible, if we will bring ourselves to face it, in the fanaticism that can do nothing with this pathetic and fugitive existence of ours but treat it as if it were the uncomfortable ante-chamber to a palace which no one has explored and of the plan of which we know absolutely nothing.

I left the house entranced. It seemed that I'd been away in a different world. I'd been allowed to enter it; I'd understood it; I'd seen 'what it was like'. To give yourself up to the bosom of fanaticism is such a comforting step. With a shrug you then deflect the moral responsibilities for your most terrible actions of inhumanity and destruction on to something else – the cause, the leader, Old Nobodaddy Aloft.

Walking up the path to the village I emerged from that strange world, surprised by the process of coming back to ordinary awareness, like that shift that you go through having been absorbed in a novel or having come out on to the street after an engrossing film, when the surroundings are not quite right for a moment.

The threadbare patches of this particular holy mantle show up quickly. The comments about Wayapí 'aspirations' and about them becoming more 'sedentary' are the result of a superficial glance and a wishful prayer. You can see, behind these comments, that old suspicion of people who move, who won't stay still, who are . . . shifty. It's not a religious point of view. It's a reaction that has to do with fear of losing control over those who move. There's nothing religious about the 'integration' and 'development of the country' stuff. That's the kind of talk that comes straight out of the mouths of generals, politicians, land speculators, and anyone else who sees a quick buck to be made out of destroying the Amazon forest. And biblical quotations are charming, but those who do it use the same repertoire. You've heard them all before.

I got back to the Indian houses and got into a hammock to chat with my old pals. It took an odd turn. 'Will the earth burn up soon?' I was asked. Years before I'd heard the myths about the end of the world, when the great fire will come, and been told of a then quite recent time when that nearly happened. They'd seen the 'red sky', and 'smoke' (or 'mist') was everywhere that year. But I'd never come across a present anxiety like this. It had been mentioned at Mariry, and again on the Araçá. Some of the younger men were to mention it again the following day when we were on the path, not long after we'd come across an agouti (a red-brown rodent, like a long-legged guinea-pig). 'The earth is going to burn up, isn't it?' Why do you say that? 'All the agoutis have disappeared.' But we've just seen one. 'Yes, but they're all ill.' And here, this night, the older men were asking me the same questions. There had been so much 'smoke' and 'red sky' at the end of last year's rains. The killing at the air-strip was thought to be a possible reason. 'Yaneyar [the Culture Hero] is angry.' If Yaneyar gets angry he may send the great fire to end the world.

That's where my suspicions began. Why were they so worried? Why these vapours of guilt drifting around Wayapí lands? And why were they so particularly pronounced here, in this settlement?

I don't know. Maybe in years to come I'll be able to give the Wayapí survivors of the future a clearer account of missionary influence. If I can't, then certainly by their time, they'll be the ones who will know. They'll be able to judge what was lost, and what of that loss was due to the influences of the missionaries who brought along their gifts of fear and guilt and shame in their fearless, guiltless, and shameless way. I'm condemning them out of hand, am I not? Who's to say my judgements are not exaggerated or misplaced? And who's to say my influence was so innocent? The survivors are the only ones who can judge that properly.

The sky on that last night was magnificent. The huge garden clearings that had been cut gave view to a breathtaking expanse of stars. I slept well, and noticed in the hours before dawn that even those horrible cockerels that the Brazilians had introduced didn't yell very loudly. Maybe they'd been missionized too. There was a grey sky and drizzle when daylight broke, but that soon cleared into a lovely day. I found myself first up – off to bathe at 6 o'clock. This place seemed to take its time to get going. I got through a lot of names with Tzako (still at the lists of names till the last), visited various houses, gave away the very last trinkets, said goodbye to the missionary helpers (and got a second breakfast of coffee and bread and butter), and to Tobias, already by that time in school at children's hour – then off.

Kere was to take me through to the road. Mikotó, Yurara, 'Maranhão' (a Brazilian given name), and Taroko came half way to go off on a hunt. Such a difficult path it was. I had a couple of bad falls. But such a joy throughout that walk to find myself at play with the language, playing with it, joking with it, as if tumbling about in clouds, doing the impossible. I felt I'd *got* the language; finally broken through. Kere and I went on for another hour or so to the road. There he waved goodbye and disappeared back into the woods.

Away, alone, at last, along that Brazilian road, that ghost road, empty and wide. The building of the road was a violent disaster that Wayapí lands will never recover from, but I could enjoy a private excitement when coming on it alone. The difficult walking was over, but most of all I could see so much more, both at my feet and around me. So much more bird life was visible, both high in the air, and along the edges of the wood. And *views* – of trees away in the distance, and of a massive sky, beautiful clear blue, with some great white puffy blocks of cumulus drifting in from the east and high cirrus motionless beyond. Each turn of the road up ahead looked like the same dead end, until rounding it I got a new vista. Each new stretch had its own character, a changing series that any of us could eventually get familiar with if we lived there long enough. I'd made it. I'd got through. The dodgy knee had held out. The footwear had held out – just – the right shoe was coming apart at the uppers. No serious falls. No snakebite. The walking now was a dawdle. It was another emergence, coming through another layer, another of these transitions where every feeling is in tremor and every sense is on edge. Coming through into what?

FUNAI

All over Amazônia, a couple of generations of Indian people had already grown to be suspicious of the word FUNAI: Fundação Nacional do Índio – the National Indian Foundation. It sounds like a charity, but it was the government department that was supposed to deal with Indian affairs. Before 1969 it was called the SPI, Serviço de Proteção dos Índios – the Indian Protection Service. It had been founded in the early 1900s by Cândido Rondon, an officer in the Brazilian army, a great explorer, atheist, and Comtean free-thinker. Comtean free-thinking was all the rage in Brazil at the turn of the century, hence the words 'Order' and 'Progress' on the Brazilian flag. Auguste Comte's stirring sentence from which the words were taken ended up with the word 'Love'. Why didn't they put that on the flag too? 'Ordem, Progresso, e Amor' would have been wonderful, Love being exactly what was missing from Brazilian politics.

For his times, Marshal Rondon's dealings with Indians were admirable. He insisted on respect for them, a certain kind of respect: they represented us at a previous stage of our development. If we are adults, in terms of our civilization, they represent us in our childlike state, so we respect and protect them rather as we respect and protect our children. Since the story all over the Americas always was and still is one of contempt for indigenous peoples, leading to their degradation and extermination, Rondon's view was indeed enlightened.

Often, contacting isolated Indians was a dangerous affair since they were for obvious reasons fearful of their lands being invaded and would kill those encroaching, and it was Rondon's SPI that

had as its motto: 'Morrer se preciso for; matar nunca' ('Die if you
have to; never kill'). There are heroic stories of SPI men coming
under attack and accepting death by arrows and clubs rather than
using their guns to defend themselves. 'Lest one good custom should corrupt the world'? Well, no.
Rondon's one good custom was no more than a trifling impediment
to the corruption into which his SPI degenerated. A major step in
revealing the scandal was Norman Lewis's 1969 article in the
London *Sunday Times* called 'Genocide: From fire and sword to
arsenic and bullets – civilisation has sent six million Indians to
extinction'. I don't think the full extent of the rot was ever written
about. It became clear that there were even incidents of SPI
collaboration with extermination raids. The Brazilian military government reformed its SPI, called it FUNAI, but apparently left most
of the previous personnel in place. In the 1970s, when I first had
dealings with FUNAI, the outfit was always run by minor generals,
one after another, whose brains were never in the slightest troubled
by thoughts of Auguste Comte or free-thinking.

The rationale that ran right through the organization was
absolutely clear: FUNAI was there, as an arm of government, to
assist in the development and progress of the country. The higher
levels of government saw Indians as an irritating impediment.
FUNAI was supposed to sort out that problem and its job was to
get the Indians under control, peaceably. Indians would be
protected from violent encroachments by frontier Brazilians, their
land would be protected, and they would be given rudimentary
health care. Well, the health care was so rudimentary that FUNAI
posts were just as much dispensaries of illness as of medicines. And
in saying Indian lands would be protected, it wasn't the Indians
that decided how much land was to be 'theirs'. Those lands so
designated were still in the hands of the Brazilian government to
do what it liked with, if, for instance, valuable mineral deposits
were found.

It was all based on a monstrous lie, a monstrous inversion of
justice, whereby Indians were described as intruders in a land that
was said to belong to Brazilians. Indians were described as an
obstacle that had to be removed. The Brazilian invaders were
described as being on a brave and worthy venture which would
transform their country for the better. Anyone in the FUNAI
organization that didn't or couldn't share these presuppositions
wouldn't be around for long.

There were clever techniques for bringing about domination over the Indians. If the group were known as *Índios bravos*, that is, if they had been resisting contact with outsiders in any even mildly violent way, then a team would go into their area, find evidence of paths they were using, construct a small shelter on the path, and leave gifts – mirrors, knives, machetes, and so on – strung up like garments on a washing line. The team would then withdraw and return some days later to examine the shelter. The trick was to wait for gifts to be reciprocated. Then the team would know it was worth the risk of going forward to attempt a face to face, or rather hand to hand contact.

If the group were known as *Índios mansos* (*manso* means 'tame'; used of animals) then these nerve-wracking preliminaries could be dispensed with. The team would find a village (perhaps from an aerial survey) then march in and start giving gifts. They'd build a post in the place that most suited them, then encourage the Indians to move near the post. For an 'Attraction Front' as this stage was called, there was plenty of funding, and plenty of everything to give – cloth and hammocks (which wear out and have to be replaced), torches (batteries wear out and have to be replaced) and above all guns (which need ammunition). Everything would be fine until it was decided that the 'attraction' phase was over. Then the funds were stopped. The Indians had then to find a way of producing something or other that would pay for the cloth, the batteries, and the ammunition. Their self-sufficiency had been effectively eroded. All sorts of dependences would have been established. They had been caught in a material gin-trap.

Was it all inevitable? When the survivors look back and see what was done, how will they mourn? With unyielding bitterness, or will their anger be tempered by resignation? At the time it would have been argued that 'development' and 'progress' were absolute imperatives. That's what civilization was supposed to depend on, after all. The great forests would be entered and occupied, tamed and made productive. The word 'destroyed' wasn't part of the vocabulary. Exploration and exploitation, domination and control; these were the guiding ideas.

The point is not to argue that there should have been no contact, no attempts at education, no teacher, no nurse, but to state that if the nature of that contact could not be guaranteed then the Indians would be better off without it. Instead of helping health, the intrusion destroyed it; instead of helping minds, the intrusion crippled them. The entire organization of FUNAI was so shoddy that it was quite incapable of carrying out its grandiose schemes. It talked easily about Indian education and about projects for social development, but it was confronting problems so delicate and so profound they would baffle the most committed and experienced educationalists and social reformers. Nevertheless, FUNAI hired anyone who might have had basic schooling and sent them off into the woods to make decisions about the future of entire cultures. Suppose we thought of the Lord God Almighty as having the temperament of an excitable teenager and the administrative vision of a school janitor. That's what the Indians were landed with.

There's one other item to add to this deadly equation. So far it goes: one monstrous lie plus institutional incompetence together with social and moral ignorance. Add it all up and the sum total produces bogus authority. It was horrible to see chiefs like Capitão Waiwai and Capitão Renato, men who would face up to the Brazilians with the stern cultural dignity of an entire Indian people, being shouted at and ordered about by a pompous half-wit invested with power by virtue of being a minor official in a decadent organization. What kind of power was this?

It was horrible to see mothers, like Japonês and Nazaré (to give them their Brazilian sobriquets), women so skilled in keeping life going and who had so often been bereaved when their babies died, being treated like silly schoolgirls, their anxieties and pleas brushed aside as if they were just minor nuisances. It was horrible to see people whose lives were informed by the decency of an integral culture being treated as if they were all in need of the kind of special care that might be offered the feeble-minded or the mildly delinquent. How did those petty officials dare think they could deal with Wayapí people in that way? And why did Wayapí people put up with that outrage?

In the early days they thought they had to put up with it, since they saw the FUNAI presence as their best hope of survival. But as time went on they learned not to be so manipulated. The road programme, which had started the final cycle of disaster in 1973, suddenly collapsed in 1976 due to Brazil's national economic crisis. The suspension of the road was a major event that gave the Wayapí a period of respite to find their feet and have a look at what was coming at them. They were not overwhelmed by immediate land invasions. The dam-building schemes, the land-grabbing, the

71

massive prospector invasions, and the large-scale burnings that went on to destroy so much of the rest of Amazônia passed this area by, for a time at any rate. They got used to FUNAI and I'm sure that by the mid-1980s they had at least to some extent learned how to manipulate the agency for their own ends. But given the political set-up and given their final vulnerability, it would be wrong to say that they'd got the better of FUNAI and that they had learned to do the exploiting rather than be exploited.

I was urged by FUNAI to make reports and recommendations. Indeed I was told I *must* present reports. I did so, seeing possibilities of resolution or at least amelioration, responding to the urgency of the situation. I went openly to those with executive power, met them honestly, and thought I was getting an honest hearing. I dutifully presented my suggestions and reports. But what I never quite bargained for was the exquisite Brazilian word *engavetado* – 'put into the drawer'. Everything I wrote, everything I said was en-drawered. I was merely carrying out required responses, genuflections in writing. Nothing was followed through.

If you persevere too much with the recommendations and reports you'll find yourself on a road that leads to frustration and anger, and finally to a *saeva indignatio* which will boil itself away to a blank and useless cynicism. So, if you want to 'cut the cackle and pursue real ends', as Hugh MacDiarmid put it, and if you find that these ends are hopeless, you have to change them. You have to accept that nothing is going to be done, and instead you have to stick to being a chronicler of the ineptitude, the stupidity, the indifference of those into whose hands the fate of Indian peoples are placed. You have to say to yourself that although you may not change anything, keeping the commentary going is fundamentally important. The real end will not be to change the course of events and turn history around, but just to try to get it down and to speak to those elsewhere, those distant from here, those survivors in some future who will be curious.

FUNAI philosophy was not complicated and obscure. FUNAI's purposes were not shrouded in mystery. FUNAI's operating techniques did not require specialized skills. It was all too easy to understand. The mistake I made was to assume that the ordinary intelligence and humanity of those employed by the organization would lead them to treat the crudeness of FUNAI's ideas and policies with appropriate nonchalance when it came to important day-to-day events and important decisions that affected the Indians. I thought they would, without a second question, step out of their silly bureaucratic postures and get down to working with a genuine concern for the predicament of those they were sent to look after. I thought that in the face-to-face dealings with real people, whom they were bound to get to know as friends, they would regard the notion of 'integration' as an unfortunate piece of rhetoric that we all had to live with, and that we all would ignore as best we could; and that they would regard the Statute of the Indian, with its description of these people as having the status of minors in the eyes of the law, as an absurd fantasy concocted by well-paid government lawyers away down there in the cities. No one with a germ of common sense or a moment's experience of Indian life would give the official views the time of day, would they?

Lusitano came from a relatively privileged background. He had a university degree, and postgraduate experience. During his spell in military service he had had specialized training in jungle survival. Educated in mind and body, he should have been just the sort of person whose humane scepticism would take him beyond the inanities of the organization whose official he was, and allow him a humane vision of what he was doing. Well, maybe.

I suppose it was Koropi who brought it all to its denouement. A young man, he was powerful, wild, and witty. In the woods he was competent and careful, and he was a mighty hunter too. He'd been 'taken' after the 1971 prospectors' invasion, and spent a year or two in one of the small Brazilian towns downstream on the Amaparí before being brought back by FUNAI. He could do a bit of Portuguese, but instead of turning into a half-way-house sort of person, he became an outright irredentist. His experience of Brazilian life gave him a special edge in being able to argue for Wayapí rights. There was no nonsense with him when it came to negotiating with the Brazilians. He knew them. He could speak a bit of their language. He had no fear of them. He hated them.

FUNAI had established a presence at Mariry: two women and a man; a nurse, a teacher, and her husband. They lived in the biggest structure right in the middle of the village. It was like a mansion: kitchen, living place, sleeping quarters, pharmacy, all built on high stilts with slat walls to give privacy – a big, high house – a structure of domination. Mariry wasn't one of those compact places, all the houses cheek by jowl. It was well spread out in a string of three nuclei connected by paths through the forest. You could be in one area and not know what was going on in the next.

Once upon a time, there was a spree in the south area. Towards the end of the day, people were breaking up and going home. At nightfall I was on my way back to the central area where the FUNAI mansion was, and on getting close heard a commotion of shouting and screaming. Koropi had arrived there out of his head with drink, angry, resentful, full of years of hatred, and armed with an axe. He had begun to chop away at the posts of the FUNAI mansion, shouting his head off in Portuguese with every foul word he could remember, threatening the FUNAI people with instant death. The FUNAI personnel had been shivering inside – a particularly frightening predicament, where the foundations of your fortress are being chopped away by your demented avenger, and where at any moment you are about to fall into his berserk arms.

Koropi's classificatory father had grabbed him at some point during the attack, and in this lull, the FUNAI people fled by the back ladder and took off in the dark to the canoe anchorage. They had a miserable night on the river and got to the post the following day. One (false) charge later directed against Koropi was that the teacher, who was pregnant, had aborted on the way. Whatever went wrong with her was known by all the Wayapí women to have gone wrong the previous day.

I hadn't properly realized the extent to which this village was now being overseen. Like Tobias the missionary, and like any Wayapí, I was living in the present, and felt that the departure of the FUNAI people was a welcome relief. I had no foreboding of future repercussions. I didn't appreciate that away down the line they would be grumbling about what had happened and working out a response. Ten days without them; ten days of . . . integrity.

Their return was like a raid by bandits. They appeared suddenly in the middle of an afternoon – a whizz-bang arrival. They certainly had the element of surprise on their side. Lusitano led the way, followed by his wife, the fugitives, and two Wayapí employees, who had their own quiet agenda for a visit like this. The fugitives came in quickly, trotting, their heads down, their bodies tense with resentment, and scuttled up the ladder into the mansion without a word to anyone. Lusitano arranged his show-down in the pharmacy room. He summoned Koropi and Capitão Waiwai – why Waiwai? – he's only a 'chief' in Wayapí terms. He had had nothing to do with the incident, and had not the slightest control over Koropi or anyone else. But Brazilian fantasy about the nature of power thought that Waiwai was going to be the key.

How I hated to see them shamed. But they took their shaming better than I would have done. They were shouted at for about an hour. (Why do these Brazilians always have to *shout*?) Lusitano's line was to be loyal to his employees, hence they were to be blameless. There was to be no negotiating, no listening; just a harangue: 'I've worked hard to get those people here. I've got you a nurse. I've got you a teacher. If you want them to stay then *you must keep your caxiris away from the FUNAI house.* One more incident like this and I'll see to it that all my people are removed.' (Caxiris referred to the sprees they go on when they make manioc beer.) On and on he went. Koropi was told he would have to apologize to the returnees he had frightened away. Apologize? Was he supposed to know the Portuguese formulations of how to say 'I'm sorry'? During the harangue came a curious blunder into social history: 'You people have only recently learned these habits of *caxiri-wasu*. You've got to learn how to deal with these new habits of drunkenness.' (*Caxiri wasu*, *wasu* meaning 'big', referred to a really serious spree.)

With his few words of Portuguese, Waiwai struggled to express his complaint that the Brazilians always came and went. The complaint was ignored. What he was trying to get across was that the coming and going brought in colds and flu, and that the village had just been through a bereavement. The previous time a FUNAI person had gone on leave she had come back with a sniffle. A minor epidemic had swept through the place, and a baby had died.

The simple home truths were that it was impossible for any person in that settlement to keep away from the FUNAI house given where it was sited. Caxiri sprees are, and always were, as central a part of Wayapí life as the manioc they make the beer from, and if Brazilians wanted to live in a Wayapí village they would have to accept that. It was not a privilege for the people of Mariry to have these ignorant Brazilians settled on them. Waiwai correctly complained of their coming and going and the concomitant dangers of bringing in illness. It is not a privilege for Indians to have people come to their villages with diseases that kill their children. The Mariry people were aware of how the child had died a few weeks earlier and were resentful of the casual way they were being treated. I found it difficult to judge, over the years, if

FUNAI people really did not see the connection between the colds and flus they brought in with them and the damage it did the Indians, or whether they did accept the connection but couldn't care less since proper control measures would have inconvenienced their travel and holiday arrangements.

After the shaming of Waiwai and Koropi, Lusitano disappeared to the north end of the village. While he was away, his wife gathered a group of women round her outside the FUNAI house and started another harangue. It was the women's turn to be shamed. She screamed at them with extraordinary stamina, bawling away like an NCO on a parade ground. Her message was that they were not bringing up their sons properly, and that various young men were not now the pleasant children she used to know. She also announced that in her opinion the young man, Namiro, who had a few weeks before been returned to his people and was beginning to adjust, was 'no good'. Later, Lusitano's gloss on this to me was that Namiro was 'introducing Brazilian sexual practices to the Indians'. Where was all this tosh coming from?

Lusitano described himself as 'knowing everything that went on' in the Wayapí settlements. He saw himself as 'sitting at the centre of a wide range of connections' where he received 'a salad of information'. It was an appropriate image. He sat there on his post, apart, getting fed a diet of rumours, gossip, spite, exaggerations, and lies, and constructed his appraisals and plans for action on that basis. Similarly, his staff at Mariry had skulked for months in their cabin-mansion, making occasional forays through the village, but most of the time peeking, peering, glimpsing. It was not standard practice, for instance, for the medical attendant to visit the houses. Babies who were ill, and any kind of walking wounded, had to attend the pharmacy. Those two ladies of Shalott sat and wove what they saw through the slats, and away downstream went a finished web of distortions and fantasies. They were fearful, isolated in the foreignness of the village. They were uneasy about their work, conscious of their inadequacy and laziness. They were unsettled by not knowing what was going on round about them. They felt surrounded by evil intent. So they wove their paranoid elaborations. That's where the nonsense about Namiro's sexual practices came from.

In the dark that night it was my turn. But I wasn't to be shamed. Lusitano tried to put it diplomatically: *not* for the sake of those 'stupid women employees he had to put up with' but for *his* sake, would I please leave? I had 'become a problem' for FUNAI. Three points were mentioned. As a 'translator' I was not on hand when most needed, that is, to save the day when Koropi went berserk. Second I spent my days getting drunk on caxiri with the Indians. Third I talked to the Wayapí in their language and turned them against FUNAI. 'The women don't like you', he announced gravely. Well, it wasn't FUNAI's village. Also, he'd have to apply to a much higher authority to have my permission cancelled, and that would require evidence. His request was refused.

We got locked into stubborn arguments about *indigenismo*, the policies and politics of FUNAI. His education had given him a formidable fluency, and his views certainly did have an edge of intelligence that was usually lacking in recitals of FUNAI dogma. There were moments when the discussion felt like a heated academic seminar. But altogether the added sharpness made the arguments not more convincing but more alarming. He followed the dogma without question.

He was firmly closed to any suggestion about the need for care in the coming and going of FUNAI personnel. 'Indian deaths have nothing to do with that. The disease is present in the population and goes in cycles, just as astronauts can go into space healthy and come back with flu.' Postgraduate training in biology or not, the sub-text here was that any other arrangements would be inconvenient for FUNAI.

On money, his ideas were tinged with originality. He wanted the Wayapí to become familiar with money. It was 'his first step' in educating them. He wanted the teacher to leave off 'stupid' FUNAI programmes of literacy and concentrate on *numeracy*. That's an excellent idea, but the manner of its implementation made it farce. He'd taken to giving the Indians money in exchange for goods they turned in (featherwork, bows, pottery), and, for instance, on this occasion he'd brought 7,000 cruzeiros to pay one person. However, the payment was months overdue; there was no foreseeable occasion when the person might use that money; and Brazilian inflation was running along in colossal figures. The bits of paper were soon to be worthless. When the argument got round to that, he changed his ground. 'We have to use money. It is the only mode of exchange that is understood by both sides.' Suddenly the Good Idea had degenerated into nonsense – a Good Idea draped in carelessness and insouciance. A Good Idea, like encouraging numeracy, takes time and effort. The exchange of money had nothing to do with the Good Idea. What it did was to make everything just so much more convenient for FUNAI.

He had worked hard with local authorities and construction businesses to get the abandoned road repaired. His efforts had paid off and road grading machines had been sent to do the job. But what was the road for? The benefit was that FUNAI people could move around with greater ease. He claimed correctly that he had worked hard to respond to Wayapí demands for a teacher and a medical attendant. But they wanted miracle workers, people with magic wands who would transform their lives. What they got was these two. And once installed, the major FUNAI effort of movement, communication, and supply was to support them.

All over Amazônia, FUNAI set their employees down amongst indigenous communities in similar cuckoo operations, dropping a large, useless, all-demanding presence into small harassed communities. The organization had not the slightest trouble in stating what it thought it was doing through these operations. It said it was concerned with the welfare and protection of Indian rights, protecting their land, protecting their health. You'd also hear, time and time again, explicit mention of the policy of 'integration': Indians were not to be left alone to follow their own ways, but were to be absorbed into the Brazilian way of life – get them into clothes, get them speaking Portuguese, get them made Christian, and for goodness sake get them settled and stop them all moving around. The word 'integration' connoted a fantasy image of benighted savages benevolently received into the arms of a benign civilization which will offer them all their hearts' desires. But strip the fantasy away and the word was revealed as a wholly negative one. 'Integration' meant removing self-sufficiency, eroding integrity, reducing land area and the possibilities of movement, exposing the people to ill-health, destroying their cultural self-confidence. Above all, it meant getting Indians to do what they were told.

Having listened to what FUNAI said, it was a good idea to take a close look at what FUNAI did. You might have found yourself pushed towards the most sinister interpretation: that the organization was used explicitly by government to see to it that indigenous life was exterminated, not by overt murder, which would be unacceptable to North American and European opinion and therefore politically inept, but through a deliberate policy of incompetence whereby, through doing as little as possible, the economic, social, and biological pressures of invasion and illness would solve the 'Indian problem' once and for all. That is to say, FUNAI was a deliberate cosmetic 'for the English to see', as they used to say during the nineteenth century when Brazil presented bogus anti-slavery measures to the outside world as a way of placating the British Navy and keeping it from interfering with the slave trade.

I'm sure there were influential government functionaries who saw it like that and were happy that the organization was left to muddle along in its hapless way. In this view carelessness and incompetence would be indications that all was well. There were also numerous cases, documented in newspapers and in reports to various welfare bodies, of corrupt and criminal behaviour by FUNAI staff – sexual misbehaviour that introduced syphilis and gonorrhoea, financial corruption where Indians were cheated for profit, and criminal collusion with outsiders involved in murdering Indians.

As regards deliberate muddling, I don't know what was said about Indian policy behind closed doors at the highest levels of government in Brasília. But it's difficult to imagine how institutional incompetence of that kind could have been so deliberately and carefully planned for. It seems too elaborate a hoax. Similarly, while degrees of corruption were found in all aspects of Brazilian public life and were clearly an ordinary aspect of FUNAI's doings, I would guess that the worst atrocities of criminal behaviour were isolated incidents. I wouldn't be convinced, without a great deal more evidence, of such extreme judgements of the organization as a whole. I'd suggest a blander view.

At all levels of the organization there were glimmers of energy where people did see themselves as trying to get a job done. At the highest level there were statements, overt and covert, about where that energy should be going in terms of social and political purposes. But when you looked at what was going on in the indigenous areas you'd see that the energy was self-absorbing. In FUNAI's forest-world, FUNAI was centre-stage. Indians were on the sidelines. Once in operation, FUNAI had next to no moral purpose, next to no humanitarian purpose, little legal or practical effectiveness, no didactic or informative end. FUNAI was primarily there to look after FUNAI. In the 1940s an American literary movement called the New Criticism made current a hard-edged word for this kind of strange, etiolated state of affairs. They described it as *autotelic*. No purpose, no meaning, no end. FUNAI was just *there*; there for itself.

Namiro

Lusitano had FUNAI behind him. Tobias had the Scottish Presbyterian Church and the Summer Institute of Linguistics. What did Namiro have? A *déraciné*, *déclassé*, or in Portuguese, *desclassificado*. He had nothing. He had been taken, like a slave, by an official in the Brazilian Air Force to Belém during that awful period when the Wayapí had been going back and forc to the Rio Cuc, fraternizing with another Indian people at Pirawiri, and falling victim to the epidemics and disruptions that were taking place then. He had become an orphan, although in a society with a classificatory terminology, when you lose your actual mother and actual father, there are still plenty of classificatory mothers and fathers around who will treat you as their own. But he had been taken out sometime, I would guess, in that spell between 1970 and 1972. If so he would have been about 5 to 7 years old.

He was taken away rather as an exotic animal would have been: a possession, partly for display, partly for use. For some time he lived on the Air Force base in Belém, like a sort of mascot – a working mascot. He had to learn to do chores. He was then passed on to a vet, and was kept there as a house boy, sleeping in a corner of the surgery. His personal development and progress had flourished along two lines: learning chores and learning religion.

A piece of Hollywood hokum went the rounds a few years ago called *The Emerald Forest*. It was based on an incident that had taken place in the forests of south-western Brazil where a boy from a family of poor frontiers-people was abducted by Indians. For the film-fantasy, it had to be a blond, blue-eyed American who was abducted. The theme appeals to profound fears where our children are in danger of being spirited off into dark primitive worlds to be forever changed unless we can redeem them. Yet so many of us seem to be able to turn the values upside down when the situation is reversed and an Indian child is taken into our world. We can be unmoved by this parallel tragedy, as if in this case we are doing the child a favour by rescuing him from the darkness of his birth. It can't be too much to ask us to appreciate the equivalent horror that relatives of the Indian child have to endure as he is taken off into a world which they accurately perceive as being implacably hostile and threatening. Namiro got precious few favours.

As the years went by his master and mistress evidently began to tire of him. He was growing up into a strapping youth, and his behaviour was becoming difficult, surly, unmanageable. FUNAI were contacted and asked to take him away. After all these years the engaging pet was turning into the adult specimen and had to be returned to the wild. Perhaps 'caged up in the zoo' might be the more appropriate metaphor, given the way indigenous peoples were being treated. I had turned up at the point when FUNAI were arranging his trip home, hence they asked me to look after him on the way. We were to travel together on the flight from Belém to Macapá. I was going back after an absence of seven years. He was going back after the absence of his childhood.

I was picked up by the FUNAI driver in the evening, to get to the late night flight. We drove to the vet's place somewhere in the middle of the old town of Belém to pick up Namiro. There was a problem. He was ready, spruced up in a white shirt and grey trousers. His gear was on the doorstep: a small case, some sort of camp bed wrapped up in brown paper, some sort of tray, also wrapped in paper, and a battered plastic carrier bag. But he also had a large cardboard box, secured by criss-crossing string, of Bibles. His instructions were to distribute these amongst his people when he got there. The FUNAI man immediately recognized that the weight of the books put Namiro well above his luggage allowance on the plane, and had to convince the passenger, who was insisting that the Bibles had to go too, that 'everything would be all right', and that the box would be forwarded by FUNAI to the Wayapí reserve as soon as possible. The box of Bibles was never seen again.

Namiro's usual posture was with his head bowed. I can't remember him ever smiling at that time nor did he look at people face to face. He gave the impression of being unable to speak either Portuguese or Wayapí competently, as if he had been brainwashed into being a simpleton. But how could anyone assess the shock he was going through? The two of us flew to Macapá and arrived at the ICOMI compound in Santana in the middle of the night. As usual, FUNAI communications had gone wrong and we were not expected. Lusitano had to be wakened to get quarters for us. Despite being disturbed, he was ready for business and a session of intense talk. The first theme, at 2 a.m., was a firm lecture to Namiro about his state of being a *crente*. This Portuguese word 'believer' is used of those who have taken up one of the fundamentalist Protestant sects, and has a born-again ring to it. Namiro got a good dressing down, I suppose partly for my benefit. 'I wouldn't have let you back, given this *crente* stuff, but you're a Wayapí and therefore have a right to know your people. But do one thing for me. Before you start any preaching, talk it over with me first.' When the lecture was over, he turned to me and explained how he was never paternalistic when dealing with Indians.

The following morning I went over genealogies with Namiro, locating him exactly. I thought I should be teaching him some Wayapí words, but either I was only reactivating a vocabulary that had gone dormant, or he was gradually letting slip his reluctance to admitting that he knew the language. He certainly had no trouble remembering people and names. I was explaining who I had stayed with in the past, who had moved where, and so on, when we came to a discussion of Parahandy, my closest friend. I gave his Brazilian name, Paulo Antônio, then the Wayapí name that Parahandy had said was his. 'Oh, I know' he said, 'that's . . .' and he gave a name I'd never heard before. I checked and rechecked. Yes it was him. There was no doubt about it. I was taken aback. All those years knowing my best friend, and the real, secret name had never come out. I knew also at that moment that I should never be able to tell him I knew.

More pieces of Namiro's story began to emerge. He had been taken on a trip to Argentina by an American missionary. He could add three figure sums. He could read simple prose, though with little idea of what he was reading, stopping at the end of every line, enjambed or not, and starting up the next line anew. He could recite the names of various countries, and mentioned the Iran–Iraq war. He'd been watching television in another room and came through to tell me that 'England has just got a new king.' (Princess Diana had had a child.)

He was indeed *desclassificado* in an accurate sense of that terrible word. His Brazilian and American minders had done next to nothing to make him a Brazilian, and he knew next to nothing about being a Wayapí. What was he? He had been well fed, kept in good health, and been sheltered, but he'd had less of a life than a Brazilian street urchin. He said that he had now 'handed himself over to Jesus' but I hardly think that gave him much of a community of identity with anyone.

The journey to Wayapí lands had changed by that time – a 4-hour journey by truck instead of a 16-hour trip up the river by canoe. We had to go to the FUNAI post, stay there, then go on to the end of the road from where we'd have to walk to Mariry, Namiro's eventual destination. We got in to the back of a pick-up truck and went roaring up the road in the usual demented way. About half way there we passed some of Yasito's group from the Araçá settlement who used to appear from time to time at the side of the road and live in a ramshackle group of shelters there. Two or three people ran out and flagged us down. We stopped and got out. This was Namiro's first moment of return.

We'd been flagged down by three young people. When they spotted him they screamed back to the others in the shelters telling them to come. Everyone came running. The truck, the Brazilians, myself, were ignored. There was nothing else to be seen but Namiro. When the older men ran up, they held him by both arms, gasped, and shouted out their appropriate relationship terms for him, turning to the others in voluble frenzy. Meanwhile Namiro went rigid. His arms were stuck straight down by his sides and he turned his face upwards towards the sky, mumbling something mechanically. There he was in his white shirt and long trousers surrounded by his people, nearly naked in their off-red loincloths, body paint, and long hair. He looked up, and away, and moaned.

There was some business to be done – young Arema was travelling to Mariry and had to be given a lift to the end of the road. That arranged, we all got on board and drove off. The scattered group stood motionless, expressionless, not a gesture, not a movement, gazing after us till we went out of sight. On the walk from the end of the road to Mariry, Namiro produced a Bible and walked with it tucked under his arm.

That evening we were both installed in an empty house that belonged to a family who had gone to the FUNAI post. When we were alone Namiro announced his plan. It had been explained to him that there was a *garimpo*, a gold-panning operation, near Aima, which had been taken over by the Mariry people after they had expelled the Brazilian *garimpeiros*. A few Wayapí had learned how to do the operation. That was the solution for Namiro. He'd go to the garimpo, get a lot of gold, and then leave for Macapá.

The following morning Namiro and myself joined a party of three who were going to hunt. He'd borrowed a shotgun and was eager to get going. Towards midday we reached a spot where we decided to split up. Namiro insisted that he was going to take a direction on his own. He was told not to, and we split three and two, Namiro going with Joaquim. Our three got back in the late afternoon. Towards evening Joaquim arrived to say that Namiro had refused to stay with him and had vanished into the forest. Was this a run for freedom? Or was it to do away with himself?

The following day Joaquim and Matam set off to look for him. Both expected that if they went to the spot where he was last seen, they'd find him there. But they came back early in the day having found not a trace. A number of men began to get ready for a full search the following day. That was Namiro's second night out. About ten of us set off the next morning, breaking up during the day to do sweeps in various directions. Part of the group met up again towards evening at some small shelters near Aima headwaters where we spent Namiro's third night out. On again the next day, again splitting up. We killed game during the sweeps and came back to the shelters to spend another night.

On our third day searching we thought we'd found tracks high on a slope, well off the path, but it wasn't entirely clear. The ground was dry. Could the imprints be tapir? Was it a tapir passing that had bent the twigs? But back down on the main path to Aima, on the far side of some ruined shelters we found clear fresh prints. We shouted for the others, and two of Namiro's 'brothers' caught up with us and went past running. I gave up at that point. They were going too fast, and I'd be a hindrance. Back at the shelters the other searchers were waiting. Some more people including three young women had arrived from Mariry bringing fruit and manioc bread. That was a much more comfortable night.

Off we went at first light down the Aima path following the tracks of the brothers. Within a couple of hours we heard hooting. They had found him the previous night and were bringing him back. He was hobbling on a stick, his feet in a dreadful state, having lost his shoes. He'd had four nights out on his own and another with his brothers. He was pale, but he was smiling.

It was a long hobble for him back to Mariry. The FUNAI people washed and bandaged his feet; food arrived from all sides; he was lavished with concern. If he'd needed a *rite de passage* for his re-entry, he had certainly invented a strenuous one. He'd become the centre of attention in spite of his stupid behaviour. But he didn't come out of his ordeal instantly transformed. The process was gradual. For weeks he refused to wear a loincloth. The Bible still went under the arm if he went off on a walk. When he did find his voice it was to make ill-natured complaints. It was the patient concern of his brothers that converted him, together with the joy of taking part in the sprees. His reincorporation was marked that day when he first put on a new piece of red cloth, got painted up by a few young women, and went off to get drunk. He didn't even know at that time that a wife had already been arranged for him.

He had been deadened by his routinized life as a slave, and it must have been a profound shock to be ejected suddenly from those routines. Whatever his initial fear of life in the forest with his barefooted, half-naked relatives, I'd have guessed at the outset that he would take to it since, for a young man, it's so interesting and eventful, especially after the kind of life he'd led before. But what he was given was much more than exciting activities and rich surroundings. He entered a community which so much wanted him there. However badly he behaved, however bizarre his manners, his people couldn't care less. His return was intensely important. After so much disruption to their community, after so much violence, death, and loss, one person had come back to them. Namiro himself had certainly been recalled to life. But more than that, for once a piece of Wayapí life had been restored to all of them.

The joy of the older men when they first saw him at the side of the road, the tenderness which came to him over the weeks from his brothers at Mariry, showed just how much he was one of them in a way an outsider like myself could never be. No matter if I could speak the language better than he could at that point, no matter if I dressed in a loincloth and painted up with urucu, no matter if I participated in their lives for years with all the anthropological charity I could muster, nothing I could do would ever bless me with the essential intensity of what Namiro meant to them. 'What it was like' for Namiro and 'what it was like' for me are worlds apart. Were the survivors able to join us, there at the Nipukú or at Mariry, it would be Namiro's welcome which would be theirs.

4

ROMANCE

Welcome joy, and welcome sorrow,
Lethe's weed and Hermes' feather;
Come today, and come tomorrow,
I do love you both together.

(John Keats)

I share a predicament with the Wayapí survivors in more ways than
one. Plainly, when I find myself in a Scottish landscape laid waste of
its trees by human activities, sitting at some ruins last used more than
a hundred years ago, I'm trying to imagine the voices of a dialect that
has vanished and the manners of ways that have gone. That's
precisely the effort those survivors will be making as they find themselves amongst the remnants of the forests of Northern Brazil.

But there's another less obvious way too. You might say that it's
one thing to try to understand an Amazonian past that is remote,
and quite another for me actually to have lived through that time
and to have had the opportunity to get to know the Wayapí face
to face. Well, there are shared possibilities and shared limits in
these two as well.

Hermes' feather

Both efforts try to grasp something about other people's existence.
The first tries to do it across time. I try to do it across cultures.
The first effort is based on the absolute primary condition that no
one is ever going to cross that barrier of time. So the survivors
can't deceive themselves that their imaginations will spirit them
across it, like some sort of science-fiction time-travellers. They're
not trying to cross it; they're trying to *see* across it. In other words,
you can't pretend about the present that you are in.

Similarly my effort is based on the absolute primary condition that I am not 'one of them' and I can never become 'one of them'. So I can't deceive myself that I'm some sort of culture-traveller who can assume different mantles like disguises, slipping out of one into another when I feel like it. In other words, I can't pretend that I don't have a past. It's precisely because the survivors can't time-travel that their question is so urgent and so interesting. It's precisely because I'm not 'one of them' that I'm fascinated by my encounter with them. Both efforts are formed by similar impossible limits.

Another way of putting it is to say that the understanding of Wayapí life that emerges – all the statements and insights, the feelings and intuitions, the imaginative constructs – all of them come into being as a result of the standpoint of distance, be that a consequence of being distant in time or be that a consequence of having come to them from a culture, a language, and a way of being in the world that is far from them.

Hence if I was to start 'doing anthropology', if I was to start making statements about these encounters with strangers, describing and assessing what the strangers do and how they live, it's important to appreciate how much of what I see and how much of what I say is my responsibility. I can't duck that responsibility by saying I'm going to be 'objective' in my descriptions – that's just a smoke-screen. It's a matter for celebration that I'm responsible for my interpretations, and a matter for delight that my interpretations are all I've got. There's no key at the back of the primer that I can look up to see if I got the translation right. I've got to make the best of it on my own and that's just as it should be.

Taking this even further, for all of us, whether we're doing anthropology or not, our interpretations of other people are the result of a living engagement between our conditions of experience and theirs. That means that whether we like it or not we are, so to speak, 'written in' to our accounts of these people.

There are remarkably entrenched pockets of resistance in academia to this way of looking at things. The defences usually go up around the idea of 'science'. Because we're doing some sort of science, a social science, it's said that we've got to have proper methods for observation which will guarantee results free from bias and from the awful spectre of subjective impressions. It's such a ponderous and unnecessary stubbornness. All of us, on all sorts of occasions, do science – we count, and measure, and weigh, and take things apart, and put them together again, and find causes, and think up remedies. We are scientists every day in the kitchen and in the garden and at places of work. We can learn how to classify wild flowers, and we can learn the secrets of geology. We learn how to observe the behaviour of animals and birds, discovering patterns by marking, mapping, plotting – science, science, science.

When you're living with people in the middle of the Amazon forest you're certainly doing a great deal of science – you're cataloguing unfamiliar objects, you're looking at the use of materials, at classifications of an unfamiliar environment, at procedures, manipulations, rituals. And learning an unwritten language from scratch is one of the most rigorous tasks any of us could be asked to do.

Of course we're doing all that, but what the science-obsession doesn't allow for is that we're doing so much *more* than that, and consequently we need all sorts of other words to appreciate everything else that's going on. We're living with people, talking, laughing, getting alarmed, mourning, helping, sulking, misunderstanding, cheering up again, and so on through whatever expanses of the thesaurus you need to make the point that what's going on is a human engagement, and not a scientific experiment. In other words it's a process of understanding, and its embrace goes far beyond measuring and verifying and finding causes.

The process is based on trust. It is based on an initial decision on our part that there is something there which is different, interesting, and worth trying to understand, not by standing apart from it and gazing at it from a distance, but by plunging into it and taking as much a part in it as one has the patience, skill, and temperament to do. Conversely, the most delicate and moving aspect of it is the reciprocal trust that people like the Wayapí offer in allowing us to take part.

The significance of our encounters is not given for us to pick up like a windfall. The significance depends on what we bring to the encounter, how long and how far we're prepared to stick with it, and how alert we are to its changing nuances. We go well beyond the accumulations of observation and fact. We are coming to terms with a relationship.

I'll offer examples of the way in which that relationship can appear with different intensities, where different assumptions are brought to it, and therefore different visions of it appear as a result. To do that, I want to return to the question of romanticizing an idyllic past, and I'll try to be more accurate about it; accurate about the question, and accurate about how the question is satisfied.

Wayapí survivors a century on will look back because a particular sense of curiosity has got hold of them. No doubt many of their friends will be more than satisfied with a visit to the folk-museum or the heritage theme park to get an image of how things were. It's sad to think that these cheap packages of the past will proliferate into the future, but what's the harm for those who are not asking the urgent questions anyway? If they want the passive comfort of a simple view, fair enough. But when the questions take hold, people change from consumer to participator. Their relationship with the past becomes alive. They expect to be uncertain about what they're looking at. They expect what they see to be protean. They expect their relationship with it to change.

When I wonder if I'm idealizing my picture of the Wayapí I try to think up miserable aspects of life there. But there's so little to think up; there's just nothing I'd want to call dingy; nothing to give the gloomy feel of Graham Greene's vultures on the roof, of T.S. Eliot's cooking smells in passageways, of George Orwell's blunt razor blades and grit-laden wind. I *try* to get to such detail. I *try* to be cynical. But what I think up glows. Am I just forgetting?

> Ô le pauvre amoureux des pays chimériques!
> . . . .
> Ce matelot ivrogne, inventeur d'Amériques
> . . . .
> Tel le vieux vagabond, piétinant dans la boue,
> Rêve, le nez en l'air, de brillants paradis;
> Son œil ensorcelé découvre une Capoue
> Partout où la chandelle illumine un taudis.

Poor lover of chimerical lands . . . this drunken sailor who invents Americas. . . . Like some old tramp trudging in the mud and dreaming, with his nose in the air, of dazzling paradises; his bewitched eyes find a Capua in those places where the candlelight reveals a hovel.

Drunken sailor and old tramp, maybe, but the visions are so compelling.

Eight of us were camping for the night during a strenuous expedition. We had gone west from Mariry, over the hills and into

Aima headwaters, a long way from home. There was unknown forest to the north, and abandoned forest areas to the west and south. The camp was three small shelters by a little stream – no clearing, although there was a space above in the foliage – a long ragged tear. Because of the slopes on either side, the canopy that could be seen through the hole seemed unusually high. It felt like deeper forest. People were tired and a bit perplexed. It was a quiet evening. I'd often been alone in the woods *between* places; say, one village four days behind and the next three days ahead, and felt a bit solitary at times like that. But I'd never felt as remote as this, even though with companions – really beyond the edges of everything.

A couple of monkeys had been killed that day. They'd been roasted and were stuck on spits over the fire for people to pick at when they felt like it. The smoke from the embers went straight up, the air so still, as the darkness began to thicken. The men were squatting in a half circle, their backs to the fire, chewing on bones, hardly conversing, low voices, laconic comments, getting ready to sit out the night. There were a few indications of their connection with the outside world – the shotguns, the knives that they cut the meat with, the faded red cloth, almost grey, that they wore round their loins. At that moment, these seemed casual accretions. What I saw was eternity in an hour, a sense of immense spans of time. The way they talked, their backs to the fire, their backs to one another, looking out into the trees, gave an image of their abiding presence in these enormous forests. Their postures showed how for centuries they had endured it all.

I was at the extremity of my world, at the end of a long thread. Back the way we had come, to the east, the path led to the village. A quick half day from there, on a good path, I could get to the road. A trek down the abandoned road would take me to the FUNAI post. Four hours in a truck would take me to Macapá and an airport – every stage getting bigger and faster and noisier. Turn the other way, however, and there were just the blank spaces on the maps. I felt that if I went further west I'd drift away into nothing.

But this was the heart of their space and their time; their forest that had supported this kind of life for hundreds of years. The emptiness of the forests to the west and the north was the only security they had. Their extremity in those days was where their villages were perched. And there, the forces from the east were gradually overwhelming them. The material self-sufficiency was being cut away: lead-shot and powder was needed for the metal cartridges, batteries for the torches and record-players, outsiders' medicines for the diseases the outsiders brought. Those were putting an end to their time. Land concessions, mineral concessions, prospector invasions, and the road were gradually putting an end to their space. At their extremity, they were drifting east into nothing. That moment in the shelters showed how much they had to lose.

These visions of a Golden Age come at you all the time. But how far do I want to push this before correctives come in? During Mary Wollstonecraft's travels in Sweden she crossed one morning into Norway and heard of an admirable way of life led by inland farmers of the far north. This is from her 'Letters written in Sweden, Norway and Denmark':

> You will ask, perhaps, why I wished to go further northward. Why? not only because the country, from all I can gather, is most romantic, abounding in forests and lakes, and the air pure, but I have heard much of the intelligence of the inhabitants, substantial farmers, who have none of that cunning to contaminate their simplicity, which displeased me so much in the conduct of the people on the sea coast . . .

Hers is a composite picture of beautiful surroundings and admirable people. We don't have much trouble identifying beautiful surroundings, especially when they are in danger of being fouled or destroyed. But are there really beautiful communities that display an 'uncontaminated simplicity'? Mary Wollstonecraft is delicately sceptical. You'll see the way she sorts through a pack of *abstractions*. (I'll mark some of the more obvious ones):

> The description I received of them carried me back to the fables of the golden age: *independence* and *virtues*; *affluence* without *vice*; *cultivation of mind* without *depravity of heart*; – with 'ever-smiling liberty'; the nymph of the mountain. – I want *faith*! My *imagination* hurries me forward to seek an asylum in such a retreat from all the disappointments I am threatened with; but *reason* drags me back, whispering that *the world is still the world*, and *man* the same compound of *weakness* and *folly*, who must occasionally excite *love* and *disgust*, *admiration* and *contempt*. But this description, though it seems to have been sketched by a fairy pencil, was given

me by a man of sound understanding, whose fancy seldom appears to run away with him.

The abstractions don't get us very far if we want to negotiate the area between fairy-pencil fancies and sound understanding. They're just not accurate enough.

Time and again the same old question comes up: 'What *is* there? What *am* I looking at?' You would think that one way forward would be to go all out for representational accuracy: just describe it; get the details down; just state, simply and clearly what's there. Try to keep the adverbs out of your narratives and the adjectives out of your descriptions, and go canny with the similes and metaphors. It would indeed be fine to throw your trust on to Calvinistic habits like that and know that you would produce a prose that was spare and exact. As a starting point, it would be a most valuable move to make. It might make anthropology more appreciative of the importance of description. 'Mere description' is one of the deadliest phrases going around in sociological circles – as if there was anything 'mere' about it. Imagine those who use the phrase referring to Thomas Hardy's depiction of Egdon Heath in *The Return of the Native* as 'mere description'.

I'm not thinking of what passes for 'presenting the facts' or 'presenting one's material' – falling back on a trawl through observations, schematisms, systems, tables, measurements, weighings, countings, stop-watch timings, and the rest of the paraphernalia of procedures and methodologies that go to produce the lumpen texts of the social sciences. I'm thinking of a lean and hungry prose that feels anxious about grasping significant details. And there's the point of Hermes' feather. All descriptions have their significance written in.

'Significance?' you could ask of leaden observations and measurements in the social sciences. 'Degree zero' might be your answer, correct though every dull detail might be – 'correct, but who cares?' 'Significance?' you could ask of Hardy describing Egdon Heath. 'Heavy with it in every sentence' you'd say. Hardy's description took the risk of being significant and got the show on the road. And it was indeed a risk. When he looked at the landscape he saw an 'ancient permanence', 'unaltered as the stars overhead'. But we are told nowadays that the heaths of Dorset and Devon are the result of woodlands being cleared by human beings for cattle-grazing. Apparently Thomas Hardy was *wrong*, as far as his knowledge of prehistory goes, yet it's difficult to imagine readers perverse enough to claim that they had been misled or that Hardy was foolish. The matter was already beyond that level of discussion.

We're always investing significance like this, and it would help if we were more aware of how much we do it, and readier to have a look at what we're doing. It's an undercover operation that's always on the go, and it would be much more invigorating to have it out in the open. All of us are off-loading our prejudices on the world all the time. We can do it in an unreflective way, or we can be a bit more circumspect as to how we do it.

Disagreements are a useful starting-point – simple fusions of vision and values which are fundamentally at odds one with the other. Here's a simple example. Yasito and Koroari, two brothers, with a fair number of people about them, had moved up the Rio Felício to a tributary called the Araçá and set themselves down there. The FUNAI staff would talk of this group as if they lived in a peculiarly awful state of *misère noire*. They were seen to be in need of special help. It was as if Waiwai's people were seen as comfortably middle-class whereas this lot had dropped into some sort of pathetic squalor. It was puzzling to think how these Brazilian outsiders could go about grading the standards of indigenous settlements, rather like local authority officials grading tenement slums. Given the technical simplicity of Wayapí life, the shared techniques and knowledge amongst such a small population, the close web of interrelations between them all, could there really be differences like this?

There was indeed something there at the back of the FUNAI descriptions – something to do with the fluctuating patterns of settlements. At one extreme was a sort of Big Village arrangement – eight, ten, maybe fifteen, family houses grouped higgledy-piggledy in a huge clearing, near a fair-sized river, altogether creating a feeling of lavish space, the forest walls pushed well back, and huge skies above. Nipukú in the 1970s was like that and so was the Mitikó settlement on the Onça in the 1980s, where the missionaries were. The houses would all be built on stilts with elevated floors made from slats of açaí palm, and a big log with steps hacked into it propped against one of the open ends to make a ladder. (If you go away for a while, or if you don't want visitors or prying children, you turn the log over with the steps pointing down the way.) That was a style of house-building they say came in from the north, from their contacts with people on the Rio Cuc and the Oyapoque River.

At the other extreme were the solitaries, the isolates – sometimes a pair of brothers and sisters who had intermarried, or a man and his family living with his wife's father and mother. The house would be remote, perhaps beside no more than a trickle of water, and it would be of the old type – four posts and the earth swept clean underfoot, none of this fancy stuff of a raised floor of açaí slats. If there was any clearing at all round about the house it would be small. The set up was much more like a temporary shelter than a 'village'. Some families would live isolated like that for years, then drift back to a larger settlement. Others would use it as a second home, and live partly in a big village, partly alone.

There were more than forty people in Yasito and Koroari's group. That's a fair-sized village. The path to get to their place began at the road and entered the forest through the middle of a collection of shelters they sometimes used there. The earth around these huts was infested with chigoes – sand fleas that burrow into your skin, often under your toe nail, and lay eggs there. No one thought of cutting a path round the huts. You ran through the shelters as quickly as possible and brushed the fleas off your legs as best you could when you got out the far side. Two hours walk took you to their settlement, and it was a bit of a surprise to arrive there. It was little more than a camp – forty-three people in half-a-dozen shelters crowded together. It did look like a pretty casual arrangement. They'd had more than their fair share of death, accidents, illness. One young mother had two hydrocephalic infants. As a group they had little to do with the Brazilians, and one or two of the men were notoriously sulky and difficult to get on with. The cumulative impression of all this got them labelled as degenerate in comparison with the other villages.

This is where the apparent rock-bed of facts and objectivity and precise description, the level we all supposedly can depend on, gets very squishy indeed. I can stand there with the Brazilian official and say 'How many houses?' – and we agree on that; 'What are they made of?' – agreed; 'How are they constructed?' – just so; 'Who's here?' – we do the litany of names; 'Let us number the ailments' – done; 'Any worse a medical predicament than the last place?' – no, much the same; 'So what do you think?' He tut-tuts with exaggerated paternalistic concern. The candles of his eyes illuminate *un taudis*, a slum. This old tramp finds a Capua, like William Blake and a companion watching the sunrise together:

> 'What,' it will be Questiond, 'When the Sun rises, do you not see a round disk of fire somewhat like a Guinea?' O no, no, I see an Innumerable company of the Heavenly host crying 'Holy, Holy, Holy is the Lord God Almighty.'

I was startled when I first came across the Araçá settlement. Many of the young adults I'd only glimpsed as children years before. Whereas I just didn't know this group, they knew a great deal about me and a lot of minds would have been made up regarding what I was doing there. I don't know whether they associated me more as belonging to the Brazilians on the post or more as belonging to Waiwai's group, but whichever way they saw it, I didn't arrive innocently at that place. I did indeed feel challenged. That night, a couple of young men, one with the manner of the young Marlon Brando, the other of James Dean, were positively hostile. The older people were distant and apparently indifferent.

There was certainly enough to start making contrasts, but it wasn't a contrast between Araçá people being essentially this, while Mariry people were essentially that, and Mitikó people were essentially something else again. I'd been two years with Waiwai's people so of course the atmosphere of my arrival here would be different, and a couple of strongly sulky young men in a group of forty-three was not excessively awkward. More to the point, it wasn't that difficult to see through the apparent material contrast: the chigoes, the mangy dogs, the crowded shelters, the lack of space. There was a contrast all right, but it was a contrast of aspect not of essence. They *were* the same people as everyone else I knew, but in a different phase. Everyone here knew how to build a house with a fancy floor of açaí slats, and if a family peeled off from here and went to live at Mariry or Mitikó, we outsiders would never notice the difference.

Everything was moveable; everything was changeable – that's the point. We're so accustomed to think of towns and villages as having some sort of permanence. We bestow that permanence on them by giving them names, and associate the name with a certain character. But there, the place names referred not so much to the human settlement but to the water it had been set by – everything from tiny trickles to fair-sized rivers.

Young people at the Araçá settlement

It's water that divided their earth. The vast continuous expanses of forest were marked and divided and given boundaries by the water courses. Hence the forest was mapped, classified, arranged, and named by water. The water and its name remained, but the human settlements did no more than occupy a boundary point from time to time. The settlement endured for a while, decayed, broke, and moved on, and let the forest return. Meanwhile, along we came, outsiders, with our presuppositions, had a look at a settlement, thought of it as an enduring thing, and gave it a description in terms of an essential quality. These judgements of ours were just doodles in the earth. It's the names that led us astray. We write our names on signposts. Their names were writ on water.

Meeting the Araçá people had all the excitement and apprehension of an initial encounter. It felt like starting all over again. My questions at the time centred on whether I was seeing a more traditional set-up than the other settlements I was used to. Was there really a much more intense concern here with shamanistic processes? Would I get a more vivid picture of the past from the older people here? Why were they still making these little oasis gardens on distant paths where they would burn down an angelim tree and plant bananas along the swathe? Why were they moving so often? That was my Capua.

Lethe's weed

I can go much further than that. All of them, not just the Araçá people at that moment, but all of them, at Nipukú, Mariry, Aramirán, Mitikó, all of them in whatever phase were, and are, my Capua. Meeting the Wayapí remains the central experience of my life. I can't find a harsh adjective to put on them. But I do have my doubts. I wonder if there was a darkness there I never saw. I was always an outsider. I wasn't condemned to them and they were not forced to have me lording it over them. Hence I wouldn't even be able to register the usual pettiness of family relationships, far less be alert to even more wizened emotional responses. There were certainly incidents that revealed the darknesses of sex, of jealousies, of envy, and domestic fear, but you couldn't make out of these any characteristic tenor of existence. Or rather, how was I to know? It was always smiles to the outsider – best face forward; and astonishing degrees of privacy can be maintained even within a cluster of open-sided houses. That said, though, and accepting the conditions of a best-face-forward relationship, it would take a lot to convince me that I'd missed some enormous sombre dimension of emotional life.

'Penned up in petty souls and desolate surroundings' says Carlo Levi in *Christ Stopped at Eboli* – a forceful evocation of peasant life in southern Italy to where he had been exiled: 'I looked into the fire, thinking of the endless chain of days that lay ahead of me when my horizon, too, would be bounded by these dark emotions.' There's a sentence to present to incipient anthropological field-workers. Test their mettle with that one. Ask them why they want to go. Ask them if they could feel like this. I don't think I could ever come near such a view, although there are more than just hints in the ethnographic literature of writers whose dispositions towards their hosts were a long way from that which could be called sympathetic. If so, then these dark moods should be drawn out from the shadows. There is no need to hide them. They deserve explicit display since they are the groundwork on which all subsequent interpretation develops.

Carlo Levi was an exile, banished by Mussolini's officials. He didn't choose to go there. He also explains vividly that the local people he was plunged amongst lived under a heavy sense of inferiority conditioned by their relationship with the outside world, particularly with Naples and Rome. In contrast, I was constantly seeing assertions of integrity that resisted that relationship with the outside world. So much connected up *within*. All the 'dark emotions' were fascinating.

'Catamenial blood', for example, – a crucial key. It makes its appearance in Carlo Levi's story in a macabre warning from a local doctor about the ingredients of secret love philtres concocted by peasant women. That leads Levi to refer to 'that closed world, shrouded in black veils, bloody and earthy'. It takes me in all sorts of other directions, opening out their world, not closing it down. Once, on leaving the FUNAI post after a brief visit, I wanted to say goodbye to a friend who lived nearby. He sent word that he'd meet me by the roadside rather than come on to the post. That sounded a bit odd, but he explained when we met that since he was deeply involved in learning about shamanic techniques he couldn't go near the post that day – my hostess, the Brazilian official's wife, was menstruating. Catamenial blood, in Wayapí reflection, was not a secret matter. It wasn't a shrouded threat. It was a matter of public concern and it took you straight to shamanism and the balance of life and death. Certainly, sexual concern, sexual tension, and sexual drama were always in the air, but unlike the elaborate screening mechanisms we're used to, the male/female dichotomy was as much a part of everyday life as the other great categorical imperatives of night and day, or the rainy time and the dry.

Catamenial blood? Greene's vultures on the roof, and Orwell's grit-laden wind? These images reflect their authors' inner feelings. What could I use? I suppose I could try the cockroaches. They were astoundingly profuse even though you wouldn't see too much of them during daylight hours. You could be lolling in your hammock during the heat of the day and be surprised by a rustling overhead, indicating that the cockroach population of the roof was on the move to the cooler slope. During darkness they would swarm over your belongings, and in the morning anything you lifted up would send a posse of them scuttling off in all directions. I'd pick up my harmonica and find cockroaches of various sizes squeezed into every note. They would eat my books and papers. Yet thinking back it's surprising to remember how invisible this massive presence became. They just weren't that much of a pest. No; the cockroaches won't do the job.

I failed to come to terms with what I took to be the most unpleasant intrusion of all into Wayapí life – the arrival at the Nipukú of their first cockerel. Oh that damned bird. Thoreau thought the sound was magnificent, majestic even, and the whole rural romance from Chanticleer to 'Fern Hill' seems to agree with him. 'Cantagalo' in Spanish and Portuguese traditions gives not a hint of irritation. 'He who blesses the morning', they say in Gaelic. 'And hark, again! the crowing cock/ How drowsily it crew' – what a monstrous hypallage. And what a monstrous tradition I'm up against. To me, romanticizing cock-crow like this is blatant idiocy. That dreadful beast took up its night residence on *my* roof ridge, and on a reasonable night would start sounding off at about 4 in the morning. At a full moon the thing could keep going all night. How I detested it. I tried wild beeswax as earplugs, but the material was too hard, cracked the skin, and gave me an ear infection. Goddam Chanticleer really was the lowest point. Everyone else adored it. Yanuari, like Thoreau, would get rhapsodic about its wonderful noise. My grief baffled them, I think, because our sleeping patterns were so different. I'm sure they couldn't care less about getting a regular eight hours. They cat-napped. Indeed on cold nights people who hadn't managed to get hold of blankets from the Brazilians would sleep in their net hammocks over small fires, and people would often be up tending the embers. Well: cockroaches and cockerels – it's all pretty trivial, isn't it. I suppose you could say that the single major aspect of gloom had nothing to do with Wayapí themselves: the rains. They came on from the end of December, through January, February, and March, day after day, the rivers rising dramatically and inundating large areas of the forest floor, making any journey a slopping misery. During such seasons various bits and pieces of your belongings get the musty smell of material that never gets a chance to dry. Grey gloomy skies. Yes, the rains were depressing. They were then, are now, and ever shall be. Even so, it's probably better to sit out the rainy season in an Indian village than in a tropical city.

Bacchus and his pards

There were fights from time to time, between men, of course – as usual. Once or twice these were the result of longstanding resentments about a man's failure to do enough work for his wife's father. Mostly they were the result of sexual jealousy. If a fight did break out it was always at the end of a spree. The drunkenness amongst both men and women was spectacular. Wayapí people really did enjoy going on the spree. These caxiri bouts were mentioned by numerous travellers in French Guiana in the 1800s. There is no doubt that getting drunk was an important Wayapí tradition.

Caxiri referred to the beige-coloured manioc beer usually made for a spree, although frequently a pink-coloured beer was made from yams. The women from one household would take on the task of preparing the beer and one of them would be called the 'caxiri-owner'. It would be made in a roughly hewn trough shaped like a small canoe, covered over with large leaves of banana palm, and left to ferment for some days. Small amounts of sweet potato would help provide sugar for the fermentation process. Also, the day the trough was being prepared you might notice a number of women with their mouths crammed with wads of manioc. They would later in the day deposit these wads in the trough. The secret is ptyalin – an enzyme found in our saliva, which breaks down carbohydrate into sugar, and hence gets the fermentation process going. They said that there's no point in men doing it – only women's mouths were 'sweet'.

Getting painted for a spree

A few sprees started late in the day and went on into the night, but usually they began fairly early. A quiet spree might just consist of a line of twelve men sitting on stools with women coming back and fore with calabashes of caxiri. The men would joke and laugh and gradually get drunk, a high point, perhaps, being when young João, who as a boy had lived with Brazilians for a time, would yell out a snatch of some dreadful song that he'd picked up from them: 'Por amor de Deus, eu não sou cachorro, não' (For the love of God, I am really not a dog).

Sometimes a number of households would get together and there could be five or six canoe-loads to get through. I didn't enjoy these days. There was nowhere to disappear to, and by the end of the day I'd be feeling at bay. I'd be surrounded by my most kindly gentle friends turned into kindly gentle incontinents – howling and incapable. Picture a moment when on one side a man was flirting loudly and salaciously with another woman, who was vomiting repeatedly. On the other side a woman was crumpled on a stool, completely out of it, weeping for some inarticulate loss. One man was sitting on my hammock holding tightly to my arms, while his brother stood in front with his face close to mine shouting friendly blandishments through rotten teeth and spraying my cheek with saliva. Another man was going round and round the hammock pretending to be a spider monkey.

The high they got from caxiri was sudden and short. They went up and down like yo-yos. They kept going by vomiting and coming back for more, and got through prodigious quantities till their bellies swelled out, tight and round. I guessed that sometimes the degree of drunken behaviour was feigned. (A young woman, for instance, made the hazardous exit from her house, down a log, without a falter, walked firmly towards the party, and on joining the crowd began to stagger and sway and moan.) Part of it was a collective ivresse where the occasion of drinking gave the signal for a general relaxation of restraints. What was remarkable was the degree of restraint that remained. They did seem to get quite incapable. They lost things, they broke things, and sometimes lost their tempers. But they were never so drunk that anger could not bring them back to some sobriety and to an awareness of any crisis at hand. They wouldn't be able to run so fast or fight so fiercely if they were in the same state as one of our drunks reeling from a bar.

I wish I knew what the ptyalin and the sweet potato were capable of. Surely the alcohol content must have been minimal. I found the beer had no inebriating effect whatsoever, although it's true I couldn't drink very much since it always gave me fierce indigestion. I was excessively bored with the sprees since I couldn't join in the spirit. But putting that to one side, getting drunk was universally important to them. In any spree one or two persons might be under some sort of seclusion for reasons of birth, menstruation, or illness. Those quietly involved in shamanistic concerns would be taking care. But no one would ever be moralistically reproving of the sprees. Everyone not under restrictions got involved.

In those days at the Nipukú a lot more dancing went on. The occasion would be named; a fish, a bird, an animal, or sometimes a plant name. Some, like the hawk dance, the butterfly dance, the maize dance could only be done at night. There were chants and songs associated with each one, and sometimes specific instruments – small flutes that would be made from reeds the day before.

One of the best took place on a December night. There had been weeks with no rain. The forest was bone dry. You could do a whole day's hunting and never get your feet wet. The party involved three days of activity, with an explosive finale. On the first day, with the women involved in preparing the beer, all the men went off to gather bales of bark from a large tree – the nyu-mi'y. It's the same bark that was used as carrying straps for baskets. The bark was cut into long strips and tied into bundles. These were carried off to be soaked in the black mud of a small stream nearby. On the second day the men retrieved the bundles, stained blue-black now, separated the bunches into the strips which emerged striped because of the way they had been tied up – a resist-dyeing technique. The strips were hung in the sun to dry. The rest of the day they spent carving flat representations of fish – pacus and piranhas – making flutes, and painting up with urucu (the red dye) and genipa (black). The fish images would be hung from the flutes that the men carried round.

At night there was a dress-rehearsal, which I found the most intriguing part of the whole thing. They had made the black strips into headdresses which hung down almost to the ground. With these on, we men began by dancing around a bit, any old how. It was all rather delicately done: no drinking; everyone on their best behaviour – and beautifully set up with the light coming from lumps of burning resin. It gradually got organized into dancing in line, the usual way, each man with his right hand on the left shoulder of the next. At one point the line went backwards towards the women standing in a group, who pelted us with lumps of grated manioc, shrieking with delight. Another spell of dancing ended with us all sitting in a long line. The 'marriageable women' (give or take a few categories) arrived in front of the appropriate 'marriageable men' handing each one a piece of manioc cake, and giving him the name of an animal, bird, or fish. The end of the dance was us all sitting, hands over our eyes, making a long drawn-out high-pitched quiet howl, while a woman walked along the line with a burning brand. 'We mustn't see the light. If we do we'll go blind.'

Everyone went to bed excited, and long before dawn people were up, restless to get going. Our time schemes have no place there. For us mornings are for starting work. Evenings are for entertainment. There the distinctions don't work. It doesn't matter which twilight it is, dawn or evening. This time it was all to start up in the twilight of the dawn. The men got their headdresses on and we took turns to run towards a small fire whistling – we were, so to speak, shamanistic tapirs – where the caxiri-owner's husband (the caxiri-owner is always a woman) grabbed our arms as we stretched towards the fire. Then to the caxiri and the dancing.

As the line swayed round, women in the non-sisters category (i.e. marriageable women) would grasp from behind the belts of men who were not their actual husbands and dance with them for a time. I was told to shout for the wife of one of my brothers (a woman who was therefore in my marriageable category too), and when she held on to my belt I was prompted with suggestive comments which I was supposed to shout at her. Later it was mostly actual wives holding on to the belts of their actual husbands.

As evening came, a few tempers had risen. Masirí had got fed up with some women taunting him that a number of men had previously had a go with his young wife. Nonato got angry when Waiwai grumbled and groused at him for not marrying Sikua. Nonato went into a long, semi-interior monologue, for everyone to hear, about Sikua making love with everybody at another settlement: 'And would you marry a woman like that? No!' Parahandy and Pau were getting ready to fight at one point. Evidently when Parahandy and I were absent from Nipukú, various men had been having a go with his wife. But by nightfall that situation seemed to have got defused.

In the dark, everyone drifted off to their hammocks. Night resonance receded. Then an awful screaming started. Parahandy was under his house, lying on top of his wife beating the hell out of her. My first reaction was 'do not interfere', but when he started to drag her along the ground by her hair, at speed, with Jimmy Peerie and Masirí making ineffectual attempts to stop him, I charged in and held him. After he calmed down, I found his wife crouched by the river, naked, very sad, with a swollen face. I left husband and wife together in their house, having given her an analgesic.

The night came alive again. Close by there seemed to be a fight brewing between two pairs of brothers. Parahandy arrived back at my hammock saying he'd gone off to eat at Siro's house, and that as we were then talking another man had slipped into his house and was making love to his battered wife. He couldn't go into his house to see, because he would be ashamed. I thought this was all rather unlikely, but who could tell in the dark? Waiwai was prowling about doing some 'hard talking', as he called it, criticizing various people not about the present quarrels and commotion but about all sorts of other old scores: laziness, carelessness, and so on. His voice boomed out of the darkness at one spot, then after a silence started up from somewhere else.

Parahandy vanished. A short time later his battered wife arrived, coming to sit on my bench. She said Parahandy was off on an amorous adventure. After five or ten minutes he appeared and they sat beside each other. He said he'd gone back to Siro's house to eat piranha. *She* said he'd been out in the cleared land having a go with Sikua. On and on the night went, but the quarrelling and the shouting were all over.

'Let's go to bed' said Parahandy. No answer from his wife sitting at his side in the dark. He repeated her name, sharply, interrogatively, again and again, trying to get her to respond. She said nothing. He changed his tone and asked very gently 'Where's your sister?' 'I don't know' she sobbed in a whisper. 'Let's go to bed now' he said. 'Yes.' 'You go first then.' Off she went. He waited then followed. And that was that. Nothing much stirred the next day, but in the late morning I could hear her giggling away.

Is all this to be seen as high jinks and hanky-panky? Or is the wife-beating confirmation of the old despair? The Brazilian officials and the missionaries saw caxiri behaviour as a sign of wild degenerate savagery that threatened their efforts to dominate and control, hence stopping the bouts was a top priority. I can see ourselves in that behaviour and that behaviour in ourselves. If you wanted to push it further and create some sort of imbalance, it seems to me it would always tilt in favour of the caxiri rather than our equivalents. You could say, if you wanted to be old-fashioned, that theirs is the incipient behaviour from which our own more exaggerated and alarming patterns of excess and violence develop (a sort of nineteenth-century view of 'them as us in a previous, simpler, more childlike stage of civilization'); or you could say that it's high time we found ways of learning from such small-scale communities the kinds of restraints that would protect us from the extremes of domestic and public violence that *our* excesses of consumption lead to. I can't see any way of saying that their behaviour represents 'savagery' while ours is 'civilized'.

You could use social science to sidestep the moral issue. You could offer a thunderingly basic 'functionalist' explanation and say that the sprees 'release tensions, sort out resentments, re-establish balance' and so on. Maybe they do. If you're a functionalist, that way of looking at it will make you comfortable. If you want to get 'structuralist' about it, you could get stuck in to your oppositions and set up schemes of restraint/excess, manioc bread/manioc beer, quotidian/ritual, and (if you're a structuralist) that will make *you* comfortable. I'm more impressed by the way that *they* were comfortable with the drinking sprees; that no one described these bouts as a threat, or an example of frailty, or of behaviour requiring censure. Women talked with pride and pleasure of their caxiri, and of how they enjoyed getting drunk, and enjoyed singing and dancing. Most of the fighting I knew of was between men. I knew of a few incidents of wife-beating, and was told of occasional fights between women. But fighting and beatings were not the inevitable accompaniments of sprees, and even if they did break out, only a few individuals were involved. All in all, they indulged in their sprees with tremendous exuberance, and took whatever fall-out came along. It's as if they knew how to handle their excesses. And it's as if we don't.

Chanticleer and cockroaches, rains and sprees; none of that can get me near those feelings of cynical disillusion. I was protected, of course. I was an outsider and as part of my particular outsider's relationship with them it was guaranteed that I was not going to be pulled round by my hair, beaten, or even threatened (well, once, only once). My judgements were not those of the reluctant exile or the birth-to-death participator. I arrived as a benevolent onlooker, benignly curious, predisposed to that outlook by anthropological charity. Does that raise the suspicion of bias? No, that's not the point. The alternatives are not between slanted subjective views on the one hand and stalwartly objective accounts on the other. What benevolent predispositions manage to do is to clear away all sorts of inhibiting habits of seeing, mean and limiting habits, quick conclusions by type and formula, snap confirmations of old reflexes. Getting beyond these clears the way for all sorts of possibilities of vision. But that's all: allowing possibilities. Nothing is guaranteed. You can't say what's going to happen in the end.

The extreme limit

There was a killing once, some years ago now – difficult to call it murder. It was certainly a matter of vengeance, of settling old scores and putting things right again. I'd never met the victim, but those who killed him were amongst my closest friends. Although I suppose the killing of one human being by another is the *ne plus ultra* of immoral behaviour, the most awful aspect of the story was not what my friends did. It was the stupidity of FUNAI. The event itself is a matter of public record – in government reports and such like – so I'm not breaking any confidences.

There were three aspects of the surrounding context that intrigued me. First of all, the event was a link to the elusive history before 1973. Second, the motives and feelings of the protagonists, together with the reactions of everyone to the killing, brought into relief the groundwork of moral authority and political power. And third, like so much else, the accusations made against the victim were mixed up with shamanism. One thing led to another.

The victim was called Sarapó. His sphere of operations had been the Rio Cuc. The Cuc is a natural connection between the Rio Jari in Brazil and the Oyapoque River which divides Brazil from French Guiana. The Cuc has two main tributaries with the beautiful names Igarapé Koroapi and Igarapé Pirawiri, names which kept on coming up as Our Wayapí told their story of their contacts with the Other Wayapí who are now to be found on the Oyapoque River in French Guiana. (Igarapé is standard Brazilian Portuguese

107

for a small stream. The word comes straight from the Tupian languages and means 'canoe-path'.)

Trying to piece together the history, it appears that Our Wayapí lost touch with the Other Wayapí late last century or early on in this one, probably after one of the many series of epidemics that swept through the area. The Other Wayapí remained along the Cuc and the Oyapoque, in contact with the French and being visited from time to time from both the French and Brazilian sides by travellers, official expeditions, frontiersmen and so on. Meanwhile Our Wayapí contracted around the headwaters of the Amaparí and were forgotten about by everyone. It was probably towards the end of the 1950s that Our Wayapí began to make contact with those on the Cuc, making their way through to Pirawiri and Koroapi from the headwaters of the Nipukú. The Other Wayapí had *things*: red cloth, of course, and above all axes and knives – iron, cold iron. Just think how much you need metal if you live in a forest. And the Other Wayapí had it. They also had disease. Time and again the story goes that when Grandfather So-and-So and his companions arrived back from Pirawiri or Koroapi they brought back fatal illnesses.

How I wish I could get back to some vision of those times when they first went through to the Cuc. How I wish I could have been with them when they made the journey, to see that moment when they first arrived on the Pirawiri. The way I heard the story was that three intrepid ones of Our Wayapí were the first to go through. They knew the direction because they were 'shamanistic', hence they could 'see' things. But what an arrival it must have been. The linguistic differences could have been no further than, say, in the terms I'm used to in this country, a person from the Shetland Islands meeting a Cockney, except that they hadn't come across each other for half a century.

The Other Wayapí had been in permanent contact both with the French and with the next people over to the west – usually known nowadays as the Wayana. Wayana language is of the Carib family – that's a huge linguistic family that stretches all through the Guianas and Northern Brazil, Carib languages being characteristically found to the north of the Amazon. (Wayapí is one of the Tupian languages, more commonly found to the south of the Amazon.)

There was a clear linguistic divide there. It's also obvious that there have been numerous linguistic and cultural borrowings from

Wayana to Wayapí, and it always seems to have been one way. Various travellers' reports, last century and this, make two points of comparison: that Wayana culture is 'richer' than Wayapí, by which is apparently meant that the featherwork, pottery, basketry, house-building and so on are more elaborate; and that Wayana think themselves superior to Wayapí. The Other Wayapí had a fair-sized lexicon of Carib words which they took from this contact. Our Wayapí often use these words nowadays but they can also state what the 'Grandfather-people' equivalent was, that is to say, the Tupi word form they would have used in the old days.

The picture is of a sliding scale – Our Wayapí coming tentatively out of their precarious isolation into contact with materially richer communities of the Other Wayapí living along the Cuc and the Oyapoque, who in turn had had decades of contact with the Wayana, seen, by outsiders at any rate, as having even more cultural confidence. Although a number of Our Wayapí did travel as far as the Wayana settlements away to the west and north on the Paru and Litani rivers, I'd guess that when they say 'We learned this from the Wayana' they may just as well have picked it up from the Other Wayapí who had borrowed it from the Wayana a long time before. That certainly goes for the Carib forms of vocabulary. The other borrowings often concerned delicate points of craft – a certain way of carving a wooden stool, a certain way of tying thatch, a certain technique used in canoe-building, a certain body-paint design.

A curious borrowing was the use by men of a couple of extra relationship terms. This was peculiar because it was so often said that this was 'taught to them by Sarapó'. Sarapó was originally neither one of the Other Wayapí nor a Wayana. It was said he was an Aparai – the name of another Carib group from downstream on the Rio Jarí. He had left, or been thrown out of there, and gone up the Jarí to join the Other Wayapí. I have no idea why he had such an influence on events, but time and again, in the stories of the misfortunes on the Cuc it was said that 'We did this because Sarapó told us to do it', or 'We did that because Sarapó said it was good.' It is significant that when the Cuc was finally abandoned (the Other Wayapí going over into French Guiana, Our Wayapí coming back to their lands), Sarapó and a small family group went by themselves right up to the head of the Jarí to a place referred to as Morokopoti, which had been variously an air-force clearing and a mission post. *Persona non grata* with everyone, he settled in that isolated spot, quite comfortably though, since he was in contact with the Brazilians and over the years got hold of cows, pigs, chickens, and ducks.

But over those years, the connections remained vivid. By that last final break up on the Cuc, it was said that Sarapó had killed at least five of Our Wayapí, and their brothers and sons were still very much alive. Sarapó had also taken away as his wife a sister of one of Our Wayapí. She was later to return with him. There were also some gruesome stories of violence perpetrated by Sarapó's sons against their sister's husband and sister's daughter – Other Wayapí whose relatives would have gone over into French Guiana. At any rate, in spite of this massive reservoir of resentment, by 1981 FUNAI had decided to move Sarapó from Morokopoti and send him to Our Wayapí on the Igarapé Onça. They took months to convince him to go. He eventually agreed, sold his livestock to FUNAI, and made the journey travelling by plane and truck.

The usual bland FUNAI documents change at this point. The pace quickens as the narrative takes form, with unexpected intensity of detail ('At 14.00 hours . . .' and suchlike). Sarapó arrived on the Onça on a Thursday in July 1981. On the Saturday there was a small caxiri party in one leader's house. On the Monday morning a caxiri-wasu began – a big caxiri party. By that afternoon Sarapó was dead. He had hardly survived four days. It was one of the older men, a calm figure, wise and pleasant, who showed up at the FUNAI post with the news. He didn't do the killing (although it was his sister that had become Sarapó's wife all that time ago). Later one of the killers arrived, emphasizing that he did it with *wood* (an axe handle), and going on to reassure the Brazilians: 'e não fica com medo porque o caso é só com Índio' – 'and don't be afraid because it's just an Indian matter'. Two men had actually done it, one holding the victim and the other beating him to death. The document ends abruptly with the usual exaggerated flourishes required of Brazilian letter writing, 'most attentively, your ever so 'umble and obedient servant' sort of thing; such an incongruous paragraph to attach to the grisly details that had just gone before. The next document is back to the usual 'report'. The old order is restored, and the matter at hand describes the ordinary workaday waste of effort in getting something insignificant done.

There's more than a whiff in the story of Wayapí people seeing the commandant of the FUNAI post rather like the Lord of the Manor who had to be told what had happened on the estate. Well, FUNAI had brought the victim in, so they were indeed deeply involved. There also seemed to be some fear, though it looked a bit offhand, that retribution might come from FUNAI. Curiously, in a matter of murder like this they were protected from Brazilian law. In those days the Statute of the Indian still stood which gave those classified as 'Indians' the status of children or wards of the state. They couldn't be prosecuted in a court of law since, as children, they couldn't be held responsible for their actions. A century after Brazil had abolished slavery, the country still had a law of this kind specially devised for Indians. All in all, then, the outside consequences of the murder were not serious. What's puzzling were the consequences on the inside.

How do human beings keep their society going? How fragile is it? While animal instincts are usually so accurate, human drives and motivations are a mess. To keep us right in the society we know here, we're held together by all sorts of economic and political institutional arrangements that we think are enormously sophisticated. They are certainly obscure, and there are so many competing views trying to tell us how it all works, how it could work better, and what the dangers of breakdown are. We are also bombarded with disparate information and have access to unprecedented quantities of knowledge. All this gives us the impression that somehow we (as opposed to them) live in enormously sophisticated societies. When we look at simpler societies from this point of view as mirrors of ourselves we think that it is they who lack something or another and we who have progressed to some superior state. But wherever you look it's the small-scale societies that seem to work. It's what's called 'civilization' that's responsible for crying 'Havoc!' and letting slip the dogs of war.

We think that our protection from havoc comes from our institutions, such as our governments and judicial systems, police and military organizations, and oh yes, our amazing scientific and technical sophistication with its basis in literacy. And I suppose that's right, in a way. We think that if these institutions disintegrated we would be at risk. And I'm sure we would be. But we then go on to reason that those societies that do not have such institutions must therefore be teetering on the verge of chaos. William Golding's *Lord of the Flies* imagines a set up where all institutions of authority are suddenly removed, and the abandoned community of schoolboys slips into a process of degeneracy where dark, atavistic manners and arrangements emerge. It's generally assumed that our civilized institutions save us from some dreadful state like that; from some primitive state that we might fall into again if we're not careful. And that line of reasoning produces our notions of savagery and primitive society. But this is all upside down. It's *we* who are the social children, living under the authority of grave, distant, paternalistic institutions of which we know little. Wayapí people, and so many others in similar circumstances, had nothing like that sitting over them (except, that is, when they were being interfered with by Brazilians). They had to know how to shift for themselves, and they did very well indeed.

How on earth did they do it? Only 150 people when I first met them and, if left to themselves, they could get on with it just dandy. No *Lord of the Flies* fantasy here at all. You could take any aspect of it you want. The one that I always find so intriguing (since I find it the most mysterious human capacity) is language. They'd been cut off for generations from a much larger population with a shared language. Wouldn't the language somehow have shrunk along with their network of social ties and interests? Not a bit of it. Here were 150 people with a perfectly formed language, now uniquely theirs, still vigorously innovative, volubly expressive, giving them access to a vivid lore of beliefs, myths, and interpretations of their surroundings.

The notion that there's a useful contrast to be made between simple-primitive languages on the one hand and complicated-sophisticated ones on the other (like modern English, modern French, modern Arabic, modern Chinese) should be one of the easiest misapprehensions for comparative anthropology to correct. But it's just so widespread. I heard in the streets of Marrakech from university-educated Moroccan students that you couldn't possibly make a grammar book or dictionary of Berber (the language found in the Atlas mountains which looked down on them, and indeed one of the languages found on their own city streets) because 'it wasn't a real language', and I've come across the same reaction in university circles here: that the people I'd visited in Amazônia 'of course didn't have a proper language'.

What's so baffling about that kind of assertion is that there's absolutely nothing you can do to *show* them how wrong they are. Talking about the wonders of a particular language is useless. You can't talk *about* a language in that way. It's even further removed than talking about music. You can always play a tape of the music, or even just whistle it. But there's no point in breaking into some Wayapí, or Berber if you were lucky enough to know it, sit back and expect them to groove away to the subtlety of the phonetics. If others want to be convinced, they have to plunge into it themselves and get some experience of what it feels like to swing off into an attempt at translation, unsure if you've got the momentum to get to the other side.

Wayapí people were not teetering on the edge of linguistic havoc where at any moment they might have slipped off into a morass of grunts and gestures. (It's we, as translators, who risk that.) They shared the same firm linguistic plateau that all other human beings are on. Similarly, as regards their material welfare, if left to themselves they did not face the havoc of starvation and famine. That's something that's left for 'civilization' to perpetrate on the world. Here again it's the wrong way round. It is we, in our complex technological societies who are, in a childlike way, dependent on everyone else around us for the very basics of our existence, and it is Wayapí people who appear as self-sufficient adults, able to look after themselves. That's why all of us who went there and lived with them admired their skills so much and became so aware of how much *we* have lost.

There is not a trace of romantic illusion in appreciating the wonders of their language. There is not a trace of romantic illusion in appreciating their superb technical skills and their knowledge of their environment. But what about the society aspect? How was havoc kept at bay there? Who decided what counted as right and what counted as wrong, what was decent behaviour and what was not, what was madness and what sanity? Who decided on punishment and revenge? Where did the restraints on violence come from? Where could appeal be made to for guidance? Why didn't it all just go to pot?

In one way the questions I'm asking are banalities. No one with the slightest anthropological experience is going to ask if you could find examples of a people without a 'proper' language. Nor would you entertain for long the idea of a people chronically incompetent in their environment (that is, a permanent hopelessness – one that is not the result of major disruption or sudden catastrophe). Similarly you can't really entertain the idea of 'a society that doesn't work as a society'. So we can say with some firmness: 'Look, it just *is* like that. That's what "human life" means – language, material culture, social codes. It's just as basic as walking on two legs.'

But it's not as basic as that. It's not as simple as basic biology. There was no way of knowing when any of us started out in our comparative anthropology that it would be at all like that. It's absolutely fascinating that it should turn out that way. And whereas anthropologists might take it all for granted, there are an awful lot of people around us who would have nothing whatever to do with the conclusion that we, on one side, and primitive people on the other, are really all much the same no matter where and when, far less accept that a comparison between us and them shows that we have lost something extraordinarily important. It's easy for anthropologists to take it all for granted, especially while being there with them in the woods, with the details of the day to get through, and the strings of immediate anxieties and decisions to resolve. While there, an appreciation of the way they held the whole show together came only in scattered moments, being puzzled by something and deliberately stopping to wonder. It's only now, looking back, that I can properly admire what was going on.

Sarapó's killing wasn't the result of unbridled savagery, nor even of a drunken brawl. He had five killings to his name and the two who killed him were close brothers and sons of the victims. The essence of the way they lived was that there was no higher authority to appeal to. There were no ponderous institutions nor grave abstractions (the Police or the Law) to take decisions or coerce. They had to sort it out themselves. An enormous wrong had been done, and the sons and the brothers sorted it out in the best way they knew. The incident was the extreme example of their singular self-sufficiency.

Without the Law

It's worth emphasizing the point about Law. Familiar stereotypes of primitive life manage to incorporate impossible inconsistencies at the same time, seeing the people so described as being at once unpredictably volatile and violent while also being fearfully hidebound in rigidly limiting codes. Again these views represent worlds turned upside down. The authoritarian, autocratic chief, signalling capricious judgements with a gesture is one of *our* inventions; another piece of fantasy. You quickly find that trying to puzzle out what the word 'chief' means is still one of the most intriguing social and philosophical puzzles that an encounter with Amazon Forest peoples presents. ('Our-Big-One' would be the Wayapí way of putting it.) The word puts into question all our notions of power, authority, influence, and rule. We're sodden with notions of patriarchies (and matriarchies now and again), of kings (and queens now and again), of dynastic power and inheritance, of status, classes, castes, races, and of all manner of hierarchies. We're therefore baffled when we come across a political set-up which is most concisely summed up in the description: 'The chief speaks, and everyone does as they please.'

Professional commentators who approach the problem do so with contrived awkwardness. 'Well, you see, the chief is a sort of distributor. Being the political centre, he's given all sorts of material goods. But anything he gets he's got to redistribute. So although he remains materially poorer he gets the benefit of superior moral and political status.' This is functionalist fantasy. There was no centring of material production, no redistributing, no displays of giving. The awkwardness of explanations like that, the embarrassing lack of fit with the life you see, is, actually, understandable. There are dozens of these explanations, including bizarre 'structuralist' ones where 'culture' takes over in the form of the chief and 'nature' breaks back through to deprive him of his power – weird bouncing dances of abstractions. The awkwardness is understandable because they are all trying to make sense of the question, 'How can you have political power in the form of a chief when nothing that the chief says has anything to do with executive decisions?' What on earth is a chief for, if not to dole out the orders? What's power without power?

I'm as puzzled as anyone else, and can't find much to say to solve the conundrum. But what delights me is that here again is something so unexpected. It throws up all sorts of questions about the nature and possibilities of human life by putting our notion of 'political power' into a strange light indeed. It's also one of the best examples I can find of the way that, when translating between languages, the possibilities of holding on to meaning are stretched to breaking point. We're at the limit again. The word is *yane-rowiyung*: 'Our-Big', or 'Our-Big-One'. It would be absolutely perverse to insist that we mustn't translate that as 'chief'. The point is we *have* to translate it as 'chief'. Everything in the habits of our language pulls us into 'chief' as if into a semantic black hole. And once in there, we find ourselves covered by layers of misconceptions. We have to go in, though. I'd insist on that. And once in there, we've got to start digging ourselves out again, through the layers of misconception, and try to find a way of reorganizing our notions of 'chief' and 'power' in order to find a way towards their notions. There's no other way but through our words.

Waiwai is a 'chief'. I think of him as a kind of moral commentator, like a stern and self-important writer of editorials in a national newspaper. Sure, he's a Thunderer when he walks about at night, or in early twilight, putting on his official voice and doing some 'hard talking' (that people shouldn't be lazy; that women should get up early and bathe in the river when it's cold, and so on). But people didn't take much notice. Certainly decisions were not his to take, and no one would think of asking him to make one.

So often you'd see the translation-mistake in action. Brazilians would come in and think that to get something done they had to negotiate with the chief, the *capitão*, as they'd translate it, and that once there was agreement with him, the rest of the village would follow. Well, you can forget your captains. That's not the way it worked. They would also make the mistake of thinking that if gift-giving or payment of any kind had to be made, the things could be given to the chief, who would then hand them around in an equitable way. Not a bit of it. Give something to someone and it was his, no matter how much you give him, chief or no chief; and no one else in the village would expect it to be any other way.

I think some of the FUNAI staff gradually got round to an appreciation of this. They noticed that there were always some individuals who were more at ease with outsiders, more confident, more willing to pick up Portuguese, and who could be relied on to do business, and who could translate orders and instructions. These became a separate little class of trusties, good intermediaries, like honorary consuls. After a while the Brazilians would do their own promotions and start calling them *capitão* too, so entering another turn into the spiral of mistranslation.

I'm not sure why we fall so easily into mistranslations and misconceptions about this. Perhaps our hierarchies and patriarchies and our sense of parental authoritarianism urges us to think that everyone simply *must* have established patterns of dominion and submission. Surely every pack of primates has its dominant male.

Even hens have pecking orders (or so it seems to us). Hence we go into all sorts of contortions trying to fit our patterns of power on to this scene and, as the effort gets more and more awkward, so the explanations get more and more bizarre.

If I could just skirt around the matter of the sexual division of labour, of the man/woman categorical imperative, of the nuances of decision around the domestic hearth – quite a lot to skirt around, you'll agree – then the picture presented by these communities is one of power-degree-zero, hierarchy reduced to a minimum, authority no more than a posture, coercion no more than a gesture. What are we looking at? Good old *Gemeinschaft*? The frozen, out-of-history, primitive society, perdurable in its synchronicity? Well, no. It's not a picture of a steady state. It's a picture of a fluctuating process that has managed, so far, to keep afloat and to get through. It's not a picture of functionalist synchronicity. It's a picture of a practised tightrope walker in motion.

But what happened there on the Cuc when the murders took place? What nightmare did they go through there? Was that an example of the fabric tearing? Was there a cry of 'Havoc' there? The entire period seems to have been a particularly sorry episode. As well as the epidemics, the settlements were being disturbed by outside interference. Both Our Wayapí and the Pirawiri and Koroapi residents (the Other Wayapí) were being ordered around by Brazilians. At one point Brazilian air-force personnel got them to clear a landing ground. I'm tempted to say that much of the difficulty came from outside pressures (the epidemics certainly did), although the Wayapí who refer to those days don't place the blame there. I saw the way they internalized their problems, diverting the causes of their misfortunes away from the Brazilians on to one another – and I mean both the way they turned external misfortunes into internecine resentments and the way that shamanism accusations took over to explain death. I think it was only in later years that they began to appreciate how much they had been victims of external forces and to learn how to articulate confidently what was being done to them.

A lot went wrong, though, and led to crescendos of resentments, accusations, and deaths. There are further curious details about the killings attributed to Sarapó in the different ways the victims died. One was said to have been shot, another killed with an axe (someone else said: no, with a knife), and a third was said to have been poisoned. Other deaths were attributed to shamanistic workings, and at this point we go beyond our furthest limits of understanding. All of us want to make a fundamental distinction between a death caused by the victim being clubbed to death and one explained by shamanistic malevolence. But in their world, club, poison, and shamanism were all part of the same world. What can we make of this? We're at the end of our road, standing at the edge of our clearing, and we're looking towards those unknown forests which we see Indian people emerge from and vanish into, but which we never really get to know.

5

FOUR, FIRE, AND GIVING

In those days Wayapí had no numbers beyond four. They had a glorious way of indicating 'a lot' or 'a very large number' which was to hold out all the fingers and thumbs of both hands and say a long word that you might translate: 'All-our-hands-together-very-good'. But four was where the strict computation stopped.

You might have thought that they would at least have gone on to five, given the digits on our hands, or even get as far as ten to account for all our fingers and thumbs. But it's not an accident that stopping counting at four is found all over the world. Four is a kind of completeness. And Wayapí indicated it like this: stick out your fingers of one hand, fold in your thumb, and separate your fingers two and two, like a sort of heavy V sign. 'Two and two make four' we say, making it sound like a platitude, but in fact we're at the heart of human logic.

I'm going to show that the heart of human logic is what articulates the heart of human organization. People have thought, in a simplistic way, that the heart of human organization is 'mum, dad, and the kids' – in our nuclear age they call it the nuclear family. They then call the next step up the extended family: an idealistic picture often of a rural people, Tuscan peasants maybe, with a dozen children running around, a beautiful old grandma sitting in the rocking chair, and uncles and aunts dropping by. Beyond that comes 'the community': the warm sociological abstraction. But what is actually at the heart of human organization is the number four.

The starting point is to appreciate that the way we use words like 'mother' and 'father', 'son' and 'daughter' in our languages is peculiar; an eccentric aberration indeed if you look at the span of human possibilities. We usually take it for granted that there's something fundamental about a word like 'father' and that it's bound to have precise equivalents in any other language. That is not the case. So many other peoples use those sorts of words according to very different principles.

Frontiersmen and roadworkers coming up the Rio Amaparí thought that Wayapí men called each other 'brother-in-law' unless they were talking to their immediate family. So when speaking in the pidgin Portuguese used when talking to Indians, the frontiersmen would shove in the Brazilian word for brother-in-law, *cunhado* (pronounced *koon-YA-do*) as in: 'Are there any more *cunhados* on the Rio Cuc?', meaning, are there any more Indians there? There's something touching about this. It's cock-eyed as far as Wayapí usage goes. But it has managed to grasp the point that Wayapí words for relatives don't just refer, as ours do, to a handful of individuals close to us. The problem is that the terms can't be translated one at a time. The words form a coherent set which, once seen in its entirety, is astonishingly easy to understand.

Our terms work by starting off with a few words for people particularly close to us, like 'mother', 'father', 'son', 'daughter'. Other words make sense through them: an 'uncle' you get at through mother or father, and 'cousin' you get at through uncle and aunt. These terms refer to genealogical links, going out like ripples from a centre. So we start with a few words that refer to a core of close relatives and move out from that, hooking on to vaguer and vaguer relationships until our vocabulary just lets us down. How many people nowadays can do 'second cousin once removed'?

Wayapí relationship words are more coherent. The complete pattern can be seen by building up layers of contrasts. Where necessary, I'll do it from a woman's point of view; that is, think of 'you' as a woman. First, divide your whole world into women and men. Hence some words refer to women and some words refer to men (see Figure 1).

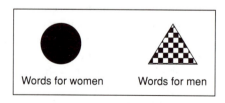

Words for women   Words for men

Figure 1. Relationship words: step one

120

Now divide your world into 'people in an older generation' and 'people in a younger'. Think of that as a 'parents' ' generation and a 'children's' generation. That leaves your generation sandwiched in the middle. So that's three generations, and words in each for women and men: six categories so far (see Figure 2).

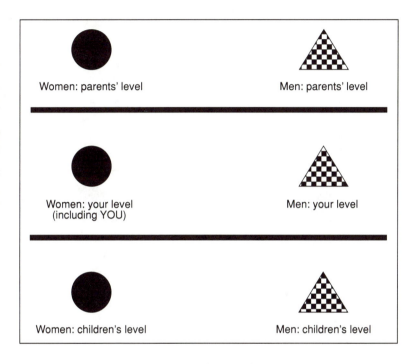

Figure 2. Relationship words: step two

Now think of your own generation: words for women and words for men. Let's have TWO words for women and TWO words for men: women like you are a word something like 'sisters'; women not like you are 'not-sisters'. Men like you are sort of 'brothers'; men not like you are 'not-brothers'. *Everybody*, every man and woman at your level, *must* go into one or other of the categories (see Figure 3).

From a woman's point of view the important point is that it's possible for you to marry any man in the 'not-brothers' category. And you can't marry any man in the 'brothers' category. You may not know who their parents were or how closely or distantly they are connected to you through other people. That doesn't matter.

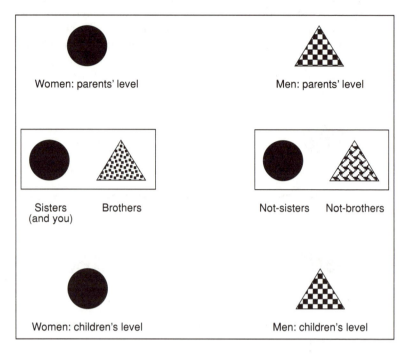

Figure 3. Relationship words: step three

All you have to know about men of your generation is whether you call them 'brother' (*kakanye*) or 'not-brother' (*emen*). Similarly all the women of your generation will be either 'sister' (*nyanya*) or 'not-sister' (*tōʻi*). The lines indicate the categories that can marry (see Figure 4).

Figure 4. Relationship words: step four

122

Your actual brother, who shares the same actual mother with you, is of course in the *kakanye* category, but so are half the men of your generation. They are *all* your 'brothers'. The other half of the men will be in your *emen* (not-brother/husband) category, and you could marry any one of them. You call *all* these eligible types *emen*, including the one you eventually settle with. So imagine the consequences at those parties where everyone gets a bit tipsy, and you've got all these husband-people around.

All those women you call sisters (*nyanya*) will be looking for not-brothers (*emen*) men to marry. All the men you call brothers (*kakanye*) will be looking out for not-sisters (*tō'i*) women to marry. If your actual brother, or any other man you call *kakanye*, has a wife, you will call her *tō'i* (not-sister). If you have a husband and he has a sister, you will call her *tō'i* as well. And if any woman whom you call *tō'i* has a brother (i.e. someone she calls *kakanye*) then you call that man *emen* (not-brother, i.e. husband).

So, to put it at it's most basic, EVERY woman in your generation is EITHER a *nyanya* OR a *tō'i* (either a sister or a not-sister) and EVERY man in your generation is EITHER a *kakanye* OR an *emen* (either a brother or a not-brother). EVERY person in that generation has to be one or the other. As a child, as you're growing up, you learn to classify everybody of your generation in that way. You learn that there are two kinds of men and two kinds of women at your level, and you have a word for each category.

Now do the same exercise for the up-one generation, and for the down-one generation. Divide them into TWO words for men and TWO words for women. The category your mother belongs to is called *mama* in Wayapí. The other woman category at that level you call *pipi*. Also, conveniently enough, the category your father belongs to is called *papa*. The other male category you call *pa'i*. (Forms of the words *mama* and *papa* appear in vocabularies all over the world.) These categories are related to one another in exactly the same way that the categories of your generation were. All the women that you call *mama* (and there will be a lot of them) address the men that you call *papa* (there will be a lot of them too) by the 'not-brother' word *emen* (the 'husband' word, if you like). And your *pipi* women address your *papa* men by the 'brother' word *kakanye*. In other words, all your *papa* people and all your *pipi* people regarded themselves as 'brothers' and 'sisters'. Also, all the women you call 'sisters' will use these *mama, pa'i, pipi, papa* words in the same way as you do (as will all your 'brothers'). But the women you call *tō'i* (not-sisters), (and

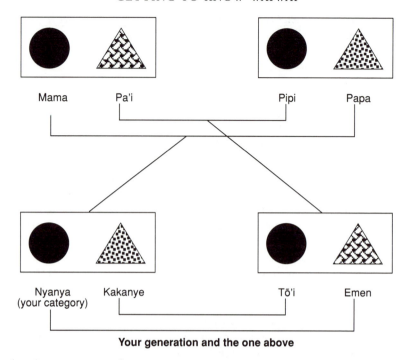

Figure 5. Relationship words: step five

the men you call 'not-brothers/husbands', *emen*) will switch the terms around: your *mama* is their *pipi*; your *papa* is their *pa'i*; and so on.

You'll also see that from your point of view, all the women in your *mama* category and all the men in your *papa* category produce all the women in the category you belong to (you and your 'sisters') as well as all the men you call 'brothers'. And all your *pa'i* men and all your *pipi* women get together and produce your *emen* and *tō'i* people, your 'not-brothers and not-sisters' (see Figure 5).

It's the same for the down-one generation: the 'children' generation. There will be male children and female children, and two kinds of male children and two kinds of female children. Your category (you and all the 'sisters') and your husbands will produce one kind; your 'brothers' (who marry your 'not-sisters') will produce the other kind. To put it in their terms, you and all your *nyanya* sisters get together with your *emen* not-brothers and produce one kind of child. Your *kakanye* brothers

124

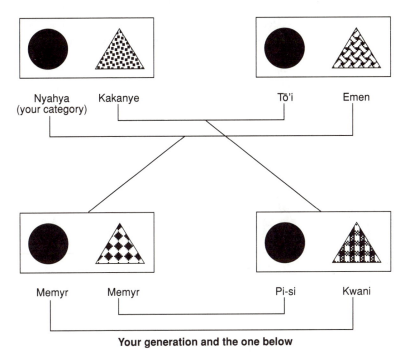

Figure 6. Relationship words: step six

get together with your *tō'i* not-sisters to produce the other kind of child (see Figure 6). These two kinds of children will marry in the same way that your parents' generation and your generation did. (Interesting, incidentally, that Wayapí women use *memyr* as we use the word 'child', not making a distinction between 'son' and 'daughter'.)

Your whole world is now divided into: (1) men and women; (2) three generations: your level; an 'up' level; and a 'down' level; (3) two kinds of men and two kinds of women on each level. That's twelve words, but look how quickly you actually make your choice. Let's say you want to classify someone and you want to choose one of these twelve words. First question: is it a man or a woman? It's down to six words already. Second question: is it my generation or not my generation? Let's say its my generation, and you're down to chosing one word or the other. That's two tiny logical steps and you're down from twelve words to two.

Doing it again – first question: is it a man or a woman? (Let's say it's a woman.) Second question: is it my generation or not my generation? (Let's say this time 'not my generation'.) Right, third question: is it the 'up' level or the 'down' level. (Let's say the 'up'.) Fine: so it's either *mama* or *pipi*.

Indeed you don't even have to think of it in terms of these tiny logical steps. It's simpler than that. You can see the jump from twelve to two immediately. You meet a woman who is up a level from you. She *has* to be EITHER *mama* OR *pipi*. You meet a man who is down a generation from you. He's got to be either a *memyr* or a *kwani*. To

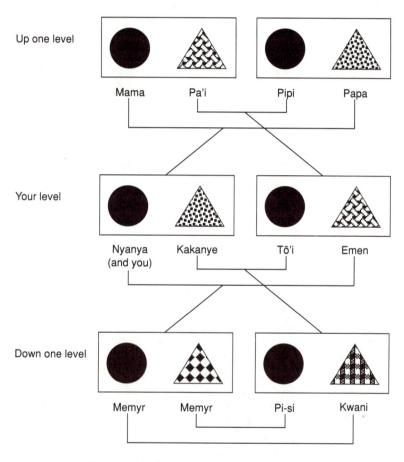

Figure 7. Twelve categories: woman speaking

126

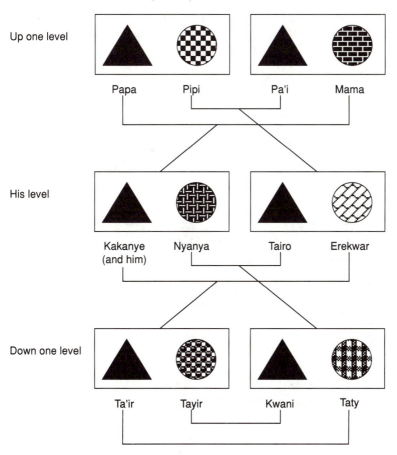

Figure 8. Twelve categories: man speaking

make that final decision, all you have to do is find one single person who has an actual relationship with you (a woman you call *mama* for example) and who knows her relationship with the stranger, and you've got your answer. If you meet a woman that one of your *mama*-people calls *nyanya* (sister), you call that woman *mama* too. And if your mother calls her *tō'i* then you call her *pipi* (see Figure 7). Men are using exactly the same set of categories, but they have different names for some of them in 'own' generation and 'down-one' generation (see Figure 8).

Now there's only one more step: two-up or 'grandparents' (*tamu* for men and *sa'i* for women), and two-down or 'grandchildren'

127

Heavy lines connect the sister and brother pairs.
Each of the two marriage pairs on one level produces the sister and
brother pairs on the next level.

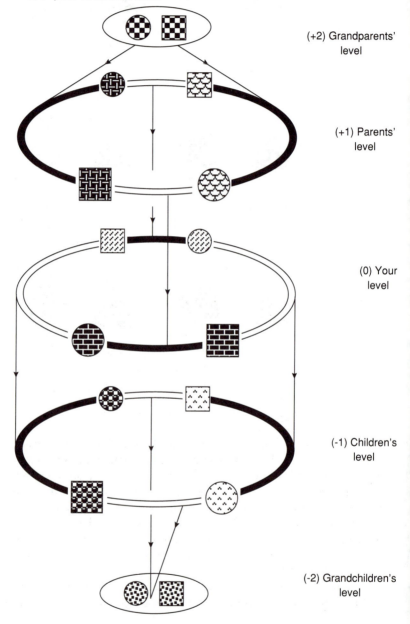

(+2) Grandparents'
level

(+1) Parents'
level

(0) Your
level

(-1) Children's
level

(-2) Grandchildren's
level

Figure 9. Wayapi relationship terms

(*pary* whether boys or girls). There's no way of saying 'three-up' or 'three-down'. Everybody in your world 'older' than your parents' generation is just *tamu* if a man and *sa'i* if a woman, and all children's children or younger are called *pary*.

Figure 9 (opposite) shows the complete pattern. This is so simple and beautiful, so compact and symmetrical. And look at the violence done when we force their words to work as our words do, for instance by translating *tairo* (a man speaking, meaning 'male, my generation, not-brother') as *cunhado* (Portuguese for 'brother-in-law') and then asking a Wayapí man: 'Are there any more *cunhado*s over there?' You can't get a one-to-one fit between our words and theirs. That's why the pattern has to be understood as a whole.

Most people with an interest in other cultures already know how to appreciate Indian artifacts, how to appreciate their knowledge and their skills. Most people would enjoy hearing their music and would be fascinated by their myths. But this wonderful arrangement of fifteen relationship words is a subtle and elusive surprise which most people miss. How on earth was it invented? What are we looking at when this constellation swims into our ken? Has it been there since the beginning? Looking at it carefully and thinking of the female words and the male words and the way they are interrelated you will see an interlocking double spiral – a double helix; DNA; life itself – all there in fifteen words.

Understanding a relationship terminology is an excellent example of the general effort at the heart of anthropology: to be able to step out of our way of seeing things and to step into other worlds. And it's a particularly acute and concise example. Unlike many shady areas, such as studying witchcraft, or beliefs about birth and death, or beliefs about souls and the hereafter, where we can convince ourselves that we've understood something when all that's happened is that we've become familiar with it, in the case of a relationship terminology you can't fake comprehension. You're either inside it, or you're not. You've got it, or you haven't. And you can achieve the radical shift in about half an hour.

We all use words like *papa* and *mama*, words that make distinctions of sex and generation and allow us to express relations one with another. But we're welded to our categories of 'father, mother, daughter, son, uncle, grandmother', which we think of according to a genealogy. It's not that easy when we're first confronted with a set of words that's dealing with similar questions of classifying people but doing so according to principles that we'd never dreamed of. Hence, when you can see that *papa* does not primarily mean 'my father', but 'one of the two categories of men one level up' and when you realize that the word can refer to even hundreds of people at once (half the males of that generation, actually), and when you can start thinking in terms of the complete constellation of terms, you've really done something exciting in terms of 'understanding other ways of thinking'.

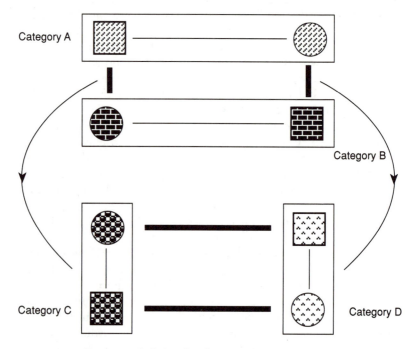

Figure 10. Relationship between two generations

There's one further step to go. We've arrived here through a series of either/or steps, in other words, through a series of binary distinctions: woman/man; up/down; brother/not-brother; either this or that. But that's just a way in; a device, like a ladder, that's no use once we're there. I've still got to show that the primary logic is not binary but a logic of fours.

Take any one piece out of the picture and you'll see it's a four. Look at your own generational level. There are four terms: two for men and two for women. Now take any two generations together (see Figure 10). Here again you'll see that Category A people marry Category B people and the result of that is that two other categories of people, C and D are produced. The males of A and females of B produce C. Females of A and males of B produce D. This diagram is the kernel of the previous one. However you look at it, it is articulated in fours: there are four classes of men and four classes of women. The one entire cycle illustrated here requires four classes of people. Once you've done one cycle, you can repeat it. If you look at the full Wayapí relationship terminology, the previous large diagram of the helix, what you're seeing is this cycle taking place twice. There are two other possibilities to think of: the cycle could reproduce itself over and over again; or it could reverse itself.

If it reproduced itself over and over again, each time you produced another generation you'd need four more terms (to correspond on that level to the fours on others: 'sister, brother, not-sister, not-brother', or 'father, not-father, mother, not-mother'). The list of terms would just grow and grow. So there's a useful economy in stopping the reproduction of terms and having terminal categories at plus two (grandparents, and everybody older) and at minus two (grandchildren and everybody younger). From your point of view, at level zero, the only really important levels are your own one together with those immediately above you and immediately below you: those who produced you and those you are going to produce. Beyond that people are just 'old' (grandparents) or 'young' (grandchildren). Hence, there's no need for the twist of fours to reproduce itself again and again. And in society after society, it doesn't. The diagram of the complete pattern could be used to illustrate examples from all over the world: from the South American rain forest, from North America before the Europeans destroyed the native cultures, from various parts of Africa, of India, of Australasia and the Pacific islands. There will be local variations to take account of, and the words themselves will be different according to the different languages (although don't be surprised if *mama* and *papa* keep appearing in the appropriate positions) but the form of the pattern will be the same.

The final piece of excitement is to find that a number of societies have made use of that other possibility, not where the twist of four repeats itself and then cuts off, but where it *reverses* itself: your level produces the level below which in turn produces your level. Or, if you prefer, the level above produces your level, which in

131

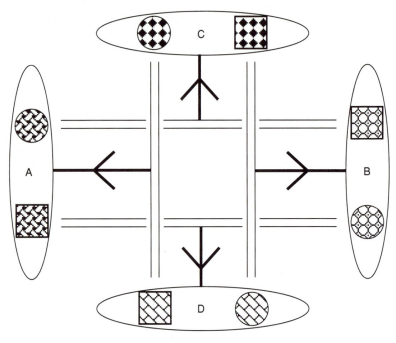

Figure 11. The four categories

turn reproduces the one above (see Figure 11). Here, the categories are related by the same principles that relate Wayapí terms from one level to the next, but instead of going down a step each time, as generation follows generation, each step reverses itself. Men and women in category A marry men and women in category B. A women produce C people. A men produce D people (while of course B men produce C people and B women D people). Cs and Ds then marry and produce A and B people again.

If we play with some names the patterns may become clearer. The four chemical bases of the DNA molecule are called Adenine, Guanine, Cytosine, and Thymine; daunting words that bring echoes of glands and sweetbreads and Peruvian dung. But if we use them as a basis for the four relationship categories, each category will have both men and women in it, and we can think up corresponding names for the four women categories and the four men categories that appear. We can have Adelina and Adrian in the first; Gwendolen and Gwilym in the second; Cynthia and Cyril in the

132

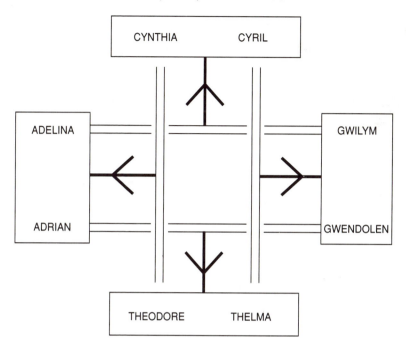

Figure 12.

third; and Thelma and Theodore in the fourth. The way it works is that Adelina marries Gwilym and they produce Cynthia and Cyril. Adrian marries Gwendolen and they produce Thelma and Theodore. In the next generation Cynthia marries Theodore and they produce Adelina and Adrian. Thelma marries Cyril and they produce Gwendolen and Gwilym (see Figure 12).

As a result, if you were Adelina (*an* Adelina of course), your mother would have been a Cynthia. Your daughter is also a Cynthia. Her daughter will in turn be an Adelina. Just as Adelina's mother and daughter are in the same category, so Cynthia's mother and daughter too are in the same category. So there's a woman line going back and fore, Adelina, Cynthia, Adelina, Cynthia – ACACA. Adrian's son is Theodore. Theodore's son is Adrian. So there's a man's oscillation too – ATATA. Directly mirroring this, there's another man's line: Gwilym, Cyril, Gwilym – GCGCG, and a woman's: Gwendolen, Thelma, Gwendolen – GTGTG (see Figure 13).

Adelina	A	Adrian	A
Cynthia	C	Theodore	T
Adelina	A	Adrian	A
Cynthia	C	Theodore	T
Gwendolen	G	Gwilym	G
Thelma	T	Cyril	C
Gwendolen	G	Gwilym	G
Thelma	T	Cyril	C

Figure 13.

The general point to notice from a technical point of view is that 'equations' are being made across the generations: for example, from a woman's point of view, Daughter = Mother, or to be more precise, your 'daughter category' is the same as your 'mother category'; from a man's point of view Father = Son, or rather 'father category' = 'son category'. This sort of set-up has been known to anthropology for decades and arrangements of relationship terms based on these principles are found all over the world.

What no one noticed was that there was *one other way* (and only one other way) of arranging these categories, producing different, and more interesting equations. No one noticed until an anthropologist, Bernard Arcand, went to Colombia at the end of the 1960s and lived with a people known as the Cuiva. These were the people who were the stars of a pioneering ethnographic film called *The Last of the Cuiva* made in 1970 by Brian Moser in the *Disappearing World* series for Granada Television.

This tiny group living in the Colombian rain forest, threatened with extinction because of the encroachment of cattle ranchers, revealed a fascinating feature in their set of relationship words. The set was based on the same principles as the Wayapí one. Unlike the Wayapí, but like many other people throughout the world, the Cuiva made 'equations' across the generations, 'folding up' the terminology into a few terms. They too ended up with four categories on the A, G, C, T principle. But they did it in a different way and produced a unique pattern.

It can be represented by leaving the Adelina/Adrian category where it was, and leaving the Gwendolen/Gwilym category where

134

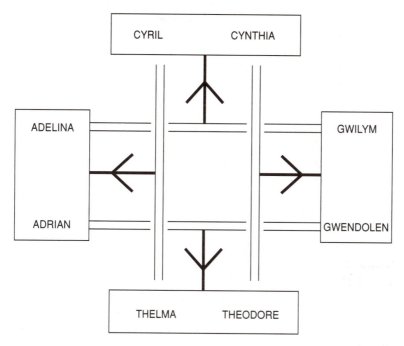

Figure 14.

it was, but if we make a minor adjustment in the diagram and put 'Cyril' next to 'Adelina', look what happens (Figure 14). The change looks insignificant and indeed the general principle of reversal is exactly the same. At a glance you might think there was no change at all. But what happens is that in this alternative arrangement the equations across the generations work out differently.

In this arrangement Adelina's daughter is still Cynthia, but Adelina's mother is Thelma. Thelma's mother is Gwendolen, and Gwendolen's mother is Cynthia. Instead of an oscillation where mother and daughter alternate, it becomes a complete circle of four. Similarly, Adrian's son is still Theodore, but Adrian's father is Cyril, whose father is Gwilym, whose father is Theodore, whose father is Adrian – another circle. Women and men go round the circle of four in opposite directions.

If you follow through different possibilities (Figure 15) you'll find endless intriguing reversals and contrasts and equivalences of relationships like this, all created out of a simple logic of four and all

135

Adelina	A	Adrian	A
Cynthia	C	Theodore	T
Gwendolen	G	Gwilym	G
Thelma	T	Cyril	C
Adelina	A	Adrian	A
Gwendolen	G	Gwilym	G
Thelma	T	Cyril	C
Adelina	A	Adrian	A
Cynthia	C	Theodore	T
Gwendolen	G	Gwilym	G

Figure 15.

balanced in repeating spirals of four. For example, Adelina's *son* is Cyril and so is her father. So the equation is made between a woman's son and her father. Similarly Adrian's *daughter* is Thelma, as was his mother. So there is a parallel equation between a man's daughter and his mother. For a woman, father and son fall into the same category. For a man, mother and daughter do. And so it goes on.

Seeing how the Cuiva think about their relationship words reverberates on all sorts of theories and conjectures. When anthropology mused about what could possibly be the 'simplest' form of social organization (in logical terms, or in evolutionary terms, or ambiguously in terms of both) there was ample evidence to show that it couldn't possibly be expressed through a set of terms based on the ones we are familiar with, pared down to a minimum; that is to say a vocabulary that reflected the kind of commonsensical image we might think up of tiny nuclear families of mum, dad, and the kids living in scattered caves.

Anthropological theory was aware that the answer had to be a formal pattern of some kind, but at the time so many writers had got stuck on binary logic, a logic of contrasting pairs, a logic of twos. The idea was that the simplest form of social organization had to be a dual one – an 'us' category and a 'them' category, where 'we' would marry 'them' and vice versa. And indeed articles were written on the theme 'Do dual organizations exist?'

But dual organizations are not that simple. If you wanted to think up a primordial society consisting, say, of two categories, the

Campbells and the MacDonalds, where the rule is that Campbell women marry MacDonald men and vice versa, you've instantly got a problem. If a Campbell woman marries a MacDonald man, what are the children going to be? They must be either one or the other, but how are you going to decide? To sort the problem out you have to introduce *extra* principles, for example that women will pass on the name (i.e. matrilineally) or the opposite way, that men will pass on the name (patrilineally), and before you know it you'll be involved with clans and all the paraphernalia of descent principles. If you didn't want to go down that line, and if you wanted to keep things simple, you would have to invent two other categories, like MacPhee and Macpherson, and arrange things according to the four categories above. (Campbell women might produce MacPhees, Campbell men Macphersons, and so on.) When it comes to social organization, four is simpler than two.

It's no accident that the Pythagoreans associated the number four with harmony and justice. It's no accident that in the psychoanalysis of Carl Gustav Jung those mandalas, the circles divided into four that people dreamed or designed, were seen as expressions of the person's striving after the unity of self and a sense of completeness, just as they were used in Buddhist traditions of meditation. Binary systems, systems of twos, dual organizations, great elaborations of contrasts like the *yin* and *yang* of the Dao, systems of left and right, the oppositions and contradictions of Marxist thought; all these seem amateur in the face of thinking in fours.

Four Mighty Ones are in every Man: a Perfect Unity
Cannot Exist but from the Universal Brotherhood of Eden.

It is no accident that Wayapí numbers stop at four. The number four is fundamental and elemental.

Fire

Fundamental and elemental – as is fire. In an earth-floored house, the old-fashioned Wayapí style, the hearth would be on the ground at one end. In a house with a raised floor of slats, a large circle of bark would hold in a base of earth on which the fire was laid. No one would waste a match. If you let your fire go out you took some from next door to get it started again. It was comforting to be so close to fire, nursing it alive in the half light before dawn or watching the flames at night when the last conversations had stopped.

Fire is so easy for us to take for granted. Old-fashioned anthropology books conventionally describe the use of fire as an 'art' – a charming and accurate choice of word. Waiwai explained that in the old days, before they had matches, starting a fire was a time-consuming process of striking a spark from stones on to tinder. When they went on journeys the women knew how to wrap up embers in leaves to carry along with them to the next stop – such delicate skills. Those who didn't have Brazilian blankets or thick Brazilian hammocks to keep them warm would place small piles of glowing embers under their net hammocks on cold nights, sometimes inches away from a sagging body, and never, apparently, had accidents.

If a number of monkeys or pigs were killed when in camp, a big fire would be lit beneath a large wooden frame and the dismembered carcasses smoked and roasted on top. Fish were treated like this too, on week-long fishing expeditions downstream to larger waters. The process is known as *moka'è*, and if you're clever with the archaeology of language, you might hear the English word 'buccaneer' coming through from this: 'a person who roasts his meat on a *boucan*'. Some dictionaries still give the derivation as coming from Carib languages. But it comes from Tupian, via French. It's the original barbecue, except that its purpose was to preserve the meat for later consumption.

Linguistic echoes like this are delightful. Sometimes, though, the reverberations are more profound, like one brief incident in that weird journey when I took Parahandy on his first trip out of the forest. He had been pestering me for weeks to make sure I took him with me when I next went to Belém. A number of Nipukú people, both men and women, had been taken down to the frontier towns by gold-prospectors or FUNAI officials, and in the settlements in the east there had been even more contact with the outside. Parahandy was intensely curious about what was out there and determined to go. I was uneasy about the responsibility, about his vulnerability to illness, and because of an understandable reluctance of the FUNAI people to agree. But then it would be so interesting, wouldn't it, to 'observe' his reactions.

Like most people, I lead a life of quiet desperation (that's one of Thoreau's phrases), and there was little of the journey that could have been described as me standing back, casting a cold eye, recording what was indeed a fascinating event. I wasn't an observer in that journey. I was an apprehensive participator. As the stages and events followed pell-mell, the observable cruxes couldn't be missed – his first sight of the road; his first sight of a truck; his first journey by plane; his first sight of city traffic. But the nuances and subtleties of what was taking place were beyond me, partly because my role as cicerone had me taut with anxiety, also because I couldn't find an appropriate medium to grasp what, for him, was going on.

If any of us want to make a decent job of our first impressions we all know how important it is to keep up the discipline of writing, or at the very least of talking. It's the only way to get hold of the vividness of the moment. Visual memories and other sensations will simply let us down later. Photographs and films won't do the job. These are freeze-dry techniques that simplify and fix the picture. The intricacy has to be imaged in words.

Parahandy wasn't talking very much. I couldn't very well keep him going on a running commentary with banal journalistic prompts like 'What's it like?' or 'How do you feel?' At the road team's base camp, where we spent a miserable night in the corner of an empty dormitory, hiding from mosquitos under sheets (and which was also his first encounter with a bed), he did say 'It's like dreaming; it's like dreaming'.

His own descriptions emerged later when he returned to the Nipukú and told of his journey to his friends. When he talked of the truck journey, he thought it was wonderful to see mirrors that the driver used to see behind. (There's a connection there with shamanism which I'll come back to.) He'd felt angry in the Goeldi Museum park when he saw a Brazilian couple kissing. Brazilian people were, he thought, by and large ugly, but he was impressed by the beauty of the Japanese he had seen in Belém. Also, he said, 'The Brazilians eat like animals.' What was this?

Friends from the Goeldi Museum came out with Parahandy and me to eat in a restaurant. The meal ordered for him was a steak, a side salad (mostly lettuce), and mushrooms. It could hardly have been a worse choice. The steak wasn't rare, but it certainly wasn't well-done, hence when he touched it with his fork he said 'blood' with quiet disgust. He giggled at the lettuce and said 'forest leaves', and said he knew very well what 'fungus' was. That dish was shared around amongst the rest of us and another of fish and root vegetables ordered for him.

He explained this incident to his friends at the Nipukú: how the Brazilians eat raw meat, like the jaguar; and forest leaves, like monkeys. The third point was made when he arrived at my house along with Siro and Teyo, all three giggling, hiding a huge fan-shaped fungus that grows on rotten trees, which he produced saying: 'Here's your food. Here's Brazilian food.'

Asking the question: 'What is it that distinguishes human beings from animals?' produces all sorts of suggestions, from nostrums to profundities, from 'naked ape' to 'zoon politikon'. In one of the most famous passages in Karl Marx's writings he says:

Men can be distinguished from animals by consciousness, by religion or anything else you like. They themselves begin to distinguish themselves from animals as soon as they begin to *produce* their means of subsistence, a step which is conditioned by their physical organization. By producing their means of subsistence men are indirectly producing their material life.

And later he continues:

. . . Life involves before everything else eating and drinking, housing, clothing and various other things. The first historical act is thus the production of the means to satisfy these needs, the production of material life itself. And indeed this is an historical act, a fundamental condition of all history, which today, as thousands of years ago, must daily and hourly be fulfilled merely in order to sustain human life.

From that *aperçu* came an endless philosophy of production: modes of, forces of, relations of, means of; production, production, production. It's a wonderfully rich insight, as long as you don't linger too long over spiders' webs and birds' nests.

But a more accurate one on the same theme came from Claude Lévi-Strauss. In his way of putting it, one of the keys that effects the passage from 'nature' to 'culture' (a periphrastic way of saying 'from animal to human') is the use of fire for cooking. It's fire that transforms food from its raw state (nature) to its cooked state (culture). Not only is he correct that cooking is uniquely human, but it's a point recognized in society after society, as it was that night by Parahandy in the Belém restaurant.

All over Amazônia you'll find myths on the theme of 'How we stole fire from the Jaguar'. It's usually in the form of an adventure where 'we' trick the jaguar and race back with the fire. Everything gets inverted. Originally 'we' were in the form of animals and birds, and, importantly, couldn't speak, but made animal noises. The jaguar had the form of a human and had the gift of speech. Having stolen the fire, we also learned how to speak. The jaguar lost both fire and speech. That's why he goes around the woods roaring in anger.

There are echoes, like etymologies, that are more or less pleasing, and correspondences, in what people say, that are more or less profound. This one is insistent and compelling. Shelley didn't know anything about Amazonian myths, but he knew the Greek ones when he wrote *Prometheus Unbound*:

> And he tamed fire, which like some beast of prey
> Most terrible, but lovely, played beneath
> The frown of man . . .
> He gave man speech, and speech created thought,
> Which is the measure of the Universe.

From Aeschylus and Shelley, and from Amazonian Indians, come two audacious suggestions: that the gift of fire came before the gift of speech; and that it's from the art of fire that all other arts and skills and sciences follow. Aeschylus and Shelley recognized that the transforming power of fire lies at the base of all human production. Using fire, humankind

> tortured to his will
> Iron and gold, the slaves and signs of power,
> And gems and poisons, and all subtlest forms
> Hidden beneath the mountains and the waves . . .

But both of them missed the more basic point; a point which is obvious to Amazonian peoples; namely, that long before these arts and skills and sciences came along, the primary use of fire, its primary transforming power, was for cooking, enabling the production of proper food. That's why fire is the fundamental art of production.

Giving

When people ask these questions about 'What makes us essentially human?', the enquiry is often based on finding differences between ourselves and animals, where somehow or another we are able to say that we have certain qualities or habits or capabilities or gifts that animals don't have. We can then survey these qualities and say 'Thank goodness we are therefore better than animals, being superior to them in this and that and the next thing'. These distinctive and superior attributes then become the essential checklist of what makes us human.

There was a time when the checklist of essential attributes of humans, such as bipedal gait (walking on two legs), language, and so on, included tool-using. Along came some zoologists working with chimpanzees who showed that chimps too were tool-users, not in the sense that, for instance, lammergeiers break the bones of their prey and get at the marrow by dropping them from the air on to particular rocks; not in the sense of thrushes using stones to break snails on. These are 'tool-using' in a sense. The point here was that *some* bands of chimps knew how to use sticks to get termites out of mounds and others didn't. In other words the key element here was learning. As long as some groups of chimps knew how to do it and some didn't, that constituted the presence of cultural tool-using. So the zoologists were able to say: 'Back to the drawing-board, you anthropologists, your checklist is wrong'.

Let's just duck the questionable assumptions. For instance, there's no need for the list of essential qualities to be a list of superior qualities; pluses for us and minuses for the animals. Animals have all sorts of capabilities that we don't have: perception abilities, awareness of sensory things, skills of locating, mobility skills. Perhaps our list of essential features should include what we significantly lack.

The checklist doesn't seem the most important problem anyway. We know perfectly well *that* we are different from chimps, and it would certainly be intriguing to have a final and definitive list of the qualities and traits that make us just so, and them just so. However far such questions go they remain questions of description and classification; of understanding from the outside. I'm more interested here in questions that deal with understanding from the inside. I'd dearly like to know, for instance, how far those who study primates feel that they are gaining an understanding 'from the inside', how far they feel they have shared the lives of those they study. I wonder if they'd ever go so far as to say they'd participated in their chimps' lives and communicated with them.

The issue is not whether we make use of the same objects as chimpanzees do, or even whether we teach each other or imitate each other in different ways according to our different cultures and so learn to use the objects in distinctive ways. What's important to try to understand amongst ourselves is what the objects mean to those involved. Meaning is use, certainly. That we *use* hoes and mattocks and axes is certainly a start. But that's hardly the whole story. As soon as you are able to say: 'This is my hoe. I will *give* you my hoe in exchange for your sack of potatoes', you have transformed the object as if by magic. Suddenly we're not talking about the *techniques* of things; we're talking about the *values* of things.

I mentioned Marcel Mauss's *Essay on the Gift* before. It was first published in 1924 and is one of the core works in anthropology. He was impressed, amongst other things, by the example of the *kula* ring in the Trobriand Islands off Papua New Guinea described by Bronislaw Malinowski in 1922. The Trobriand *kula* valuables were of two kinds: necklaces and armshells. The necklaces went in one direction and the armshells in the opposite direction round a huge network of exchanges that involved islands hundreds of miles apart. You couldn't call this 'trade'. These items were in no sense of the word 'sold'. Their practical value was nil. (Many of the armshells were too small to be worn, for example.) What was going on? What was all this exchanging for?

Malinowski saw that the flamboyant ceremonial *kula* exchanges were reflected at all levels of the society. *Kula* exchanges were the most dramatic and obvious, but behind them there was an enormous fabric of formal exchange procedures involving various degrees of political and social relationships: gifts given to chiefs; distributions made by women to women after mortuary ceremonies; all the way down to the domestic sphere where obligatory gifts of yams went from brothers to their married sisters. 'The whole of tribal life is permeated by a constant give and take', said Malinowski.

Marcel Mauss saw the key to the whole matter in his *Essay*. What is it, he asked, in the thing given that requires reciprocal giving from the person who receives? He saw that the dynamic of giving and reciprocating was a profoundly moral matter. Indeed in Mauss's vision, the exchange of objects is *the* fundamental expression of human morality. The obligation to give, the obligation to receive, and the obligation to repay are together the groundwork on which human beings maintain responsible relations between one another. The failure to give, and indeed the refusal to receive, are tantamount to a declaration of war.

Mauss had a profoundly moral point to make. A main theme of the essay is to contrast the morality of gift exchange in the societies he looked at with present-day economic and market forces which he referred to as 'constant, icy, utilitarian calculation' . . . 'One might even say that a whole section of the law, that relating to industrialists and businessmen, is nowadays at odds with morality . . .' 'It is our western societies who have recently made man an "economic animal".' He insisted that we should learn from these examples of exchanging: *'Ainsi, on peut et on doit revenir à de l'archaïque, à des éléments* . . .' which an earlier translation rendered: 'Hence we should return to the old and elemental'.

I saw the old and elemental once in the most fleeting way – two slight moments so discreet that they were perhaps meant to be imperceptible to the outsider. High up the Igarapé Onça two young men with their two young wives, each with two children hardly more than toddlers, had settled by themselves well away from any of the large villages. Each man had married the other's sister. They lived in one oblong earth-floored house, a separate hearth at each end. I arrived to visit and hung my hammock with the man I knew better. In the morning both men went to hunt. Both got a single peccary. Both hearths cooked up a stew. Our end had its meal ready first, and as we began to eat a child from this end was sent with a calabash of stew to the other end. This was deposited in the pot cooking at that hearth. Later, as we at our end lolled in our hammocks, a child came from the other end with a calabash of their stew which was taken by the woman at this end and put into her pot. Nothing was said. The exchange wasn't, of course, an 'economic' act which distributed scarce resources. It was a moral act, expressing the obligations of the relationship the people were in.

The obligations of giving and receiving are certainly old and elemental. But there's nothing idyllic about them. Mauss mentions the dangers of getting involved in exchanges that might go wrong, unwanted obligations, and the fears and anxieties that such obligations engender. The exchanges need not be dignified. They may be done with reluctance and resentment. And the force of these obligations can be exploited cynically.

One of the most damning details of the European invasions of the Americas is that you can hardly find a case where first contact with the native people was hostile. There was no excuse for the subsequent brutality. Here's what happened when a Portuguese expedition made the first European contact with those who lived in what is now called Brazil. The men on the shore were Tupian. Contact was made on a Thursday morning, 22 April 1500, at 10 o'clock. It was described by Pero Vaz de Caminha in a letter to his monarch, Manoel I of Portugal. The first contact was marked by an exchange of gifts:

We caught sight of men walking on the beaches. The small ships which arrived first said that they had seen some seven or eight of them. We let down the longboats and the skiffs. The Admiral . . . sent Nicolau Coelho on shore to examine the river. As soon as the latter began to approach it, men came out on to the beach in groups of twos and threes, so that, when the longboat reached the river mouth, there were eighteen or twenty waiting.

They were dark brown and naked, and had no covering for their private parts, and they carried bows and arrows in their hands. They all came determinedly towards the boat. Nicolau Coelho made a sign to them to put down their bows, and they put them down. But he could not speak to them or make himself understood in any other way because of the waves which were breaking on the shore. He merely threw them a red cap, and a linen bonnet he had on his head, and a black hat. And one of them threw him a hat of large feathers with a small crown of red and grey feathers, like a parrot's. Another gave him a large bough covered with little white beads which looked like seed-pearls. I believe that the admiral is sending these articles to Your Majesty.

When strangers meet in amity they *know*, whatever their culture, that they should exchange gifts. In this case, and in hundreds of others like it which go on to this day, it was a cynical manoeuvre from the point of view of one of the parties, since the Europeans had an agenda very far from one of friendship, trade, or reciprocal interaction.

I mentioned before the well-tried procedure that FUNAI expeditions used for making contact with isolated Indians that they feared might resist violently were they to be approached. It was developed during the days of the defunct SPI (the Indian Protection Service) and, although its aims were questionable, it's worth appreciating how courageous those who took part were since they put their lives at considerable risk. If, for example, an unknown group was located by surveying the area from a light plane, and if it was decided that these people should be brought under government supervision, an expedition would set out over-land in the direction indicated by the aerial survey looking for paths used by the Indians. At selected spots on the paths gifts would be strung out like objects on a washing line. The team would then withdraw. They would return from time to time to examine the string of gifts. Perhaps at first the Indians would remove some objects, such as knives, but would smash others, like mirrors. More gifts would be left, and again the team would withdraw. The strategy would be repeated until the team found objects left in return. The return gift, the act of reciprocity between those who have never set eyes on each other, was the sign that the team could risk going forward and try to make personal contact. They might even risk entering a settlement. The power of the gift breaks the suspicion, the fear, and the will to resist of the isolated people. They are 'pacified' by being enticed into the obligations of gift-giving.

Now and again, if we're on their side, we can squeeze a wry drop of satisfaction when we see Indians exploiting the procedures rather than being exploited. In 1556 Manoel da Nóbrega, leader of the first Jesuits to set up in Brazil, wrote an imaginary dialogue between two missionaries where one of them, pessimistic and contemptuous of the heathens he was trying to convert, says:

> The worst thing of all with the Indians is that when they come to my tent by giving them one fish-hook I can convert them all, and with another I could unconvert them again, for they are inconstant . . .

Malinowski's account of the Trobriand Islands revealed an array of gift-giving procedures, varying in scale and in public importance. The major, formal procedures were named. Particularly as regards the *kula* exchanges, there was a complicated vocabulary to describe the various kinds of gifts given at the various stages of the cycle. I think in some ways I'd have found life easier if I had been living amongst an elaborate formality like that. You can't live in the forest for long without having to come to terms with the basics of giving, receiving, and repaying, the difficulty being that although you know that the procedures are a matter of course, you have no idea how to do them. You've been asked to dance, you can't refuse, and you don't know the steps. Are you going to make an awful mess of it?

There are peoples in the Amazon forest who live in large communal houses, shared by a number of families. There are others (famously the Gê-speaking peoples of Central Brazil) who construct circles of houses round a generous space with a communal men's house in the centre. Still others have individual houses set up in a random pattern but maintain communal eating practices. Wayapí villages had none of these formalities. They were reluctant communities. People felt drawn to a communal life, but living together was a constant source of tension, as if certain protocols which might ease the strain were missing. There was a restlessness, an unsettled way of being, where families sometimes split off and went to live on their own. Sometimes it might have been two 'brothers'; sometimes a 'brother' and 'not-brother' each of whom had married the other's sister, like those who exchanged the peccary stew; sometimes it might indeed just have been a man, his wife, and their children.

I've explained how settlements were impermanent. Of course there were thunderingly basic material forces at work to induce their movements. However well a house was built it would get decrepit in a few years. Cockroaches and scorpions would have moved in. The thatch would get ragged. And finally termites would get going on the poles. Also the habits of slash-and-burn agriculture encouraged people to move their gardens. But materialistic reasons aren't enough to explain the movements. The gardens and settlements could easily have crept around the same area for years. You could burn your house down and build another just to the side of it. You could clear the bit of forest right next to your three- or four-year-old garden that's getting overgrown. But that's not what happened. A family that wanted to go would choose a spot two, three, four days' walk away. They would go to and fro, visiting the spot over a couple of years, living in shelters there, clearing and planting a garden before making the final break. It often happened that following one family's move, others came and set up near them until gradually over the years another village was formed.

Looking at their movements over the years I've known them, and hearing them talk about the past, I get the feeling that in an ideal Wayapí universe there would be a large population living unmolested in unlimited areas of forests, where each household would be self-contained, isolated, far enough, but not too far from neighbours – rather like the most prosperous suburbs we see around us in our major cities.

Nipukú, during the 1970s, was one extremity: a single clearing, all the houses cheek by jowl, everyone in sight of everyone else. It was impossible to enter or leave the village unseen. This was a community responding to the surrounding crisis. The intensity of contact was at its height. Enormous changes were taking place. Epidemics were sweeping through the area. Hence Nipukú was a protective huddle.

Mariry during the 1980s was composed almost entirely of the previous Nipukú people, but, by contrast, the settlement was scattered: a nucleus of three houses crowded round the FUNAI house; two others within sight a hundred yards away to the north; then an area of forest and a few minutes' walk to a self-contained cluster of five houses round Waiwai's place. To the south of the FUNAI centre it was maybe half a mile, past a couple of gardens to a clearing – two families and two big houses there, then beyond that, perhaps a half-hour walk to a single house shared by two men and their families. The whole arrangement was much grander than Nipukú; much more settled; that much more at ease with itself, although all the old tensions still simmered on.

The principal problem of communality was food sharing; not garden produce, but what was brought in from hunting and fishing. The most dramatic result of a hunt was killing a tapir, the largest mammal of the region (curiously classified by our discipline of zoology in the same order as horses and rhinoceroses because of an odd number of toes). If near enough the village or if able to attract the attention of someone else, the hunter was supposed to start a long drawn out howl to indicate that a tapir had been killed. When the news got to the village everyone who could, would set off to where the animal lay. The hunter whose kill it was would sit by as the carcass was cut up by others, and he would shout out who would get which bit.

If there had been a particularly successful pig hunt, say five or six white-lipped peccaries, then all would be shared around the village. Similarly if a fishing expedition came back after an absence of a week or so with a large amount of smoked fish, that too would be shared around. But mostly hunters out for the day scuttled back into the village, their kill on their backs, with as little fuss as possible. Fresh fish from a day's outing would be left in the canoe for the women to collect later, rather than have the fisherman march through the village with his catch dangling from his arm. If it wasn't clear what someone had brought in, a child might be sent to find out. Of course, if I'd been out with the hunters it was always acceptable for Waiwai or Yanuari to come across and ask me, loudly and directly, what and how many had been killed.

The firmest formal arrangement was the obligations a young man had to his wife's father. Part of the process of marrying required the young man to live near his wife's father and work for him, clear gardens, and give him game and fish. You can see the obvious attraction for a young man to marry in his home village: he wouldn't have to move. Because so many older people died in the epidemics of contact, many young men found they could dodge these obligations, and if, say, a Capoeira man (from the east side of the area) managed to marry a Nipukú woman (from the west side) whose actual father was dead he would take her back to his original home in spite of the protestations of other Nipukú men, including of course Waiwai, that he wasn't doing the decent thing.

Apart from that particular formal arrangement, obligations of giving and sharing were more or less the kind of familial ties we would recognize. Although everyone on your generation was *classified* as one or other of two kinds of men and two kinds of women, you may have found yourself, as a woman, in a closer relationship on a daily basis with another woman you call 'not-sister', rather than with a number of other women in the place you might have called 'sister'. Your closest ties were with those who shared your house. Hence, if the man hunting for your house brought in one middle-sized bird, say a jacu (a 'guan'; about the size of a farmyard hen) then you may have had to let your obligations for that day shrink down to those sharing the same roof with you. But each time, each day, you had to decide that, and perhaps even if only one jacu came in, surrounding houses might have felt that they deserved a morsel too, especially if they had given you something yesterday or the day before. When supplies of fish and game were not lavish, it was a permanently awkward matter to have to decide how much your house was expected to share around those outside your immediate circle. You knew you were under constant scrutiny. Everybody had their eyes open to see what was coming into the village from the hunt, and everybody was keeping a look out for the subsequent movement of every calabash and every plate. Nevertheless, even at Nipukú, I'd have needed a gang of private detectives to keep track of the food sharing between houses. It was done surreptitiously, usually a child trotting off next-door with a plate.

From that perspective you can see how important the caxiri sprees were. Like the famous potlatches of Northwest America, they were the major expression of giving and receiving. Manioc was plentiful for those who had been provident. There was nothing furtive about the supply. Everyone knew how much there was in everyone else's gardens. The effort required was labour; gathering the tubers, peeling, scraping, squeezing, and then preparing the canoe-loads of beer; and how convenient for the men that the major expression of material exchange was entirely dependent on women's work. Sometimes the women from two or three households would take part in preparing a caxiri-wasu (a big caxiri), but it was always known that there was one particular woman who was the caxiri-owner for that occasion.

From the purblind view of FUNAI officials and missionaries the caxiri sprees were expressions of primitive debauchery. But if you appreciate Marcel Mauss's vision of the old and elemental you'll see in the sprees, through the medium of fermented manioc, the heart of communality where the most ancient protocols of exchange are fulfilled: the obligation to give; the obligation to receive; the obligation to repay.

It's not just a matter of appreciating the significance of a particular institution that appears here, there, and everywhere. It's not as simple as that. *Le don*, 'The Gift', in Mauss's view is a moral disposition, a moral feeling, a moral tone, not a particular procedure. So: you won't be able to do a cross-cultural survey, looking for 'The Gift' as an item on a checklist of attributes as you might ask: 'Do they have bows and arrows or not? Do they use hallucinogenic drugs or not? Do they cremate the dead or not?' You can't sensibly ask: 'Do they have gift-exchange or not?' That's not an accurate question. The general principles of exchange are going to be there wherever you look, but they are going to appear in a myriad of different forms, all the way from the high drama of the *kula* ring down to those 'little, nameless, unremembered, acts', not of kindness, not of love, but of *obligation*, like the exchange of peccary stew from one end of a house to the other. Hence the question is not: 'Are these principles there?' but: 'Are you and I capable of seeing them?'

If you compare societies cross-culturally you will easily see how these patterns of giving and receiving ebb and flow in varying intensities, where, for example, the description of the Trobriand Islands presented by Malinowski might be taken as a benchmark against which to compare other degrees of formal exchange procedures in other societies. Similarly, when you consider the example of a single society like the Wayapí, you can see in their singular lives different intensities of formality and elaborateness appearing in different contexts, all the way from the crescendo of a caxiri spree to the diminuendo of an exchange of peccary stew.

Food was the principal medium of these exchange procedures. (There was a series of creaky anthropological arguments that described women as the prime commodity circulated as a form of exchange through marriage arrangements.) How, then, was I to fit in to these formal patterns, or rather the lack of them? I couldn't live by sprees alone. What was I, without a household, to do on a daily basis? I couldn't possibly have arrived with sacks of rice and beans. It was impossible to carry in enough supplies to be self-sufficient. I had to throw myself entirely on them for food, do what I could in my role as 'master of the remedies' as I once heard myself described, and volunteer for as many hunting or fishing sorties as possible. In the close community of those years at the Nipukú it wasn't that difficult. My house was right in the centre of the place and I was fed by everyone with no apparent awkwardness. Everyone would know what I'd been given and would soon come with something if I'd been left with an empty stomach on a particular day.

But it was much more of a strain at Mariry where those nearest felt the greater burden, and where the rest wouldn't know what I was getting. The cuckoo in the nest was a much more anxious problem for my few immediate neighbours. And it was a much more anxious cuckoo they were feeding, too. It all worked out, though. The near neighbours were often relieved of their burden by the more distant people. Siro or Joaquim would arrive with a pineapple or a hand of bananas from their distant houses to the south and Nonato would regularly come through with a plate from Waiwai's area to the north; all this even though my role as 'master of the remedies' was now redundant since FUNAI had a pharmacy and a medical attendant in the village. (I wasn't supposed to give out any medicine but Yanuari, my 'father', and I had an understanding, and I'd manage to slip him extra analgesics or indigestion tablets when he felt he wasn't getting proper attention.) There were no formal obligations to feed me. This was The Gift modulating towards those very 'acts of kindness and of love', or so I like to think of it.

There's a question of professional ethics here. How should those who call themselves anthropologists and who arrive amongst such people as Wayapí relate to their hosts? When the missionaries set about learning the language and finding out about the ways of the people they are trying to convert, their policy is to pay for it. There are anthropologists who take the same line: pay your way, if not with money then with beads. One hour's talk equals so many bags of beads or so many dollars. And you'll probably find they call their hosts 'informants'. As soon as you set a standard of exchange where value can be numbered, a precise quantity of beads or a price in money, you've let yourself off the moral dilemmas. You've also, of course, let yourself off the relationship. That kind of exchange has nothing to do with the morality of The Gift. It's to do with the requirements of 'icy, utilitarian calculation'. I'm not prepared to turn my friends into paid informants. I'd rather take my chances with the impromptu arrangements of each day and deal with the concomitant anxieties as they come, worrying about being hungry and worrying about my obligations to repay.

Although I didn't pay 'informants', I was a useful conduit for outside goods. When it came to getting outside things from the Brazilians the morality of The Gift was left far behind. The idea was to get as much as possible by blunt and persistent requests. The shopping lists were long, but if you think about the items you could have predicted them: shot, powder, and percussion heads for brass cartridges; knives, machetes, axe heads, and files; hooks, fishing line, and wire; aluminium pots; torches and batteries; matches, cigarettes, mirrors, soap, shampoo, brushes and combs, toothbrushes, razor blades, talcum powder, scent, lipstick, nail-varnish, safety-pins, needles, coloured thread, nylon ropes, and postcards of other Brazilian Indians. That's a very modest list of requirements and luxuries.

Two other items were particularly important: red cloth (they could *always* do with more) and beads. Why beads? European invaders have for centuries been ingratiating themselves with indigenous peoples by giving beads. The appetite seems universal. It bemuses me, I suppose because I can't see the attraction of jewellery in my culture. When I see people fussing about their diamonds and pearls I find myself saying: 'Aye aye – beads'. All Wayapí adored beads. I had arrived at the start with three or four kilos of small *rocaille* beads in dozens of small sachets. When I first produced them at the Nipukú people ran from all corners of the village, crowded round, uttering their gasps of surprise which they do by letting go a glottal stop. They had hardly any of their own then, just some large dull ones from the French Wayapí in Cayenne.

No one ever asked for beads in exchange for food. What happened in those early days was that the discovery of the beads produced a flurry of headdress making. They made beautiful circlets mostly from toucan feathers. These were to be swapped for beads. We had now left far behind both gift exchanging expressing relationships and 'getting things from the outsider'. We were now into a mode of serious trading, one valued artifact to be exchanged for another. I hadn't been ready for the intense interest in the beads; I didn't want to trade; and I was glad to get rid of them once and for all. On later visits I gave all beads away immediately and made sure that everyone knew there were no more.

There were no formal rules about how to give things away. I found it an awkward business and I just had to get on with it. It had to be done in the 'getting things from the outsider' mode and the demands could get quite intense. Right at the end, at Mariry, came the final crisis of giving everything away. I'd made a list of what I had, and a list of who to give to. I thought the prize gift was the ·22 rifle, worth about US $150 in those days, together with the ammunition, and a pouch to carry the bullets. I reserved that for Matam. I was enormously fond of him, and owed him a lot. We'd been on dozens of hunting outings together. And more than that, he knew, and I knew, that I also owed him my life. Eight years before, at the Nipukú, it was he who had spotted me unconscious in the river, and who had got me out from under the branches of a submerged tree. If he could forgive me loading him with adjectives, Matam was fierce, independent, clever, and tender; lots of different moods. Fine: *we'd* done the hunting; *he'd* get the gun.

I got him as he was passing my house one day, and went through the negotiations of giving the rifle away. Once you go through something like that, what you *don't* get when it's over is: 'Oh, thank you very much. Very grateful, indeed. Just what I've always wanted.' To hell with that. I had a $3 aluminium pot sitting there too, ready to give away to someone else, and as soon as the matter of the rifle was settled, Matam started on about the pot too. He really, really wanted it.

That was the pattern. Young Piko'i had become a sort of major-domo shortly after the night he'd threatened to kill me. Nothing serious – he'd been drunk, and asked and asked and asked for beads till he, not I, got fed up with the conversation. He went berserk, jumped out of the house, and pounded up and down outside, shouting that he was going to finish me off. He began with a macaronic threat, half Portuguese, half Wayapí: 'Tu quer *rapar*?' ('You want *rapar*?' that being Wayapí for 'arrow') and went on in Portuguese: 'Eu vou pegar espingarda. Eu vou tirar en tua cabeça.'

('I'm going to get a shotgun. I'm going to shoot you in the head.')
I got a bit scared when it came to the shotgun threat since I'd seen
two drunken shotgun attacks during quarrels. So, when he moved
off, presumably to get the gun, I ran after him, and gave him a
violent hug. That seemed to calm him down, but when I let him
go, he started up again. Some of the other men came and dragged
him away, still screaming that he was going to put an end to me.
Two days later he moved in, hammock, bits and pieces and all,
never left again, and was utterly charming for months on end.
Right then; for all the charm he was to get – scissors, machete,
trainers, soap – I deluged him with gifts because he'd been so
endearing. After this, he noticed a miserable piece of red cord I'd
noted as something for . . . for who? . . . for Wei? for Kuretari?
. . . I can't remember. And Piko'i began to *beg* for it.

During those last days, one after another of my friends glided in.
I thought to begin with that they'd come to be close, since I was
going. But each began to ask, again and again, for the few little things
I'd got left, or to repeat requests about what to bring next time, or
what to send. I felt the strain growing. Surely they could see that I
was getting grumpy. In came Matam and started up yet again. He'd
already got the gun. He'd been refused the pot. This time he really
got going: 'GIVE ME . . .' What was it? I don't remember. A small
plastic container? A piece of red cloth? A bar of soap? God knows
what it was – some last trinket that I'd noted for someone else. I
refused, and grimly explained: 'I have already given you this and that.
I still have to give to so-and-so and to so-and-so. I don't have many
things left to give.' Composed, but earnest and determined, he
bounced on: 'Why do I ask you for it? Because I REALLY REALLY like
it. See? I REALLY REALLY want it. That's why I ask you for it.'

What a performance – utterly disarming. He had fallen in love
at first sight with the object. Nothing else mattered but to possess
it, hence the determination. My feeling in those situations (that a
sense of friendship was being cheapened by cupidity) was an
indication of how loose and inaccurate my emotional directions can
be. There I was worrying about the nuances of friendship, expect-
ing to be comforted by little signs and little reassurances, in the
middle of serious competitive negotiations about important objects.
Since I haven't the slightest idea what it's like to want a plastic
container so much it should be up to me in these circumstances to
make the effort to keep good-humoured throughout whatever
acquisitive onslaughts my friends put me through.

It was a major difficulty; and it never quite went away. At its heart was a lingering suspicion about what was at the back of motives and relationships. Had there been formal obligations and formal procedures there would have been no doubt. Were I to have taken the escape route of putting everything on a monetary scale, measuring and paying, the doubt could have been sidestepped. But this way I never quite knew.

I certainly do still have to learn the lesson of adjusting my feelings to keep my equanimity about the asking. They deserved and will deserve as much as I can possibly give them, and more. After all, the demands are just to do with trinkets; just objects and money. I can surely put up with that. What they have done for me by caring for me, feeding me, and allowing me into their lives puts me into a relationship with them that is far beyond the trinket mode. It's the obligations at that level I'd better attend to. I will try to return to the old and elemental.

A grain of sand

There, then, are three simple images: holding out your fingers in a fat V sign to make two and two are four; Parahandy's disgust at a rare steak in a Belém restaurant; and exchanging bowls of peccary stew between one hearth and another. The gestures and incidents seem homely and banal, but behind them are eternal verities.

> To see a World in a Grain of Sand
> And a Heaven in a Wild Flower:
> Hold Infinity in the palm of your hand
> And Eternity in an hour.

It would be splendid to be able to say that anthropology teaches everyone how to appreciate such significance in the commonplace. But I don't know if we could bear to live with the visionary gifts of William Blake every day of our lives. Wouldn't the intensity be too demanding? Perhaps the more modest and accurate claim would be that since the central concern of anthropology is with *other* cultures, with *cross*-cultural comparison, it can therefore offer richer and more inspirational opportunities for making something significant out of the quotidian.

'Significance is not given; it has always to be created.' Yes, but perhaps it's more complicated than an 'either/or' like that. It's not just that you *either* have the experience but miss the meaning *or* that you get down to work and find the answer. I find the meanings constantly fluctuating; glimmering, growing, and fading again. Something that looked important yesterday re-emerges as pretty banal today. Some other details do explode like a star-burst and change the view of the world. Four did that. So did fire. So did giving.

Four, fire, and giving: the elements of our thought, the fundamentals of our production, and the foundations of our morality. They are the measures of our universe. Why only three? you might ask. What about the four mighty ones? the perfect unity? Well, the fourth has been there all along. Shelley saw it. So did the Amazon Indians in those myths about the jaguar. Swinburne put it as a question: 'Who hath given man speech?' Language; that's the fourth one, and that's been the leitmotiv from the start.

6

REMEMBERING

We take it for granted that literacy is a necessary skill in our world. We take it for granted that those in our societies who lack that skill are disabled, and that they would function a lot better were they made literate. As the Wayapí came into contact with the Brazilian world it seemed an obvious step to teach them how to read and write. Here was a genuine gift – innocent, free of charge – that the invading world could give them. They would benefit enormously from it and would be better able to negotiate with the world that was going to engulf them. Alas, that gift is neither innocent nor free.

When I scribbled in a notebook, they called what I did *ekosíwar*. They also used that word for the designs on the skin of the anaconda and on the skin of the jaguar, as well as the kinds of abstract pattern they would make on pottery and baskets, and on their bodies. Anaconda and jaguar designs have all sorts of associations with knowledge and culture, given the place of these two creatures in beliefs and myths; but by the time I'd been around for a while, and by the time the missionaries had got to work, the specific kind of writing that I did was recognized as something separate. As Brazilian and missionary contact increased, our kind of writing, that particular kind of ekosíwar, came to be seen as a desirable skill. They wanted to learn it. Early on, though, I don't think it was as clear cut as that. Our writing wasn't seen as a practical skill for recording. It was looked upon as a way of seeing and creating knowledge.

After a few months at the Nipukú I went to the FUNAI post to get medicine. The awful news on coming back was that Tora had died; a young man about 16 years old. He had vanished in the woods and it had taken them two days to find him. His death was a mystery. It was announced one morning that a number of people were going to visit his grave. I was asked to come along, but first said I'd go another day since I'd promised to do thatching with Parahandy. There was a bit of a hubbub about this. Parahandy himself said I should go. I saw I'd misjudged the request, that it was important to go, and that the journey would be called off did I not agree to it.

Twice, before we set out, Waiwai checked that I was taking my notebook and pen. The group included Tora's mother and her infant, her two older sons and an older daughter. Tora's actual father was dead but his mother's new husband (another 'father') came along. So did three of the mother's brothers (from the 'not-father' category): Waiwai, Kuyuri, and Kasiripin. We went south into a hilly area unknown to me. Tora's grave was on a ridge. A small shelter had been built over it and small bundles of tobacco, urucu dye, and food had been hung from the roof poles. We went down to his death spot, half way down a steep slope. Kasiripin was beside me. Waiwai was someway off, looking away from us. 'Did he bring his book?' asked Waiwai, quite audibly. This was one of these peculiar formal conversations where the exchange took place through an intermediary. 'Did you bring your book?' asked Kasiripin. 'Yes,' said I. 'Yes,' said Kasiripin. 'Well, start writing,' said Waiwai.

Tora had been found naked, his tanga round his neck, and his waist string round his wrist. His bow and arrow had been propped up against a tree nearby and his knife was found stuck into the earth at his side. One knee was broken. He had a wound in the crook of one arm, and a large wound in his stomach. How and why had he died? Animals, snakebite, and Brazilians were all ruled out. Waiwai began his formal questions again: 'Has he finished writing?' 'Have you finished writing?' . . . 'So now he knows.' 'So now you know,' repeated Kasiripin.

I had feared, because of the formal build-up, that something like this was going to come. I could do nothing but disappoint them. The evidence baffled me. In those early days I didn't know of the suicides that took place from time to time during sprees, where men and women would hang themselves with their tangas from roof poles. Years later, at Mariry, someone said that Tora had indeed hanged himself. But how? And why wasn't he found hanging? I was hoping at the time that they would tell me what had happened, as indeed they did later. An agreement began to emerge that

Yurupari, a principal forest demon, had done it. Some weeks further on, that turned into a shamanistic accusation – that Sarapó, the *éminence grise*, still at that time living on the Rio Jari, was responsible. But there and then my writing was supposed to produce the explanation. Parahandy, who had not come on the visit, asked immediately when we returned: 'Did you write there?' And all that evening and into the next day or two the questions still came: 'Do you know *now*?'

In those early days no one ever suggested that I should teach them writing. It seems to have been regarded as some secret skill of mine. Perhaps my failure to produce an explanation altered their appreciation of what the skill was. Perhaps it took away something of the mystique. I just don't know. At any rate, years later their expectations were different. The missionaries near the post were getting on with their schooling, and Waiwai was also determined that the young people of his group be taught. What precisely Waiwai thought the skill would do for them I can't say. But are we so sure about what the skill can do for us?

'And today we start with the letter A'

It became FUNAI's policy to teach them how to write. I'm sure this was indeed intended as an enlightened and progressive move. It went along with other crackpot schemes like introducing cattle-raising and rice-planting – both of these being ways of making Wayapí people into productive members of the Brazilian market economy. Like everything else FUNAI did, the teaching was pretty pathetic. The teacher was casual, did a class when she felt like it, and that only with children. The FUNAI idea was to teach them to read and write in Portuguese.

Literacy was a missionary ploy too. The Summer Institute of Linguistics missionaries were trained in a strict teaching technique. They followed a disciplined timetable, worked hard, and were concerned to teach everyone, adults and children. Moreover, the missionary idea was to teach them how to read and write in Wayapí.

Both efforts filled me with dismay; the hopeless inefficiency of the first that was going to promise them so much and give them so little, at the cost of having to maintain these incompetent people in their midst; and the enormous grip that the second was beginning to have on them precisely because of its discipline and expertise. I was frightened by these literacy exercises because it was so difficult to appreciate what was going on.

I'd have been reassured had Waiwai and his people been indifferent to the offer. In *Phaedrus* Socrates tells the story of Thoth, the Egyptian god who invented writing, trying to convince Ammon, the King of Egypt, that this was a wonderful accomplishment. Ammon would have none of it, arguing that it would impair memory and lead to a bogus wisdom. And of course Socrates himself left nothing written. Mostly, though, people are impressed by the skill and are prepared to see a preternatural power in it, like the story of the Norse god Odin hanging himself for nine days and nine nights from the World-tree Yggdrasil, the tree of mystery, and getting as his reward knowledge of the runes and all the magical power that came with that.

Illiteracy is usually seen as a handicap that contributes to the miserable condition of so many of the wretched and dispossessed of the earth. So, at the simplest level, what is there to worry about if the missionaries and the Brazilians started teaching them reading and writing? It's just a skill, like learning to play a musical instrument, or learning to drive a car. It would be an additional skill that would enrich their lives. What could be wrong about that?

It's a naïve view by any standards. We all know that literacy is not just one skill among others. When you call someone illiterate you assume something about fundamental human capacities. Hence, in our way of thinking about it, we have upped the stakes immediately. It's widely held that literacy skills affect cognitive processes: that they allow for more rational, critical, and logical thought. Literate and non-literate is, at this level, well beyond mere skills. We're now at the level of different mentalities.

It was a pretty poor show that the anthropology profession took up the distinction as an equivalent for the earlier nineteenth- and twentieth-century distinctions between primitive and civilized. Non-literate people were even said to be stuck at a certain stage of cognitive development (which we, of course, were supposed to be well beyond). They were said to be stuck at what psychologists called 'pre-operatory thought'. Fine; let's for one moment accept this nonsense. Given these presuppositions, if illiterate primitives are in this benighted state, can you bring them out of it? Presumably the answer is yes, by teaching them literacy. And if you follow the argument through to this stage, it's now clear that you're doing an awful lot more than just giving them another skill. You are transforming the way they think. You are civilizing their minds.

Why would you want to start interfering with peoples' minds, especially if what you encounter is a more-or-less self-sufficient society that gets on perfectly well without you? The answer is that it's not just their minds you want to change. The Spanish conquistadores gave their religion to everyone they overcame, then took their land and their liberty. That's what they wanted. The religion was just an excuse. Similarly we give them our literacy not just because we want their minds to be like our minds. We want their *lives* to be changed too. It's their society we're after. It's the control and authority that we want.

William Blake, the mystic poet, engraver, and painter, saw the predicament in his weird images. He was steeped in balanced ambiguities, and saw that knowledge and reason were not all they were cracked up to be. He too saw it as a 'Tree of Mystery', like Yggdrasil that gave the runes, but in his vision it brought spiritual death:

> Soon spreads the dismal shade
> Of Mystery over his head:
> . . . .
> And it bears the fruit of Deceit.

This was the Tree of the Knowledge of Good and Evil. From this knowledge come all the systems of false morality and false churches. Under the rule of 'Reason' we hide in 'forests of night', forests, for Blake, being massive accumulations of such errors. The parson, like the missionary, manages to trap the farmer, surrounding him:

> With cold floods of abstraction, and with forests of solitude,
> To build him castles and high spires, where kings & priests
>   may dwell.

And it's in these forests of the night, these forests of Church and State, that the tygers of wrath burn, destroying them with all-consuming anger.

> . . . his tygers roam in the redounding smoke
> In forests of affliction.

Blake is doing as much in his fierce visions to condemn our despotic assumptions about literacy and reason as Karl Marx did later in his fierce economic commentaries on the moral degeneracy of capitalism.

In today's world of markets and development, of capitalism and multinational corporations, the illiteracy rate in this or that country is taken to be one of the clearest markers of its backwardness. (In this way of looking at things you can immediately notice the conflation of mental backwardness with material simplicity.) Economic development and prosperity are inhibited because of the lack of a literate workforce. From the basic literacy skills follow the basic work skills that will allow the powers that be to put everyone to work in factories and get the place on the road to prosperity.

This is where the complications begin. If you argue that way, you've committed yourself to the view that literacy skills produce *something else*. In this case the 'something else' is what's being called economic prosperity; to be more precise a certain specific kind of economic arrangement. But how do you know it's going to produce this? Suppose the skills you give the mass of illiterates produce not an army of compliant factory workers and docile civil servants but a band of eloquent revolutionaries who start writing about, and teaching others about, all sorts of other possible visions of prosperity? The answer is that the programme is not just one of 'teaching literacy'. What's being offered and what's being controlled is a package that socializes and institutionalizes people in the specific direction required.

Paulo Freire recognized that, in his *Pedagogy of the Oppressed.* Literacy and literacy programmes were not, for him, simply a matter of supplying people with a skill. It was a way of 'raising the consciousness' of those involved. In other words, far from solving an economic problem and allowing capitalist organizations to flourish, Paulo Freire was offering people a way of become more aware of their own predicament and capable of questioning it and protesting about it and resisting it.

Freire's approach lifts the veil on what's going on. There's not just *a thing* called 'literacy' that people either have or don't have. Acquiring literacy is part of a process of education by which people are moulded and socialized in various possible ways. In other words, people can be put through different kinds of procedures and regimes to make them literate. There is an excellent example from nineteenth-century Canada where literacy skills were taught by reading aloud – a common way of teaching. The case studied here showed that pupils from different ethnic backgrounds, with different accents, would be 'corrected' and taught a standard pronunciation. The teaching process was here being used as a way of controlling and eradicating what were seen to be deviant speech habits. The social consequences for those who were not educated into the standard patterns and who continued with their ethnic forms of speech are blatant.

It's not, therefore, a single skill that is being taught. People are being processed through, and made to conform with, the specific institutional arrangements that dispense the literacy. Literacy programmes don't take place in an institutional vacuum. They certainly did not in Fidel Castro's Cuba, nor in the Nicaragua of the Sandinistas. In Brazil, up until the military coup in 1964 that overthrew Goulart's government, there were exciting efforts up and running in the North East, inspired by Paulo Freire's views. There, the literacy programmes were a fundamental part of an enlightened political initiative that wanted people to find a way of fighting against those who oppressed them. Literacy was presented in a context that got people engaged with questions of land tenure and health care.

It's at this point that Freire's point of view does not seem to be radical enough. All specific literacy programmes hope to mould people in specific ways. And all specific programmes do so. But it's not done, as Freire still maintained, by changing people's mentalities, but by organizing social institutions in certain ways. Hence it's not the skill or lack of it that is in question. It's the surrounding paraphernalia that makes the difference.

So: I'd throw out, as dangerously trivial, the anthropological efforts to resurrect the old-fashioned primitive/civilized distinction as illiterate and literate mentalities. I'd want to go as far as querying any kind of *intrinsic* benefit of the skill of literacy. It's not the literacy that 'raises the consciousness'. The 'literacy' or 'illiteracy' is neither here nor there. Everything depends on what goes along with the educational process. Conversely, you can achieve your social goals by educational means that don't depend on literacy. You can hone people's self-awareness and increase their political sophistication without ever throwing alphabets and books at them. When you do begin to bombard them with letters what you've brought into play is a vehicle for carrying across the values and the expectations and the social forms you want to implant. The important question is: what, precisely, are you loading your vehicle with? Like religion for the conquistadores, literacy is just one possible vehicle for having your way with vulnerable people. That's why both the FUNAI efforts and the SIL efforts were, in their different ways, sinister.

With the inducement of a quasi-magical technique of knowledge, one ill-trained young woman, with hopeless materials, was able to start imposing a daily discipline on the children at Mariry, where at certain times of the day, times set by the outsiders, children were to be at a certain place doing certain things. I saw them gather for their first day, in a specially built hut, and heard that leaden opening: 'And today we start with the letter A.' I comforted myself with the hope that the operation would be so badly organized that it would disintegrate. The enterprise was inappropriate, inept, and suspect. Furthermore the Mariry people were being duped, with an empty promise of better things, into complying with this silly regime. Meanwhile, two or three days' walk away, through the forests of affliction, Tobias had them in the grip of his presbyterian discipline, enticing them, with the lure of the reading-and-writing magic, into the dark tabernacle of The Book.

I'm all for Ammon. At least that view would water down the exaggerated presumptions we make about our own intellectual powers, our cognitive development, our grasp of logical and rational processes, all because we can show off in writing. I'm more struck by the limitations of what writing can do, how it inhibits us, how badly most of it is done. Conversely, I so appreciate how much Wayapí were able to do and remember without it. Look at the way so many of them in those days got the hang of quite passable Portuguese, better than my efforts in Wayapí, without ever having put pen to paper.

If we had our books and our archives and our notes and our files removed from us forever, what a mess we'd be in. I'm supposed to have read a lot, but how much can I recall of the content of what I've read, far less recite it? If you can do the whole of 'Tam o' Shanter' at a party it's considered a small miracle. I write books and articles, but I don't keep them in my head. I look back at them with an uneasy sense of detachment. 'Did I write that? How could I have thought that up?' It's like stacking up attics, lumber rooms, forgotten warehouses of stuff that sit there getting dusty.

All this knowledge that has no immediacy. That's the principal result of our literacy skill – a storage system.

Since they had *nothing* of that kind of back-up, it made their way of storing knowledge so precious (and ours so cheap). All they knew they carried in their heads. It's like carrying all your belongings with you, having no need for rooms and cupboards and chests of drawers. It's eminently self-sufficient. But if you forget, it's gone. Your store of knowledge is as finite as your living memory. Siro, who was so good at the myths, was like a National Library. If he had died in a flu epidemic it would have been as great an intellectual loss as if one of our storehouses of texts was burned down.

'Dark sayings of old' (Psalm 78:2)

If you were suddenly whirled away into the world of Amazonian myth you'd be as alarmed as if you were lost in the forest for the first time. All the rules would have gone. You'd have no bearings. You'd find yourself in a bizarre world where narratives didn't seem to be narratives. You'd probably start saying that myth narratives were like dreams or demented visions. You can get a hint of such dislocation if you start reading Claude Lévi-Strauss's *The Raw and the Cooked*, where, in cerebral spheres dangling in an ethnographic void, myth after myth is presented for processing through a structuralist blender. Never mind the structuralism. That was an intellectually frivolous fad of the 1960s and 1970s. If you ignore the 'analyses' and concentrate on the myths you'll start getting something of the feel of being set adrift in a very strange world. But although you do get hints of the strangeness, the presentation of the myths as neat little packages on the page is not the way you find them. They are not as domesticated as that.

The myths come at you very slowly, at first just fragments that you hardly notice, as when a certain liana is called 'japu-bird's snot'. You just note that down as the name, and learn to recognize the liana next time. You perhaps won't find out for months that there's a long story wherein, at a certain point, the japu-bird sobs uncontrollably, hence its snot is all over the woods. There are lots of these bits and pieces, and at this level you feel you're building up an interesting folklore.

Masirí and I, on a run to the post, were camped at the Sabão. We were sitting on rocks in the river with a full moon up.

'What's that, papa?' asked Masirí, indicating the moon. I was puzzled by the question but managed the phrase: 'A big star, perhaps?' 'No', said he, 'that's a man who had sex with his sister.' 'Why is that?' 'Oh, I don't know. Ask Siro. He knows.' Months later I got the story:

The origin of the moon

Long ago in the grandfather-people-time a woman was visited every night in her hammock by a lover she did not know. She wanted to find out who he was so she hid a calabash of black genipa dye under her hammock. When the lover arrived she reached down into the bowl and covered her hands with genipa, then caressed her lover's face. Next morning, she told the other women what she had done, and they all looked around to see who the man was. It was one of her brothers. He was so ashamed that he left the village. He shot an arrow away up until it stuck in the sky. Then another so that it hit the nock of the first arrow. Then another. Then another, until he had made a chain of arrows all the way to the sky. He climbed up, and there he is today. You can see the marks of the genipa on his face.

It looks like a simple narrative. But think of the questions you could ask. What do the words 'brother' and 'sister' mean? They are not simple equivalents of our words. So is this what we call 'incest sex', or just 'inappropriate sex'? Why black genipa dye instead of red urucu? What's this business of making a chain of arrows by shooting one into the nock of the other? (It's a detail that appears all over Amazônia.) These are the kind of questions that intrigue you even when you're learning the simplest story, and even when it's presented in a neat package on the page.

So much goes missing when the myths have to be presented in this way. Myths aren't merely texts; they are performances. The texts that appear on the page are the result of an extraordinarily convoluted processing. The researcher takes the person called 'the informant' to one side and, with pen-and-notebook and tape-recorder as tools, squeezes out the myth, like a confession or a police interview. It's then transcribed, translated, written-up, edited, and printed.

166

But telling a myth is an animated, vocal event – not, though, as far as I know, a great public event. Myths are not declaimed, like a theatrical show, to a large audience who attend specially for the event. It's a domestic performance, usually involving older people telling youngsters. But even in the most intimate circumstances other people are around, listening in, participating, correcting, asking questions, laughing, and oohing and aahing. What we see on the page is a package in a narrative form that we are able to find comprehensible, accustomed as we are to newspapers and novels. The performance is on the one hand more vivid, accompanied by noise effects, mimicry, and gestures, and on the other hand more difficult for outsiders since it can be so condensed – the teller can assume that the audience knows so much both of the story line and of the particular details that for us require glosses.

The easiest part for us is that so many charming fragments have a *Just So Stories* point made at the end. Most of these explain details about animals and birds: 'Why does the tapir have a curly tail? Because when they were all climbing up an arrow chain to the sky the tapir was too heavy and fell down landing on its bum.' 'Why does the trumpeter-bird have a grey back? Because it had sex with the anambé-bird's wife and when they all got drunk the anambé got angry and pushed the trumpeter into the ashes of the fire.'

The *Just So* aspect is always there. 'And that's why . . .' is a fundamental modality of myth. But no sooner have you got used to that than it starts getting complicated. When one of the really good story-tellers gets down to it, he'll launch into a long epic, and someway through his narrative, one of the *Just So* fragments you already know suddenly pops up as part of this intricate story, and you realize that there's a lot more going on than just *Just So*. Here's an example that starts with a *Just So* and quickly moves away into all sorts of layers of associations. I heard the precept: 'Don't kill butterflies.' 'Why not?' I asked, and was treated to the story of:

The Day we Killed the Butterflies and the Sky Fell Down

Butterflies look after the lianas that tie the sky to the earth. That keeps the sky up. There used to be hundreds of butterflies. Then the grandfather-people killed them. The grandfather-people were like small boys then. They caught them in baskets. No more butterflies.

So the sky fell down. It came down to the level of the top of the forest. The dark came. No sun; no moon; no daylight; no food since they couldn't hunt at night.

'Why did you kill the butterflies?' said Yaneyar, the culture hero. 'Make caxiri-beer,' he said.

So they lit resin candles and went off to the garden to get manioc to make the beer.

'Dance,' said Yaneyar, 'dance the Jupará.'

So they took the resin candles and went to cut poles to dance with. They made cross ties for the poles and hung feathers from them – macaw feathers, hawk feathers, eagle feathers.

Then they danced the Jupará. While the men danced Yaneyar sang the Jupará song.

Then Yaneyar said 'Let the sun appear'.

Then the sky rose. It went far up. Away up. The sun appeared. Day came.

Nowadays we don't kill butterflies.

All the different dances had names: of animals, birds, fish, insects. This name, the Jupará, refers to what in English is called the kinkajou; a small nocturnal creature related to the racoon. Everyone still knew how to decorate the poles and dance the Jupará. At this point the myth had slipped into another dimension where there's a direct connection between the story and the dance.

There was once an influential dogma in anthropology that stated that myths had their counterpart in rituals and rituals their counterpart in myths. The images in this case would be taken as an example of that thesis. But putting it in that way makes it all far too systematic, as if in some way if we were all to dance the Jupará we'd be thinking about butterflies and propitiating the forces of nature in order that the sky didn't fall down again. It's just not like that. The connections aren't systematic, in the sense of a clear logical rationale of connections presented as a kind of theology. They don't form architectonic structures. The connections are fragmentary, aleatory, gloriously random.

But that doesn't mean that they're fragile. The exuberance of the connections makes for an endless tangle of associations. Again, calling it a 'network' of associations would give it an inappropriate tinge of order. The details tumble around one another. The myth and ritual association in this example is just one strand, one liana, in the convolvulus tangles. The narratives *are* confusing. They do seem like a jumble of bits and pieces. Fragments appear in one myth and crop up in another. One person would tell the myth in one way; another person in the same settlement would have a different story line. But, like imagism, or surrealism, or any of the *isms* that have been part of the century I live in, getting used to the idiom is the simplest remedy to our initial confusion. Just be open to it, relax into it, become familiar with the idiom and so many of the problems disappear. When you come to hear your fiftieth myth the frown of puzzlement has vanished from your brow.

I can see three principal difficulties that we have to overcome. First, being baffled by the narrative style; second, being baffled by the particular details that compose the narrative; and third, a self-inflicted difficulty where we feel urged to find some sort of order in what we are looking at.

Narrative

The narratives may be fragmented and straggly, twisting around in forms unfamiliar to us, but the redeeming quality that allows us to connect up is the oldest trick in the narrative book: *What happened next?* Once we get used to the narrative lines, the bizarre becomes the expected; or rather, nothing is too bizarre. Anything can happen. Hearing the gasps of delight from the listeners confirms that the more bizarre the turn of the plot the more it is enjoyed. These are their winter's tales, which are not supposed to be credible, consistent, or concise.

While getting to the stage where you can enjoy the bizarre narrative lines, you'll have learned one important lesson on the way: that the initial bafflement is not due to the particular version you've confronted being a corrupted or partial version of a more perfect, complete, rational, logically coherent narrative that lurks somewhere in a missionary's travelogue of two centuries ago. That's the last hope of the baffled mythographer. There's no easy salvation somewhere back there when Amerindians were more logical and rational and architectonic in the way they constructed their story lines. You've got to accept the narratives as they are, in all their crazy, fragmented incoherence. It was ever thus.

There certainly are common themes that come up again and again all over Amazônia, although it's perhaps more appropriate to catalogue them as fragments rather than themes; fragments that are shuffled around into different patterns like a kaleidoscope. 'Getting fire from the jaguar', for example, is a common story, but sometimes the fire is given, sometimes stolen. Sometimes, even, fire is taken from another creature.

However exhaustive our catalogue, I think it unlikely that we'd ever exhaust the possible variations constructed from those fragments. The variations and transformations just go on and on. Those with a purist itch will keep looking for some kind of complete, definitive version, but that kind of search is a blatant result of literacy, where the most complete *text* is the version that has the greatest authority. In the woods, there are no texts; just people's memories.

Natural History

The second difficulty is the most obvious one and is the one most often overlooked: not the inner difficulty of form but the outer difficulty of content. It's simply that since the myths are a reckless cornucopia of images taken from those particular natural surroundings, how can we hope to slip into a shared familiarity with those who have lived their entire lives in the forest and whose intimacy with it is so complete? They can let their imaginations run along with the details. When the story mentions a particular bird or a specific liana they know *exactly* what's being referred to: how the bird behaves, where it is to be found, even what it tastes like; how the liana hangs, what tree it hangs from, and what they used it for last time. We can't share the immediacy of the plants and animals, the shapes and the sounds, the clues about what's dangerous, what's noisy, what's stealthy, about what's likely to happen in a specific situation; or rather, to approach such an immediacy requires enormous efforts on our part. Hence, besides being baffled by the bizarre story line, we are hindered by our patchy and superficial knowledge of the great woods.

What follows is a variant of one of the most widespread myths in Amazônia: the mythical twins. You might want to say that this myth is principally about the origin of fire, an interesting variant here being that fire is taken from the urubu-vulture, not from the jaguar. But this story is also about: the origin of otters, herons, piranha-fish, pacu-fish, cooking, the surucuá-bird's tail, the cácá-hawk's red throat, the jacu-bird's red throat, the toucan's red beak, the owl's wooden leg, and why the owl eats mice while various other birds eat fish, not to mention the origin of hills and mountains.

Yaneyar's Twins

Yaneyar [the culture hero] used to be here a long time ago. One of our Old People let his flute fall on the ground and it broke. Yaneyar was angry. He stood up and went off without saying a word. He went off down the path.

He had a wife. She was sleeping. She was very drunk therefore didn't know. Her husband had gone off, gone off. She didn't know.

She woke up. 'Where's my husband?' she said. 'Your husband went off,' said our Old People.

She was pregnant with twins. 'Is this the way your father went off?' she asked the twins inside her. 'Yes,' they said. There were some yellow leaves. 'Get those and show us, mama,' they said. She plucked them. They went on. 'Get those and show us, mama.' She plucked them again and was stung by wasps on her belly. She slapped her stomach.

'When you're properly born you will be able to see things,' she said to the twins. The children didn't speak again. They were angry, angry with their mother.

She went off down the path to the jaguar's place.

The jaguar's mother arrived – a huge jaguar. She hid the woman in a huge pot. Then all the jaguar people came. First came the ocelot, then all the different kinds of jaguar; puma, bush dog, margay, jaguarundi, 'red' jaguar.

'What's that smell, mama?' one of them said. 'Oh, just a pet of mine.' Then another: 'What's that smell mother?' 'Oh, just a pet of mine.' 'I will kill it and eat it.' 'No, you won't. It's my pet,' she said. Then another. Then another. Then the tikiri-jaguar, the biggest of all, said 'I will eat it.' He lifted off the cover of the pot and killed the woman.

'You should cut open the belly and take out the children,' said the mother jaguar. They did so, and put the twins out in the sun to dry.

'You should gather the bones together,' said the jaguar mother. They gathered the bones and took them away to the foot of a pepper bush.

'Listen to the curassow-bird calling,' said the jaguar mother to the twins. 'Off you go and kill it.' They were still very small. Off they went. Then the curassow-bird sang: 'At the foot of the pepper bush are your mother's bones.' They went back and told this to the jaguar mother. 'It's a lie what the curassow-bird told you. Off you go and kill it.' They went off again, and the same thing happened. They went off to look for the bones and found them below the pepper bush.

'Let's set up mother's bones,' they said. They put them together. The little brother was crying. 'Don't cry,' said the big brother to the little brother. 'Mama, mama, mama I want to suckle your breast,' cried the little brother.

Poro-toto, poro-toto, poro-toto: all the bones came tumbling down. The bones were stinking. 'Let's leave mother's bones there,' said big brother. 'You'll just have to do without your mother's milk.' They threw the bones away.

They were both angry. They wove a fire-fan. They made the water in the river come up very high. 'We shall get rid of the people who killed mother,' they said. The jaguar people went off into the forest leaving the jaguar mother alone. They came to a tree bridge. When they were all in the middle of the log, big brother cut the log with the fire-fan. All the jaguars fell into the water. Each species of jaguar turned into a different species of otter, giant otter, macaw-otter, river otter. The twins threw the fire-fan into the water and that became piranha-fish. They threw in a piece of manioc bread and that became pacu-fish. Then they got the jaguar mother and threw her in. She became a kind of heron and flew off.

Then they climbed a bacaba tree because there was so much water. They plucked unripe bacaba fruit and let it fall into the water. Papa-KOM, went the bacaba fruit into the water. Papa-KOM, papa-KOM. Then TISH. Ah, that was the bacaba hitting the ground this time. Then they knew the flood had subsided.

They climbed down. It was completely dry. 'I want a drink of water,' little brother said. The water snail arrived. 'What do you want, grandchildren?' he asked. 'Little brother wants a drink,' said big brother. 'Mmm. Touch my bum, then,' he said. Pasooooo. Lots of water came. That's the way little brother got to drink. Then the water stopped. Then the trahira-fish appeared. 'What do you want?' he said to them. 'Little brother says he wants a drink of water.' 'Touch my bum, then.' Pasooooo. Lots of water arrived again. Then this water finished.

There were lots of pacu-fish lying in the dry river bed. 'How do we eat them?' asked little brother. Big brother sent the surucuá-bird to take fire from the urubu-vulture. He stuck his tail into the fire but that was no good. He didn't bring any fire back. The twins then sent the cácá-hawk. The cácá-hawk swallowed some fire and has a red mark on its throat. It didn't bring any fire back. They sent the jacu-bird. It also swallowed some fire and it too has a red throat. It didn't bring back fire either. They sent the toucan. He just stuck his nose into the fire.

Then they thought to themselves, 'How do we get fire?' They made the owl's legs out of inajárana-tree wood. 'Off you go and get the fire,' they told the owl. The owl went, and managed to pick up a piece of burning wood. As it flew off the urubu-vulture managed to hit him on the head and he fell to the ground, still holding the fire. The caracará-falcon, who was the urubu's pet, went to see if it was dead. 'It's still *alive*, it's still *alive*, it's still *alive*,' wailed the caracará. 'Would you still be alive if I hit you on the back of the head?' said the urubu. 'Look it's dead,' and he stuck a finger into its eye. They left it. The owl wasn't dead. It got up and flew off and brought the fire back. The twins had fire then and cooked the pacu-fish.

They invited the birds to come and eat – the white egret, the various storks (jaburu-moleque, passarão), the heron, the spoonbill, and the kingfisher. 'Come and eat,' said Yaneyar's twins to the owl. 'No, I'm eating already,' said the owl. 'Very well,' said the twins, 'you'll do without this sort of food. You will not eat fish.' So the owl doesn't eat fish, only mice.

When the birds had finished eating, they flew off. 'Where's our father?' said the twins. So they went off to find him. On the way they made stone. They made huge hills stand up.

'That way, no other people will be able to follow us.' They went to the end of the earth and climbed into the sky.

How many exegetic clues do you and I need before we can begin to appreciate the imagery? How many kinds of jaguars (and otters) are there? A fire-fan looks just like a piranha fish, actually. And once you've opened up your finger on a piranha fish's teeth you'd have no trouble understanding why Yancyar's twins cut the tree-bridge with a fire-fan. You can guess about the colours of the birds, but it would be helpful to know what the wailing cry of the caracará-hawk is like. Also, when you get to the episode of the owl, you would have to know (a) that inajárana-tree wood is often used to make handles for utensils, and (b) if you want to test whether an animal you've shot is dead or not, since it can be dangerous to handle one with some life still in it, stick a finger in its eye. I was baffled, when I first heard the story, about the list of guests that were asked to come and eat at the end. I had no idea what the names of those birds referred to, and those telling the story didn't know the Portuguese words. Much later I was able to piece the list together: egret, various storks, heron, and so on – all fish-eaters, of course; all so obvious once I knew.

'I must put my pyjamas in the drawer marked pyjamas'

The third difficulty is that self-inflicted one where we fuss about getting everything tidied up into some kind of *order*. Amazonian myths defy classification into neat sets such as 'origin myths', 'heroic exploits', 'legend and history', 'homely tales'. Categories like that are not so much types of myths as aspects of all these narratives. When I first began to hear these stories and when they'd appear in what were apparently fragmented transformations and deformations one of another, I wondered whether there might not be a great dark mythical pool, like some sort of subterranean cistern, that people dipped into from time to time and pulled up a single libation for that moment's telling. I thought that if I heard enough over the years I'd eventually exhaust the repertoire and I'd find that all the myths connected up in one endless circular stream, like some kind of Möbius strip, and that any particular myth was just an extract plucked from the continuum.

It *is* tempting to think of everything connecting up in one vast imaginative reservoir. But I don't think it can be as simple as that. Or at any rate, I never knew enough to get an inkling of such unity. There are indeed certain clearly recognizable themes that keep coming up all over Amazônia: the origin of fire, the origin of death, the great fire, the great flood, the mythical twins, the origin of cultivated plants, the creation of particular animals and birds, the personifications of stars and constellations, recurrent dramatis personae such as Jaguar, Anaconda, Vulture, Opossum. Some go through obvious variations (such as fire sometimes coming from Jaguar, sometimes from Urubu-vulture). Some are remarkably consistent: the origin of death appears again and again as due to 'our ancestor' answering the call of the rotten tree having been warned not to. And all over Amazônia appears the image of the ladder to the sky being made of one arrow being fired into the nock of the first, then another, then another, until the chain of arrows is made.

Over and above these common themes, what is so exciting (or bewildering if you want to have everything tidily in its place) are the infinite variations that appear – alterations, adaptations, transmutations, contradictory versions – and every now and again something apparently unique. As regards a story that appears strikingly original, I'd guess that the novelty is due to my knowledge being limited. Time and again the myths you gather end up echoing off other myths elsewhere.

The urge to classify them, to tie them down, to get them into some kind of order, to find definitive versions, to grade them according to pure and less pure, corrupted and more corrupted versions, all that effort is just a projection of our intolerance of phenomena that do not conform to our expectations of domesticated form. It's a particular fussiness of the social sciences – finding principles of *order* – like legions of Mrs Ogmore-Pritchards from *Under Milk Wood* in their dust-defying bedrooms, whose husbands must put their pyjamas in the drawer marked pyjamas, and who won't even let the sun in until it's wiped its shoes.

An example of the clumsy imposition of our categories is the curious quest by professional commentators for a 'supreme being'. Did the So-and-Sos believe in a supreme being? Can we find evidence for such beliefs in their myths? Perhaps the question is partly motivated by our own monotheistic believers looking for reassuring reflections of their own notions amongst the peoples of the Amazon. Perhaps the question is a lingering carry-over from nineteenth-century concerns about stages through which human thought was said to develop; a scale from polytheism (many gods), through henotheism (one supremo, but lesser gods tolerated), to monotheism. Once again, I just don't think you're going to get very far by holding to hard and fast distinctions between a set of categories like: (1) a deity; (2) a supreme being; (3) a creator (who makes the forest, human beings, the animals, etc.); (4) a culture hero (who teaches human beings skills and gives them cultivated plants, and so on); (5) an ancestor or two.

The principal figure in Wayapí myths is 'Yane-yar' (Our Master). But Yaneyar fills all five categories quite easily in various myths. Moreover, after months of getting used to 'Yaneyar said this, or did that, or created the next thing', where I thought of 'him' as a central character, I suddenly had to make sense of statements such as: 'There were *lots* of Yaneyar, of course.' Siro, for instance, added as a codicil to 'The Day we Killed the Butterflies and the Sky Fell Down' that it was one Yaneyar that made the sky fall and another Yaneyar that made the sky rise again. When Waiwai is telling the story of Yaneyar's twins, by the time we're well through the tale, the decisions and orders that big brother and little brother are giving are put in the form: 'Yaneyar said this and Yaneyar did that.' The solitary supreme being, so firmly fixed by the parallel figure in our imaginative traditions, burst into a whole society of clones, men Yaneyars, women Yaneyars, child Yaneyars, only to reconstitute itself again into a single supreme character as the context spiralled through other myths.

It's the deep grammar of our theological imagination that makes this so difficult for us to grasp. If we hear of a central mythical character called 'Our Master' and get myth after myth about his exploits, it's just too easy for us to slip our 'God' category or our 'supreme being' category on to that. And the cramps of our monotheistic imagination don't allow such an entity to fragment into families and societies and then reconstitute into a singular being whenever the context changes. Furthermore, 'God' for us is a proper name, and individuals with proper names just don't behave like that.

What we're failing to notice is that there are all sorts of other entities in Amazonian myth behaving in just this way and which we accept quite comfortably: 'Jaguar', 'Urubu-vulture', 'Owl', and so on. In one myth 'The grandfather-people steal fire from Jaguar.' We have no difficulty personifying the jaguar in that particular context. When another myth comes along, like 'Yaneyar's twins' for example, producing an entire society of jaguars, we don't bat an eyelid. We have to allow examples like these to break down our imaginative grammar and free us so that we can think of 'Our Master' or 'God' in this way. In some contexts it will be 'Yaneyar-as-singular-person'; in others 'the Yaneyar-people'.

Living words

Once you see it, it's not difficult to move from God to Jaguar. But there's more than this going on. Can you imagine living in a language where plural forms are not indicated simply by adding on a letter like 's', 'a book' to 'three books' or changing from an 'o' to an 'i', 'libro' to 'libri'? Can you imagine no differentiation in ordinary speech between singular and plural? Every noun in the language would follow the paradigm: 'I caught fish today.' Not: 'I caught *a* fish', or 'I caught *three* fish'; but just 'fish'. We're now beyond the level of trying to understand particular images and particular concepts. Here we've got to face up to the relationship between the forms of language all of us are brought up in and the forms of thought that drift in our minds.

I take it for granted that there is no such thing as a 'primitive language'. All languages work equally well. All languages are there, in the world, perfectly formed. There's no point in saying that English has more words than French, by pointing to the relative size of English to French and French to English dictionaries, and then going on to claim that English is somehow more complicated or more sophisticated than French. Numbers of words, size of vocabulary, are not what is in question. Those people with the most limited vocabulary in English are sharing the same formal, grammatical excellence with the most eloquent, whatever purists may say about solecisms and non-standard usages. All languages in the world show the same level of astonishing grammatical sophistication – or at any rate, I'll say again that I take that for granted. It would take some pretty careful and detailed work to convince me otherwise.

'How on earth do they manage without our plurals?' you might ask. 'How on earth do we manage without their inclusive and exclusive "we"?' they might respond. Imagine you are part of a group of three people talking. One of your companions says to you: 'We will now go to eat.' What does 'we' mean? Wayapí has two quite different verbal forms and accompanying pronouns, one which means 'We, the two of us, but not you, will go and eat' and the other which means 'We, all of us, including you, will go and eat.' 'Why don't you get mixed up?' they might ask of us. We'd have to admit we sometimes do; and we'd explain that if a confusion occurs we sort it out in some other way. They would then tell you: 'My friends, that's just what we do with any confusion that might arise about our plurals'. No human language can claim a superior essence, a superior form, a superior logic, a superior grammatical sophistication that gives its native speakers both a surer grip on reality and a surer vehicle for communication.

What is not clear, as far as I can see, is whether or not different languages with very different grammatical foundations may constrain peoples' ways of thinking about and relating to the world around them to such an extent that it can be clearly stated that 'they', with their language habits, think in a very different way from 'us', with our linguistic habits. I'm going to come back to this question later when I get on to the existence of shamans and rabbits and other apparent beings. The general question is referred to as 'linguistic relativism' where it's held that in some way or another 'language determines thought', so that if you're brought up speaking and thinking in Chinese certain fundamental linguistic categories will constrain you to conceptualize the world in a way different from those of us brought up to think and speak in English.

I'm sceptical, first of all because of the enormous possibilities we all have *within* one language to manipulate and mould concepts in all sorts of different ways, and second, and more importantly, because of the miracle of translation. It is, astonishingly, the case that all languages are reciprocally translatable. You can always, to some extent, find your way in to another language. Certainly all translations are acts of faith. When you do a translation, no matter how good you are in the other language, you can never be quite sure about what you've achieved. Translating is like taking a piece of music that is played on one instrument or in one arrangement and playing it on another instrument or transposing it into another arrangement. No matter if you are supremely confident about your musical accuracy, what was there before and what's there now are different, irremediably different. And there's nothing you can do or say, or play or hum, to account for that difference. It's just there – *un grand peut-être*:

> The grand Perhaps! We look on helplessly.
> There the old misgivings, crooked questions are . . .

We can never be sure about translation. Nevertheless you can always give it a try. It's up to you how you accept the uncertainty: either as a gloomy impediment or as a creative opportunity; either as midnight's doubt or as the dayspring's faith. I enjoy it, as I enjoy the risks of climbing mountains. It might be a steady scramble up a hefty bit of Portuguese, or it might be trying to find fingerholds in the sheer smooth face of Wayapí. But however far you're prepared to take the risks with other languages, it's important to realize that the same uncertainty is around us at all times *within* our own shared language, whenever we talk to anyone, whenever you and I talk together in the same language. We all take risks when we make the attempt to understand each other. We're translating all the time, between different cultures and languages, and also between our isolated selves, ego to alter.

That's why 'linguistic relativism' arguments miss the point. The problem is not that different languages produce different forms of thought. If we're baffled by what we encounter, instead of rushing to the conclusion that we have found an alien mode of thought, we might instead consider whether or not we have managed an adequate translation. If we find that their 'deity/supreme being/ culture hero' can be both an individual and an entire society and if we're puzzled by that, the problem is that we haven't been able to loosen up our own language categories to take account of the movements that their categories are going through.

Seeing and believing

The questions don't stop with the technicalities of translation. What have we done when we translate *Yaneyar* as 'Our Master'? Have we revealed something or occluded something? We can ask how we are going to image *Yaneyar*, and we can look at the kind of picture our translation conjures up for us. We might then be able to assume a more-or-less correspondence between our sketch and their conception – a sort of 'that will do for the moment' state of affairs. The closer we think we have come to their notions, the more another question emerges: if this really *is* the picture, do they really believe it? Is that liana really japu-bird's snot? Is the moon really a man that had sex with his sister? How can we assess what these myths mean to them and how these myths inform their view of the world?

Sometimes the answer can be clear. There are examples of Indians being driven by their myths into the most direct action, as we too have been by ours. On the Atlantic coast of Brazil, before the European invasions began, there were a number of Tupian speaking peoples. Common to many Tupí groups was the belief in a land-of-immortality, an earthly paradise, where the culture hero (often called by the name Maíra) had departed to. Periodically shamanistic leaders and prophets would encourage entire peoples to move off in search of this place. Usually the impetus was in response to European invasion and interference, although there is evidence of such migrations having taken place before the arrival of the Portuguese.

About 1540, forty years after the first European arrivals, several thousand Tupinambá left the coast of Brazil in search of the land-of-immortality. In 1549 300 of them arrived at Chachapoyas in the northern Andes of Peru, having crossed nearly the entire continent. The Spaniards, who had by this time successfully destroyed the Inca empire, had occupied Chachapoyas, and the Tupinambá were taken into custody. During their interrogation, before they were dispersed as slaves, they told of the marvels and splendours they had seen on their travels up the Amazon river.

These descriptions were taken by the Spaniards as convincing evidence for the existence of El Dorado. Starting with some gossiping in 1540, the Spanish invaders, who had been establishing themselves firmly in Peru and Ecuador, had become more and more obsessed with a rumour that told of a place, fabulously rich in gold, where the king was powdered in gold dust every morning, hence 'el Dorado: the Golden Person'. A few expeditions had already come to grief in the deep forests to the east trying to find the place with the gold-powdered king. The descriptions given by the Tupinambá were used as a pretext for mounting yet another sortie to find the fabulous kingdom. It's an exquisite contrast of inspirational myths, revealing the heart of the different cultural values: the Tupinambá searching for a land beyond evil, the Europeans searching for a land of endless money.

Are myths charters for action, then? You'd be unlikely to find many examples as dramatic as that one where a mythic epic turned into an actual one. But you'll certainly find echoes and associations going to and fro between myths and the real world, the vivacity of the links ebbing and flowing as the contexts change. It was Bronislaw Malinowski, one of the founders of twentieth-century anthropology, who made the point about mythic charters most forcefully:

> Myth fulfils in primitive culture an indispensable function: it expresses, enhances, and codifies belief; it safeguards and enforces morality; it vouches for the efficiency of ritual and contains practical rules for the guidance of man.

This is one of those infuriating statements where you could look at every second word and find it both right and wrong. The trouble with it is – exaggeration. It freezes 'primitive culture' into a caricatured pose. The function is not 'indispensable', as if human life would grind to a halt without its myths. It doesn't 'codify', unless what's meant is 'mix up into a bewildering enigma'. It's a pretty weird way of 'safeguarding' anything, far less 'enforcing' such a protean business as morality. There's hardly much 'efficiency' vouched for. And would you look for practical rules in the stories you've just heard?

But at the same time Malinowski's 'mythic charter' view does emphasize that the myths are packed with lore. The *Just So* aspect of Wayapí myths was certainly a natural philosophy, which they talked about on a daily basis, and which gave immediate vividness to the natural world around them. The imagery and symbolism was, in a loose sense, their science. It was an idiom of animals, birds, snakes, fish, trees, plants, rocks, water, rain, thunder, stars. That liana *is* Japu's snot. The caracará falcon *is* Urubu-vulture's pet. The cayman *is* Anaconda's stool. The saki monkey *was* the first animal created, just before the small anteater. On and on go the associations. I'd say 'enhances' is the most accurate word Malinowski used in his description. The associations combine imagination and mnemonics. They don't so much classify and codify, as tie together in long strands, criss-crossing, one reminding of another, and that one of yet more; not rigidly structured, but sinuously anastomotic.

181

Explaining

I wouldn't want to go much further than that. I wouldn't want to try to produce a single coherent explanation of what myths are, why they are there, and how they are understood. There are, for example, symbolic approaches to myth that rely on psychoanalytic insights, saying that the images 'jaguar' and 'anaconda', 'fire' and 'flood' mean something specific and universal. If you feel Freudian you'll want to reduce these images to some sort of preoccupation with sex. The trouble with this particular line is that sexual preoccupations in Amazonian myths are anything but hidden, and it seems odd, when there's so much sex explicitly going on anyway, to argue that there's even more going on in a hidden way.

There are two other interpretations of myths that are worth noticing in passing. Both try to approach the question from one single point of view which will work for all societies. A standard, pedestrian approach in social anthropology was to say that myths reflect social structure. Analysing myths gives important insights into other aspects of society. For example, the description of certain relationships between figures in the myth, perhaps as 'brothers-in-law', and the various actions that took place, might parallel or invert actual relationships in the society and the kinds of obligations and consequences that follow from such a relationship. 'Myths reflect social structures; social structures are reflected in myths.' It's banal and tautologous. I'd be more interested in Freudian fancies.

A second approach, popularized during the 1960s and 1970s, was Claude Lévi-Strauss's structuralism, demonstrated in his four volumes of *Mythologiques*, where he claimed that myths take empirical oppositions, binary contrasts that are given in the natural environment (such as fire/water, raw/cooked, up/down, honey/tobacco, noise/silence, light/dark) and construct out of these what he called 'logical propositions'. What he meant by those propositions was not a particular statement of belief such as 'We got fire from the jaguar', but just the arrangement of oppositions in itself. The idea was that the human mind would endlessly work away churning out these logical patterns which were all just 'transformations' of one another – endless rearrangements of contrasts which are made, indeed constrained, as he would put it, by a universal binary logic.

For Lévi-Strauss the myths were 'meaningless', 'le sens du non-sens': 'the admirable syntactical arrangement of a discourse which says nothing at all', as one of his best critics put it. In other words, it didn't matter what the myths meant to the people who told them to each other. They were 'meaningless' anyway. They were only useful as examples of how the human mind, if left to ruminate by itself, would keep on producing interminable structures of binary contrasts.

That haughty, lifeless view from afar has nowadays been spliced on to the previous standard anthropological approach; the one which looked for reflections of social structure in myths. Nowadays the structures of binary oppositions are held to reflect, not fundamental structures of the mind (Lévi-Strauss's blank claim), but the structures of the society in which the myths are found. In other words, structuralism was brought back to its sociological home. The societies themselves are now held to be constructed out of bundles of binary contrasts.

I'm sure binary thinking (thinking in opposites, thinking in contrasts) is indeed a fundamental technique of human mental capacities. Heraclitus made that explicit. So did the *yin* and *yang* of the Dao. We all find ourselves thinking in opposites. But it gets a bit limiting if the only commentary we can make on the life going on around us is to point out the binary structures.

All these approaches have an original point to make. The trouble is that they assert themselves so intolerantly, like a sect, claiming that 'I am the way, the truth, and the life' to the exclusion of all others. The sectarianism of ideas in academia is one of its most dreary aspects. There's no reason why you can't be a Freudian in the morning, a functionalist in the afternoon, a structuralist in the evening (and a critic after dinner). I'll accept any of them and all of them to the extent that they are convincing in any particular case. But there's no one way of unravelling the myths.

There's no point, then, in looking for a specific answer as to what myths mean, as if there's a hidden layer that has to be turned up. The general human preoccupations in the myths are obvious, not hidden, and we all share them. Time and again, up come images of creation and images of destruction, beginnings and endings, coming into life and being destroyed. It's such an obvious cultural universal. All of us want to know about beginnings and about endings. We're all curious about our personal backgrounds, whence we came. It's there too on a scholarly level in my society through academic researches into archaeology, evolution, and geology. And it's there in their myths about the creation of this and the origin of that and why this happens and why that is just so.

If I was urged, and reluctantly agreed, to produce some sort of general statement about what myths are, what myths do, what myths mean, I would be prepared to suggest a kind of unity in the phenomenon. But it's not a narrative unity, where you could exhaust the corpus by gathering more and more stories until you came to the end. Nor a more formal unity of types of stories. There are lots of different stories and lots of different modes to tell stories in. It's a unity of random and exuberant associations. For me, the stories that are told offer a privileged access into the way they think about their world. Hence it's not 'myth' in the abstract that I want to understand. If I could feel imaginatively at home in the myths I would, linguistically, practically, environmentally, cognitively, and perhaps even emotionally be as close as I could get to understanding the world from their point of view.

And having gone on that journey, I'd find myself back where I started in the most homely context shared by us all. However difficult the stories may be to understand, however unfamiliar the idiom and the details, there is one aspect that we can take full part in, be our responses sophisticated or naïve: that is, the sheer fascination of narrative itself, the delight of anticipation and 'What happened next?' We all love winter's tales, to drive away the time.

7

SUBMITTING

It's time to get down to the heart of the matter. It concerns the enigma of *pajé*, as they call it in Brazil, taking the word straight from the Indian languages. I'm convinced that a hundred years on in the Portuguese of that time there will be an easy turn of phrase to say that in the old days Wayapí people had lots of *pajés*, lots of 'shamans', lots of 'medicine-men'. Well, it wasn't quite like that.

Paye, pajé, and *shaman*

The Wayapí word would normally appear in the form *i-paye*, and cognate forms are found in numerous indigenous languages. Like so much else, the word lost its integrity by being made to work in another language. Portuguese and Spanish took over that sort of vocabulary just as they took over the forests. And just as they destroyed the woods, so they bulldozed their way through the grammars of the languages they obliterated. The word-root *paye* appears in Portuguese as *pajé* and is taken to be the equivalent of shaman. You'll find people calling themselves shamans in the loopy fringes of my society here and now. But *pajé* wasn't simply a kind of person like that. It wasn't a NOUN. You can't just say: 'Apeyawar was a shaman.' It wasn't just a role or an office. *Paye* was a whole way of being in the world, an outlook on the world and a relationship with the world, that everyone was involved in.

Our philosophical persons

The processes of shamanism were central to Wayapí life. If there ever was such a thing as a key word to their world it would be *paye*. Because of that, I often feel it should be kept secret. They'd often become reticent and guarded if the subject came up with outsiders around. And no wonder. It's so clear that our culture doesn't deserve to have mysteries of this kind revealed. If anything about *paye* or related matters came up amongst the Brazilians on the post, the FUNAI men would assertively describe themselves as Christians. That left Wayapí people silently labelled as heathens.

Academic discussion can be equally benighted. On a subject like this even the best of those who consider themselves wise can end up behaving like moral hooligans. Moses Finley, for example, who wrote so many inspiring pieces of work on the ancient worlds of Greece and Rome, should have known better than to say the following. It comes from a lecture he gave at a women's college in Cambridge in 1972; a memorial lecture for the classics scholar Jane Harrison.

He recalls that nearly a century ago Jane Harrison had written that savages (as she called them) wearied and disgusted her, although she had to spend long hours reading of their 'tedious doings'. Moses Finley goes on to devote the lecture to looking at the relationship between anthropology and history. He scouts around various anthropological writers and picks up a remark by Godfrey Lienhardt (whose best-known book is on the Dinka of the Sudan). In one of his articles Lienhardt mentions the example of people who speak of pelicans as their half-brothers, and points out that the bald translation is inadequate since it leaves an atmosphere of fairy tales and nonsense. Hence, to make the image understood Lienhardt suggests that 'it would be necessary to give a full account of views about the relations of the human and non-human quite different from those we entertain, but not, therefore, necessarily less reasonable'.

This is not good enough for M.I. Finley. He mocks this use of the word 'reasonable':

> There is a sense of the word 'reasonable' that can comprehend pelicans as half-brothers to men, but there is another, far more important sense, understood by everyone of us, which renders that form of words simply unreasonable.

Why 'unreasonable'? Because, according to Finley, 'everyone of us', like Macaulay's schoolboy, knows that *development, change,* and *progress* have all brought us civilized folk away above the tedious doings of savages. And the two shining examples of development and progress are *political institutions* and *literacy*.

186

Behind the genial notion of progress is a glimpse of hidden, unspoken feelings – feelings that are the grounds for basic dispositions. The robust declaration of Jane Harrison is not shocking. Flagrant prejudice like that becomes pathetic when it is grounded on flagrant ignorance. But M.I. Finley's exposition is more stealthy – so reasonable, so assured, so poised, and so deadly.

Superstition, Science and God

I find his argument an unsettling *trahison des clercs* for two reasons. First it's unexpected, given the general nature of Finley's writings. Second, if someone like M.I. Finley can harbour such views, where can one look to with hope? Here is the argument in another form, spelt out in more detail, this time by Perry Anderson, reviewing Carlo Ginzburg's *Storia Notturna*, a book on witchcraft. Again it's disturbing, again for the same two reasons.

Anderson thinks Ginzburg has gone too far in emphasizing the continuity of popular beliefs, giving them a coherence and meaning that they don't deserve. They are really just 'folk shards' or 'the mental rubbish of peasant credulity' (in Trevor-Roper's phrase). Perry Anderson quotes Ginzburg's own words from an earlier work – commenting on a contemporary Italian cult near Salerno, in which a local woman periodically assumed the personality of a dead nephew. The quote is supposed to show that Ginzburg wasn't so gullible in his younger days:

'In wretched and disintegrated conditions, religion helps men and women to bear a little better a life in itself intolerable. It may not be much, but we have no right to despise it. But precisely because they protect believers from reality rather than prompting or helping them to become aware of and change it, such popular cults are in the end a mystification: to overvalue them in populist fashion is absurd and dangerous.'

Perry Anderson approves of that earlier view: 'It would be good to hear that voice again' says he, and goes on:

One much-needed word has disappeared from the vocabulary of *Storia Notturna*: superstition. It is salutary to recall that a Hungarian scholar, describing the poor, sparse societies in which it once dominated, could speak of 'the misery of shamanism'. That judgement is too strong for what was once a coherent set of beliefs, giving moral shape to a world. But superstitions are the scrambled relics of belief, no longer comprehended.

Who gets to draw the line between what is a 'coherent set of beliefs giving moral shape to a world' and 'scrambled relics'? Radio, television, and public debate all around me are flooded with God-talk. The three monotheisms that encircle the world (Judaism, Christianity, and Islam) appear in ever more strident and intolerant forms. Presidents and Prime Ministers, judges and police chiefs, journalists and media pundits are all up to their ears in God-talk, in rites and incantations – heaps of scrambled relics – and yet their kind of behaviour and their kind of talk are considered respectable. It's only the vulnerable and the oppressed that get tagged 'superstitious' and 'unreasonable'.

Notice the vocabulary used to describe the predicament: credulous savages and peasants are mired in superstition since these beliefs and rites are a form of *mystification* that stands between them and *reality*. Development and Progress allow us to stand with our feet firmly on a rock-bed of Reality and Truth.

There are a number of words in our ordinary vocabulary that get their power from their relation to reality and truth. 'Dreaming', 'magic', 'illusion', 'appearance' are examples. All these assume that there is an identifiable experience of what is real of which dreaming, magic, illusion, and appearance are modifications. Hence alongside all these modifications there is a corresponding experience of disappointment: when the modifications are put right again; when everything is straightened out and put back to normal. What appeared to be the case is revealed in its true colours; the illusion is seen through; the magical loses its magic; we awaken from dreams, or perhaps they 'come true'. These are the gifts of development and progress.

The basis of our development and progress is *science*. Scientific thinking and scientific knowledge is, most exactly, what 'thinking' and 'knowledge' are. Indeed it's difficult for us to appreciate notions of 'non-scientific thinking' or 'non-scientific knowledge'. Terms like these seem to be self-contradictory. If we *do* manage to be tolerant of these phrases, we demote them to a second-order status. Non-scientific thinking is flabby. Non-scientific knowledge is suspect. We're still living under the shadow (or the bright lights it would be said) of the enormous plausibility and power of what's referred to as scientific thought.

Of course all sorts of grandees and world leaders, politicians and scholars can claim to be thoroughly reasonable, thoroughly civilized, thoroughly scientific, thoroughly in touch with reality, and still have ample space for God-talk. Our God-talk is kept in a special sacred compartment where none of the ordinary rules of credulity and incredulity, of reasonableness and unreasonableness, apply. Hence all of us, we civilized folk, share together the benefits of development and progress, and the God-talk comes as an extra. Indeed God-talk devotees would go as far as to say that their religiosity makes them even more civilized and dignified than their sceptical brethren. Civilized sceptics might disagree, but even if they thought the God-talk was cretinous, they would rarely get round to describing their religious coevals as savages and peasants. Civilized God-talkers and civilized sceptics unite in thinking of themselves as the beneficiaries of development and progress, and both congratulate themselves on being far removed from the mental rubbish of peasant credulity. That's what science has done for us all. Old Lafew in *All's Well that Ends Well* saw the predicament:

> They say miracles are past; and we have our philosophical persons, to make modern and familiar, things supernatural and causeless. Hence is it that we make trifles of terrors, ensconcing ourselves into seeming knowledge, when we should submit ourselves to an unknown fear.

Art and ethnography

But there are different voices. There are those prepared to explore unknown fears. It's not the God-talkers that show how to go about dissolving our boundaries and getting ourselves within reach of others. It's Art that shows that way. As soon as we start discussing aesthetic experience the direction is set. Some scientific strands of thinking might feel drawn to place aesthetic experience in the same relationship with 'reality' as magic and dreams, as illusion and appearance. But since the nineteenth century aesthetic experience has been rescued from such a second-order status and been given back its integrity. It's difficult to argue nowadays (except in some hide-bound recesses of the social sciences) that art and poetry, metaphor and symbol, are modifications and refractions of what's 'real' or what's 'literal', and that what we should be doing is making the effort to get through them, restoring the literalness and getting back to reality.

Appreciating the power of metaphor and the integrity of art parallels the ethnographic appreciation of unfamiliar cultures. What's required is a similar disposition to be open to strangeness. 'Submit' was Lafew's word – to learn to submit to the beliefs and practices, to those 'things supernatural and causeless'; not to reduce them to familiar trifles. The most important lesson anthropology has to teach is that there's simply no point in making statements about how reasonable or unreasonable 'savage' thought might be, about what Dinka may or may not say about pelicans, or about what peasants near Salerno do or do not believe unless you're prepared to take the plunge and participate in their lives: *convivência*, as they put it in the Romance languages. That means going there. That means making the decision that it's worthwhile to spend years of your life living with them; as Ezekiel, when he came to them that dwelt by the river of Chebar, *he sat where they sat*. It means when you're there, dressing as they do, eating what they eat, sharing their daily activities, and above all learning their language. It's no accident that our philosophical persons who pontificate about superstition and who pride themselves on their development and progress always do so from the outside; always from the armchair, or, at their most daring, from the verandah.

Parsing the world

Commonsensically you'd think that the principal problem for us in trying to understand shamanism is the gulf between believing and not believing. How can we possibly understand what we don't believe? Well, that *is* the ultimate problem but it's not the initial one. The problem we start with is that we are not at all clear what we are looking at. We see only through a glass darkly, and not face to face. The reflections are dim because the languages don't fit together easily. Hence, when exploring this kind of enigma, the first paths you have to follow are linguistic ones.

When I suggest that we think of *paye* primarily as an adjective, as a quality, and not as a noun, that sounds like a minor grammatical adjustment. But it's not an easy move to make. It's not a surface adjustment. It sets about interfering with deep categorical habits. It's one thing to interfere with a person's beliefs. But it's more unsettling to disturb the very foundations and props and scaffoldings that got the beliefs up and running in the first place. The problem of shamanism will eventually come round to the point that they believe in this and that, and we don't. But long before we get to that question we've got to be brave enough and skilful enough to throw off all the grammatical certainties that our habits of language afford us.

Imagine: you're sitting by their camp-fire, on your first day. Even better, make it a day soon after 22 April 1500, when Pero Alvares Cabral made his first landfall on the Brazilian littoral. You know not a word of their language. You have been communicating by gestures and smiles. Your notebook is empty. Your pen is poised. A bird flies over and settles on the branch of a tree nearby. It's black with a white front and an immense coloured beak. You've just seen your first toucan. One of your new friends points to it and says '*tukan*'. (We took the name from the Tupian languages.) So the first entry in your new notebook is their word for that bird. *Tukan* will henceforth mean 'toucan'.

Look at the enormous assumptions you've made. Suppose you were forced, later, by example after example, to face the fact that what your friend had said wasn't short for a statement like: 'That is a toucan', but short for something like: 'Oh look, it's toucanning again', or 'My goodness, there's flying – toucanly this time', how are you going to deal with that? It's not a problem about belief. It's not a disagreement about what's there. It's a radical difference in the way another language negotiates with the world.

Our philosophical person who dealt best with this example went by the resounding name of Willard van Orman Quine. Doing a severe kind of philosophy he nevertheless looked cross-culturally for examples, and I find his anthropological insights refreshing and sympathetic. (How could he see so far from his armchair?) In this case he concluded that, be it a toucan or a rabbit that appears, be it *tukan* or *gavagai* that our companion says, you and I have no choice but to write down our noun-ish translation. We simply have to assume that all human beings are going to see toucans and rabbits in the same way we do and that they are going to name them; different words certainly, but according to the same linguistic form. That kind of naming is our entering wedge into the other language. It gets us in. That's why Waiwai began his language lessons for me by naming leaves and tree-trunks; lists and lists of names. But the point of these playful examples of toucans and rabbits, simple though they may be, is to show how linguistic structures can bend and sway and make you conceptually giddy, as if they are made of ropes rather than girders. Once you see that even this kind of naming is based on massive assumptions of perceptual and linguistic communion, you are warned not to take these assumptions too far. If the radical translation of 'toucan' involves so much, how are you to deal with the radical translation of 'Beauty is truth, truth beauty'?

Our language world is heavy with nouns – substantives, abstract singulars, concrete plurals, names. It becomes particularly obvious when we define ourselves. When people ask 'What do you do?', inviting a verb, we answer with a noun. 'I am an architect; I am a miner; I am a poet and tragedian.' We're uneasy with the fluidity of verbs. We're more comfortable with the obduracy of nouns. We're more concerned about what we are than what we do.

Because we cast *ourselves* in nouns, constantly, endlessly, we go on to impose this idol of the forum on everyone else we meet. We want to find reflections of our status differentiations and role differentiations wherever we go. 'Chief' and 'Shaman', potentate and witch-doctor, are two of our main inventions which we have foisted on to primitive life. 'Chief' we get wrong because, through imposing the word on them, we also impose the role we are familiar with. We dump our notions of executive and coercive power on to the person recognized as 'chief', and are then baffled when we find that the chief has no power. 'Shaman' we get wrong because we can't see beyond the specialized human role to the quality from which the role is moulded; a quality that inheres amongst many aspects of the world; that emerges from all sorts of places; and that envelops us in all sorts of ways.

What's in the name?

It's easy to spot the role, and most outsiders (government officials, missionaries, and scholars) just stop there. If you look at it cross-culturally, as it emerges from the literature, it's a wonderful collection of credentials. SHAMAN: curer and curser, doctor and demon, mediator between the spirit world and the human world, ritual specialist, conjurer and seer, prophet and priest, thaumaturge and psychopomp (that is to say, miracle-worker and soul-guide).

Of all these, though, the principal role that a *paye*-person is expected to carry out is that of curing.

You can see a remarkable consistency in many of the beliefs that surround the phenomenon right across the Americas and back beyond the Bering Straits into Asia, where the very word *shaman* comes from. The shaman will have spirit helpers, small animals perhaps, like caterpillars or maggots, invisible to the rest of us. He might do his curing work by approaching the sick person and blowing tobacco smoke on the patient's body while chanting and rubbing hands up and down the body, or he might do a general cure for the village by constructing a shelter somewhere nearby and going into a trance there. In Siberia and Inner Asia a drum was characteristically used during a shamanic seance. In South America rattles are used. These are the original maracas – gourds with seeds or pebbles inside attached to sticks. At the Nipukú it was said that the Other Wayapí in French Guiana still used rattles and that 'We had them too, long ago'.

In many parts of the Americas, and particularly in the Western Amazon, various hallucinogenic drugs, often extracted from lianas, are used to induce a visionary state. Wayapí people had no knowledge of these. They used tobacco. I'd guess that the chemistry has to do with ingesting abnormal amounts of tobacco while breathing abnormally. 'Hyperventilating' would be the technical term. As with hallucinogenics, the effect is to alter normal consciousness. The state that is induced is not only clairvoyant. It's transcendental too. Time and again the detail of travelling upwards appears. 'Do you see that tree there?' said Yamaira as we paddled back up the Nipukú river after a fishing trip – a monstrous tree it was too. 'That's where Yiseiwarai went when he was last here. He built a shelter near there to shamanize. He was singing. He sang "sumauma-tree". He sang "angelim-tree".' And you'd hear talk too of journeys to the sky.

The time to start learning these powers is when you yourself are ill. A *paye*-person will come to your hammock and blow smoke on you. As you begin to get better other spirit *paye*-people will come too – Anaconda, for instance, will come and blow on you. If you are very careful, if you stick to your hammock, take great care about what you eat, and if you're not disturbed by noise (by children playing around you or by dogs yapping) you'll begin to learn. To make sure that your surroundings are peaceful, it's best to go and stay in a shelter away from the village where you will not be disturbed.

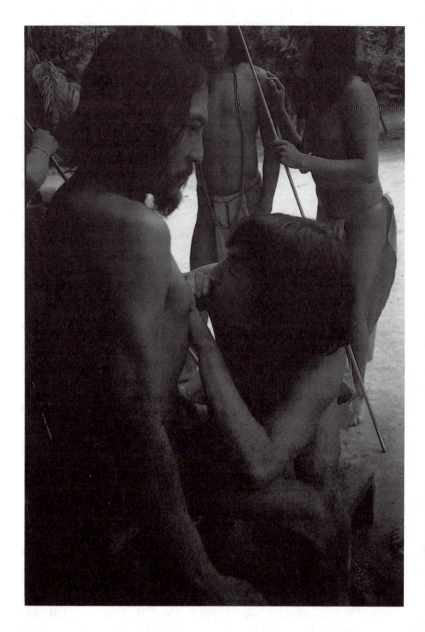

Blowing smoke – pretending to shamanize

The spirit creatures will visit you there. You'll begin to see them. Tapir, Peccary, Jaguar, Armadillo, Monkey, Anteater, Blue Butterfly, Vulture – they will all come. They don't come as animals. They come as people. 'Who are you, grandfather?' you ask. 'I'm Tapir', answers one; 'I'm Armadillo', answers another. That's how you know who they are. 'What's wrong with you, grandchild?' they ask. 'I'm ill, grandfather. Blow smoke on me', you say. And gradually you begin to see.

It is the spirit creatures that give you your helpers, small animals or insects. These are like pets. They stay inside you. While you've got them you've got to be very careful not to do anything that might cause them to go away from you. If you lose your helpers you can't be *paye*. As well as giving you your helpers, the spirit creatures teach you songs, and they also give you mirrors for your eyes.

The point of the mirrors is that you *see* and *know* what is not ordinarily visible or known. Just as in the languages we know, the Wayapí words for *seeing, knowing*, and *understanding* are intertwined. Seeing through appearances to another reality is a mark of being *paye*. The anaconda is a huge snake, certainly, but only if you're *paye* will you be able to see it in human form. And along with that seeing goes all sorts of knowing. *Paye*-people were diviners. They could find things that were lost. They could guess the weather. They could say in which direction game could be found. Going back through the genealogies I'd collected trying to find out who were the first of Our Wayapí to break out of their isolation and find a way through to the Other Wayapí on the Cuc River, they named the first three men to do it. Three tantalizing names were all that was left to mark that moment of truth which was going to have such far-reaching consequences for the people round the Amaparí waters. The aspect of the decision that most intrigued me was 'How did they know where to go?' The answer was 'Because they were *paye*.'

You can see already that if you begin by privileging the curing role, you're quickly carried ever further outwards from that centre by ripples of beliefs and ideas. You start with these male healers and their peculiar gifts. You see how they learn to follow specific techniques in order to achieve their ends: techniques of blowing, singing, getting into a visionary state. You notice how those men who are most renowned for their curing seances sometimes make a point of living on the edges of a settlement or even going off to live remotely, taking wife and children too. Keeping apart helps them maintain their talents since care and moderation are so important. It's not essential for them to live apart, and it's not only *paye*-people who do so. Many households peel off from the main groups for a season or two and take to solitary places. And, frequently, renowned healers will live amongst a settlement and may even be one of the few 'Our Big Ones' (or 'chiefs' as we would put it). However, 'Our Big Ones' don't have to be *paye*, and *paye*-people aren't usually chiefs.

The curing role is the most obvious aspect (which strikes us) of more general doctrines of disease and health. Time and again when people died it would be explained that it was not the illness that killed. Death was blamed on the ill-will of *paye*-people. 'If you fall ill with influenza an enemy *paye*-person will "see" and "know" and will send invisible darts which will penetrate your body. That's what kills you.' Who these enemies were was often a matter of conjecture and disagreement. If the Other Wayapí, or the Wayana, or the Aparai downstream on the Rio Jarí were blamed then there wouldn't be any trouble. Indeed watching meteors at night, you could laugh about it. Meteors were said to be shamanistic darts flying over us, sent by the Other Wayapí on the Oyapoque River on their way towards the Aparai. But if one of our own people was accused the matter could get deadly serious. All very well to be the village doctor; but it's not much of a role or an office to be the village killer. This is the first crux, where the notion of *paye* as a role begins to stretch thin. It's being asked to do too much.

Dark words

The ambiguity came tumbling out one night sitting with Maraté in the ragged little settlement that was attached to the post. Houses in that settlement were more in the style of the Brazilian frontier. They were more substantial, making use of planks and slats; more private. There was no communion of fires here. Maraté had set himself up there temporarily, on an extended visit, and he had built himself a small shelter-type house at the edge of the village, just the kind that should have had an open fire on the ground at one end. It strikes me now, thinking back, that the lack of fire was deliberate. I remember we talked in deep darkness, unable to see each other's faces.

He was there to learn how to become *paye*. There was a particularly well-known *paye*-person nearby. I had known Maraté for years and had seen him go through some of his greatest tragedies. He had lost two wives and three children, and this move was an attempt to find out what on earth was happening to his life. 'So how do you go about becoming *paye*?' He went through a fairly standard list of prohibitions and precautions: don't kill game; don't carry a basket on your back if you have to travel; keep away from women who are menstruating; don't have sex ('because if you do the beautiful people will be ashamed and won't come near you – the spirit people, Tree people, Anaconda people – they've got long hair; they're dressed like Brazilians; you get to have sex with *their* women'). And eat cold food only; white tapioca bread is best.

As he went on his account became more feverish. When you are *paye* you have feather headdresses, beads round your arms and legs, a mirror on your chest, fish hooks in your teeth (for taking out *paye*-darts from victims), shoes, and gloves. (Shoes and gloves? Brazilian fashion was beginning to enter shamanic reality.) All these are invisible. He went through the various people considered to be shamanistic, and graded them in order of power. 'So-and-so has removed darts from victims and let everyone see them. He also taught such-and-such's second wife how to be *paye*.' (So women *can* be *paye* after all.)

The argument then was turned up another notch. He talked of the two wives he had lost over the years, and immediately blamed . . . let's call him Sora. None of the others on his list of shamanistic people presented any threat at all. Sora had been singled out. I reminded him how years before, at the Nipukú, it was so often Aparai shamanizing or Other Wayapí shamanizing that was blamed for the deaths. Well, said Maraté, that was all wrong. Sora had tried to seduce his first wife all those years ago. When she had turned him down he had later killed her. 'And it wasn't just her. Do you remember *this* person and *that* person who died? It was Sora who did it. Sora did it all.'

And who, precisely, is shamanistic and who isn't? Many years before deciding to take up this apprenticeship, Maraté had tried to fight back. When his second wife died, a child-wife, he knew who the culprit was. Before she was taken to be buried he gathered together: a piece of her big toenail, a small piece of skin from her heel, some strands of her hair, and a small piece of her loincloth. After her burial he boiled the bits and pieces from dawn till midday and then emptied it all on her grave. This took place at Nipukú, but he managed to make Sora, 80 miles away, ill with a skin disease. Indeed he'd nearly managed to kill him. You'd want to call what Maraté was up to 'shamanizing', but you wouldn't have called him 'a shaman'. Sora was supposed to be 'the shaman', not Maraté.

Being very fond of Sora, I found this talk alarming. It really began to look as if his days were numbered. All these accusations were backed up the following day by one of the more Brazilianized Wayapí who lived permanently at the post. Again this young man went at the matter with vehemence:

'Why are X, Y, and Z in good health? They are Sora's imme-diate relatives. Why is it only my immediate relatives that die around here? Sora says it's Aparai *paye*-people from away over there on the Rio Jarí who are doing it. W [another "great" *paye*-person, the speaker's elder brother] says it's Anaconda. I say it's Sora. I've lost three children. Why me? Perhaps *paye*-people are angry. Well, I'm angry too. Do you remember, long ago, at the Nipukú, there was so much malaria? But *no one died*. Wayapí didn't die of malaria. Now they die. It's not the Aparai who are doing it. It's *paye* here. And who? And who? Well, if Sora's immediate relatives died I wouldn't be angry. But it's just mine. That's why I'm angry.'

There was a FUNAI plan on the go to take a number of Our Wayapí to French Guiana to meet the Other Wayapí. Sora was one of those to be taken. I was urged to do what I could to see to it that this didn't happen. If he got there, said the young man, he'd learn monstrous powers and Our Wayapí would be finished.

I want to come back to the point later, but let me say now, in case academics not as wise as Willard Quine are listening in, that while this talk of boiling up bits of your dead wife, and accusing your neighbour for deaths that occurred years before, all seems dreadfully 'unreasonable' to those of us living in our comfortable civilization, it is not at all unreasonable when you and I come to the agony face to face in the dead of night with the great woods around us. The question: 'I wonder if this is "reasonable"?' simply does not arise. That's not what's at issue. The point is: here are our closest friends, in extremes of grief, trying to make sense of what is happening to themselves, and producing pictures that are quite beyond our grasp. The urgent question is not 'Are they being reasonable?' but 'Can we find a way to get in there?'

Quiddities and qualities

When you're still hobbling along with the language, sentences come at you that you try to translate. You've heard the word *paye*, and you think it means *shaman*. Then you start hearing all sorts of things: that various trees are shamans, that the tapir is a small shaman, that the deer is a fairly important shaman, and that the anaconda is a vastly powerful shaman. Indeed the anaconda is such an important shaman that when you see a rainbow, which happens to be the anaconda's soul, you must not point at it with your hand and arm. If you do so, you risk paralysis. If you want to indicate a rainbow, you point at it with your lips.

If a shaman is the local doctor, if that is the shaman's role, what is the role in society for a tree, a tapir, a deer, and a huge water snake? This is where you begin to see that your grammar is letting you down. Of course they are not saying that a certain big tree 'is a shaman'. They are indicating that the tree 'is shaman-istic', that it too has the quality shared by the well-known healers. Hence, when they say 'Sora i-paye' rather than translating that as 'Sora is a shaman' you'd do better to say 'Sora is shamanis-tic'. Similarly you can say that the anaconda, the various trees, and so on are all 'shamanistic'. You've moved on from the role, from the essence, to an attribute, to a quality, which is found all round about you.

Thinking in terms of a quality allows thinking in terms of degrees – something or someone can have a lot of it, or a little of it, can have it for some time and then lose it again. Yanuari explained that he used to be shamanistic but he lost the gift after a dreadful fall while climbing a tree to get a monkey he'd shot. He broke his back, and his legs have now withered. He says the fall also broke the mirrors he had in his eyes, hence he's now only *very very slightly* shamanistic (not a *tiny, tiny shaman*).

'Knowledge itself is power.' Shamanistic power, which is all around us, accounts for misfortune, illness, and death. Certainly it's a quality that includes the power to heal and the power to harm, but it's more completely to do with knowing and seeing: with a whole other way of understanding. Those who have learned how to grasp this power can see beyond the everyday appearances of people, animals, and the rest of the natural world to another reality. It sounds familiar, doesn't it? Our most worthy philosophical traditions have struggled for centuries with questions about appearance and reality, efforts that look forced and over-elaborate when you realize that Wayapí people take it for granted that the world is not as it seems to be.

Looking at parts of speech has taken us a long way from 'the shaman is a witch-doctor'. Starting from a simple noun 'shaman', *paye* has waxed like the crescent moon into an entire cosmology. *Paye* is a way of looking at the world. To be more precise, I think the most important point to hold on to is that the other reality yonder, revealed by shamanistic knowledge, has been thoroughly humanized. It is full of creatures all of whom appear as people we talk to and learn from. The world of these creatures and the world of humans becomes shared. That is to say, the heart of that shamanic reality reveals a human relation between ourselves and the natural world.

Animism and phlogiston

If the first key was a point of grammar, the second key is the animal spirit-people. It is a detail that opens out an enormous perspective on a way of being in the world, one that presents us, here and now, with a genuine challenge; a challenge as to how far we can go to meet it and appreciate it. It's been a received idea in anthropology since last century that primitive cosmologies entertain the view that 'everything lives' – that animals, trees, plants, rocks, water, are alive as we are. The word for this is 'animism', from the Latin *anima*, the soul. In one way it's a most appropriate word since it includes connotations of air, of breath, of life. Hence we might be able to see everything in the world around us as 'animated'; not inert, or distanced from us, but endowed with vigour and liveliness as we are. In another way the word is a disaster.

Once again, it's to do with nouns, these sumps of meaning. We owe the word *animism* to Georg Ernst Stahl, who taught at the University of Halle at the end of the 1600s and the beginning of the 1700s, and went on to become the personal physician to the King of Prussia. He taught practical medicine, anatomy, physics, and chemistry, and is best known to our world for the theory of 'phlogiston' which was held to explain how matter burned. What on earth can phlogiston have to do with animism? The point is: the form of reasoning that backs up the ideas is the same in both cases.

A brief digression, then: why do things burn? Stahl thought up the ingenious notion that matter possesses a certain thing, a certain essence, a certain element, which he named phlogiston. This stuff will be released on burning. The more of the stuff a certain kind of material has to begin with, the more of this stuff will be released when the material is burned. A certain *thing*, in this case with a Greek rather than a Latin name, has to be present to explain why matter burns. Why can't you set fire to a piece of metal? Because it has hardly any phlogiston. Why does wood catch fire? Because it has a lot of phlogiston. It took nearly eighty years until Antoine Lavoisier, just as the French Revolution broke out, explained the principles of combustion in terms of oxygen (an acidifying principle, as he called it) in the air reacting with the material. Phlogiston was merely a thing, a pseudo-thing; just a noun.

But nouns run on. When Georg Stahl thought about living things, he accepted that the physiological changes seen in living organisms were due to chemical processes. But those kinds of explanation, in terms of chemical laws and mechanical laws, were not enough to explain what life was and how life went on. Something more was needed. Material was one thing, but in order to be alive, an organism required a quantity of a substance, a 'life-force' which he called (in Latin this time) *anima*. Another noun, another name, another pseudo-thing, is invented. *Phlogiston* is 'burning stuff'. *Anima* is 'living stuff'.

After the chemists came the anthropologists. They were after stuff too. The term 'animism' was taken up in anthropology by E.B. Tylor in 1871 to describe what he saw as the origin of religion: 'belief in spiritual beings'. The theory was that primitive people came to the notion of spirits through experiencing dreams and visions. Noticing, for example, that you can meet dead people in dreams, primitives thought up the notion of an immaterial soul which was separate from the material body. Once human beings saw themselves in this way, it was a short step to attributing a similar duality, of material thing and immaterial spirit, to all sorts of aspects of the natural world – to animals, trees, rocks, and so on. Rain and thunder, for example, could then be explained as the goings-on of these spirits.

Tylor's notion of animism has long been out of fashion in anthropology. It's a pity it was dropped since he certainly was on to something important. 'Animism' as a signpost pointed in the right direction, albeit that the notion needed refining. It should have been sharpened up. But instead, the signpost became deformed into a very blunt instrument indeed. It got tied up in discussions of classifying religions. Once you get it into your head that everybody in the world can be classified according to their 'religion' (whatever that word may refer to), you can start producing colour-coded maps of the world where huge areas are marked off as 'Here Be The Christians' (colour them blue maybe), and the next tranche, perhaps in red, is 'Here Be Islam', and so on through as many religions as you have names for. But what do you do with 'tribes', as they are still called, who have never been touched with a religious label? You call them 'Animists' and colour them, what? green? Animism becomes a thing, a condition, a sort of non-religious religion, synonymous with 'heathen'.

But E.B. Tylor was indeed on to the core of it. It's astonishing to do student course work in anthropology, writing essays on the history of anthropological thought, for which you've got to look through nineteenth-century tomes, where it appears easy to spot the prejudices, and yet where you can learn so much. You can read Sir John Lubbock, for example, in 1882 on what he ponderously calls *La Couvade* (where on the birth of a child, in all sorts of societies, it is the father, more obviously than the mother, that goes into seclusion and has to observe restrictions), and having written your essays you can walk straight into *La Couvade* in your first few weeks in the Amazon woods. Similarly, you can gen up on Tylor's 1871 notion of 'animism' for your exam paper and find yourself face to face with it a few months later. That surprise is rare nowadays. As the world gets more and more homogenized, and as the discipline of anthropology gets more and more self-absorbed ('let's study ourselves'), the enormous ethnographic richness presented by the nineteenth-century ethnologists appears more and more as antiquarianism. It's a disappointing turn in the present fashions. The richness is still there; far away, perhaps, but there. All that's required is the disposition to go and encounter it.

Tylor's term became blatantly useless when it turned into a religious tag. But even before that there was an inherent difficulty in it. Nouns make us think of discrete essences, of quiddities, of an essential whatness. So if *that* collection of beliefs over there is what's called 'animism', then it must be something different and distinct from *this* collection of beliefs that we're familiar with. Behind the term lurked the grounding idea that whereas we know what is alive and what is not, they don't. They attribute life to what we consider inert. Animism extends the notion of 'being alive' into areas where we know the term to be unacceptable.

There are two clear strands tied up in nineteenth-century theories about animism. One is the notion that primitives think that all sorts of things round about them are simply alive. The other is that all these things have a soul or spirit in them that makes them alive. Wayapí conversation shifts between both points. I don't think either is particularly obscure, and I don't think calling either the one or the other 'animism' marks any great divide between us and them. As regards the first (the alive business), we just take it for granted that animals are alive. We would say the same about plants, although we might, if we thought about it, say 'alive in a different way'. 'Tree dies', Wayapí would say when we'd hear the distant boom of a tree keeling over – an eerie event since there was seldom any wind to do it, and a terrifying experience when it happened at night close to the shelter when journeying. Well, we talk easily of our house plants or farm crops dying. There's no great difficulty there.

La Couvade and Anaconda

The second aspect of nineteenth-century animism (the soul and spirit business) emerged vividly in Wayapí conversation when the parents of newborn children went into elaborate precautions as regards what they could do, what they could eat, and where they could go. It's to birth precautions like these that nineteenth-century anthropology gave the name *la couvade*. One of the principal reasons Wayapí people gave for taking these precautions was that the well-being of the child had to be protected from Anaconda.

Babies were constantly carried close to their mothers in slings. If present-day psychoanalysis is accurate in saying that the first loss the growing individual has to endure is the loss of the mother, then being carried in this way should lay down enduring sediments of psychic reassurance. *Arrimage* I heard it called in French: like stowing everything onboard ship, making everything *secure*. There's a similar word in Spanish: coming close, snuggling, cuddling. 'Arrímate a mi querer, como la largatita se arrima a la pared' (Cling to my love, like the little lizard clings to the wall) as it is sung in a *Fandango de Huelva*. It's an appealing and comforting sight wherever babies are carried like this. Furthermore, as if to presage psychoanalysis, Wayapí imaging of this was precisely of psychic clinging.

The soul of the child is not properly attached to it, they said. If a toddler fell over and began to yell, the mother would pick it up in one arm and then scoop up the soul from the ground with her free hand, blowing and lifting a number of times. If the child didn't stop crying she would return to the spot and 'lift up the soul' again. It would be fatal for the child to be taken to the river for a bath since Anaconda would take the fragile soul.

It wasn't just the body of the child that was clinging to its parents. The soul clung on too. If a toddler's father went for a walk in the woods, leaving the child behind with the mother, he would still have the soul attached to him. So he would blow and scoop to make sure the child's soul got over fallen logs or streams. He would also avoid large trees in the woods since they were shamanistic. Hence, as further protection for the child's soul both parents would keep well away from the river. Friends brought them water in calabashes for washing. They had to keep away from the power of Anaconda.

'Anaconda' is probably a Sinhalese word applied to a python of Sri Lanka and South India. It's irritating to be stuck with a linguistic mistake instead of an evocative Tupian word. The name was applied in error by English speakers to the snake known in Brazil as the *sucurí* or *sucuriju*, straight Tupian words. The particular Wayapí word is *moyó* – simply 'great snake'.

The anaconda is an awesome creature; the largest snake in the world, said to reach 12 metres, although the largest authenticated specimen, held in a London museum, measured 29 feet (just under 9 metres). I thought the massive diamond-shaped head looked particularly threatening since the eyes were not prominent, giving it a wicked, purblind look. But, in spite of exaggerations of size, and unsubstantiated stories of attacks on humans, the anaconda is not dangerous. It has no venom fangs, although the jaws are toothed and are enormously strong. It feeds on fish, caymans, aquatic birds, and mammals that come to the river bank to drink. It grasps the prey with its mouth, and, if it has caught something large, wraps itself round the victim. The prey is often drowned. The tremendous power of constriction then breaks the dead animal's bones, crushing it and preparing it for swallowing.

This is the creature, with its beautiful skin markings, that was the most potent centrepiece of Wayapí imaginative life. It would come to the Nipukú at night – shamanistic Anaconda that is. People identified its approach by a high-pitched whistling sound. I could never confidently isolate what they said they were hearing from the perpetual night background noise; a great blanket noise of whistles, chirps, and croaks.

Anaconda was the 'owner' or 'master' of water, and menstruating women didn't go near the river since the smell of blood would make Anaconda angry and the woman would get dizzy and die. In the village, there were no obvious precautions taken. Menstruating women would discreetly stay in their hammocks. Away from the village the anxiety was more obvious. In a temporary camp near Aima, preparing an area to make a garden, a woman went into seclusion and her husband strung up a raggedy blanket to act as a screen between her and the nearby water, protecting her from Anaconda.

Anaconda was the most impressive character to emerge in this area of the imaginative world. In many other Amazonian cultures the jaguar has pride of place both in myth as the giver of all sorts of cultural gifts and also in shamanistic thinking as a possessor *par excellence* of that kind of power. But in Wayapí cosmography it was Anaconda that was referred to again and again as 'vastly shamanistic' and the force most feared.

I'm tempted to set up a simplistic opposition between Yaneyar on the one hand, the Our Master complex of ideas that was constantly referred to in the myths, and Moyó on the other, Anaconda that was constantly referred to on a daily basis in discussions of danger, ill-health, and mortality. Binary contrasts like that are the currency of structuralism, and I'm wary of such contrived reductions. But I'm puzzled by the lack of any obviously shamanistic themes in the myths I found. It's the same imaginative world. Animals, birds, and trees appeared in the same way as *dramatis personae* both in the idiom of myth and in the idiom of shamanism. But amongst all the violence and killings and deaths in the mythical stories I haven't found a single one where shamanizing is said to cause anything, where shamanistic practices are illustrated, or where any character is said to have the powers.

In the best Anaconda story, the snake comes to the house in human form, teaches the sisters of the grandfather-people how to do genipa dye designs on their bodies, and then proceeds to seduce them. The brothers find out and kill Anaconda. The corpse gets filled with maggots and from them appear tiny people who are given food and brought up by the grandfather-people until they turn into the Aparai and the Wayana, the two neighbouring peoples. 'So you see, Yaneyar didn't make the Wayana. They're just from Anaconda's maggots.' There's not a word in the story of any shamanistic powers.

The way I make the contrast for myself is to think of the myths as encyclopaedias, histories, morality plays, pictures, illustrations, entertainments, that make of the surrounding natural world a vivacious spectacle. The myths are a great carnival of associations with the various Yaneyars and Grandfather-People and Jaguars and Anacondas playing the Pantaloons and Harlequins, the Inamoratas and Columbines. To that we are all spectators. Shamanism by contrast images the hand-to-hand struggle of keeping alive that we go through every day, victims as we are of illness and accident, and always threatened with death. We are surrounded by *paye*-power which is exercised by people, by the various spirit-owners of large trees, of various animals, and above all by the Owner-of-water, Anaconda.

The picture is not one of 'animism' as opposed to 'non-animism', but a congeries of ideas, some of which we all share, some of which we don't, including what counts as alive and what does not, notions of spirits and notions of souls, differences and similarities regarding human life, animal life, vegetable life, and mineral life. It doesn't work very well to abstract a particular set of features from this assortment and label them 'animism', thereby allowing us to say 'they are animists and we are not'. The more important distinction is to notice what human beings are thought to be in a relationship with, and what they are not. It's not the nature of life that is in question, but the nature of our relationship with our surroundings. This is why the presence of the owner-spirits is a key point.

No one ever said that artifacts (bows, baskets, pots, dwellings) had owner-spirits. The lovely ubim leaves from a dwarf palm that were used for house thatch did have an owner-spirit out there in the forest that you had to be careful of when you gathered them. But the thatch itself didn't have an owner-spirit. Artifacts, then, are the only things that both we and they would agree were inert objects.

It's astonishing to look around me here, whether living in the city or in the countryside, and try to see something that is not human-made or human-managed. The trees are all planted. Fields and hills are ploughed, grazed, or burned. The very weeds in derelict sites are the result of human intervention. The waterways and rivers are managed. They once quarried the cliffs. But there in the Amazon woods, the human environment stopped at the settlement's edge and at the garden's edge. Human beings lived in tiny islands amongst the vastness of the forest. A path would disappear in a season, and the signs of an abandoned settlement site would be obliterated by the forest in ten years. The only congener of the forest left for us is the ocean.

My world here has been living for centuries according to the monstrous presumption found in the first chapter of the Book of Genesis where human beings are given dominion over every living thing that moveth upon the earth. You can see a monstrous transformation of the same presumption into contemporary political terms in Rudyard Kipling's 'Recessional'. Here the vision of the British Empire is expressed in tree metaphors as 'dominion over palm and pine'. (The people under the palms and pines were, in spite of what George Orwell said, 'lesser breeds without the Law'.) By 1897 Adam was an upper-class Englishman. But whereas people are more willing these days to be frank about the appalling presuppositions underlying imperialism, they refuse, tediously and stubbornly, to make similar adjustments regarding our relationship with the natural world. Humility and respect are not the characteristics that spring into prominence when considering our relations with animals and trees.

But if you lived in a tiny island in the middle of the rainforest and if your most powerful tools for interacting with your environment were a machete, an axe, and a bow and arrow (let's forget the shotguns just now) the assumptions of dominion that we take for granted would be absurd. Again and again when I try to submit to shamanism, I find myself coming to a stop when I try to appreciate the material conditions of their lives. I did indeed find so many of the ideas and visions difficult to grasp and difficult to enter into. But imagining spirit-owners and Anaconda-people was not too difficult. I could share the talk and make an effort to share the visions. On the other hand, the way their lives were integrated with their environment made them, to me, intangible. I could go and live there and take part, but I could never know the full force of what it is to have my life determined by these conditions.

Out there, in their world, before the processes of acculturation overcame them, there was no social world set over against a natural world. There was no culture as opposed to nature. There was no human fantasy of dominion over the natural surroundings. There, the human world was part of the forest, and it shared it with jaguars and anacondas and fish and birds. The shamanistic beliefs revealed these relations with the world, 'relations of the human and non-human quite different from those we entertain, but not, therefore, necessarily less reasonable', as Godfrey Lienhardt had tried to explain at the start. It isn't so much the particular beliefs that are incomprehensible to us. It's not that they were 'animists' and we are not. The difficulty is rather that we have, for ourselves, through the material conditions of our lives and the relation with the natural world that comes from that, made their kind of relation with the animals and the trees and the waters profoundly incomprehensible.

None of us can get ourselves back to the ecological integrity that was expressed through shamanistic processes, where each person is in a life-and-death relation with their surroundings. If you get an inkling of that kind of integrity you can also appreciate the the full awfulness of the Brazilian government policy of 'integration'. Integration into what? Into the 'national society' (that empty abstraction), which means destroying that relation between them and the forest. It's the process which takes place through acquiring and depending on material goods. 'Integration' meant shotguns and radios, hence an umbilical cord to the outside society to get hold of lead-shot and batteries. That meant cash. That meant producing to sell. That meant an earthquake in their relation with their surroundings, breaking it into scrambled relics. It was a policy of disintegration, perpetrated on them, destroying the material conditions of their lives but leaving them with the lingering beliefs which would serve as requiems both for loved ones and for lost ways of being.

That's why there's no point in thinking we can reinvent the relation in a piecemeal way. When we look around and find that there are no *pajés*, no shamans, no witch-doctors, there's no point in play-acting such parts in parlour seances and meeting hall displays, claiming thereby to be returning to those elemental sensibilities of relation with the spiritual and natural world. The fancy dress taken from picture books and the *bricolage* of procedures – these are the real scrambled relics; the scrambled relics of a middle-class, first-world credulity that hasn't managed to grasp the enormity of what has been destroyed, root and branch.

Understanding and believing

I began this chapter with linguistic difficulties. These we can get used to. The mysteries of language are inexhaustible, but with practice we can become nimble in getting over the obstacles. Yet, however far I think I'm getting into it, shamanism is the principal aspect of their lives that retains an immediate capacity to shock. Sometimes I get excited about it, sometimes frustrated, sometimes frightened. It's like trying to get to know a bit of land and finding that the area you're walking in isn't obeying the usual rules. You think you're learning your bearings, but you keep on getting lost and emerging in the wrong place. If that happens then either the land really is weird, or there's something going askew with the way you're taking your bearings.

Approaching the FUNAI post for the last time, walking easily along the abandoned road, I met Yiseiwarai on his way to hunt. He'd always been talked about as being greatly *paye*. I had missed him this time in all the settlements I'd visited. We hadn't seen each other for years although he'd heard that I'd come back. We talked about the thunder earlier that day and he said that was because Yaneyar was drunk. This set him off on a bizarre line. He asked about aeroplane travel, how high I'd got in my previous journey, if I'd seen Yaneyar when I was up there. Did I do my writing in Yaneyar's place? was the next question. When I said I'd probably not been high enough to see Yaneyar, he said he'd been away up there himself the previous day. That short meeting on the road made me see how far I still had to go to. Was he just having me on? Was he really cranky in a way others were not? Was there something here that I would, eventually, grasp? Or was this a final impasse? I couldn't and still can't decide amongst these possibilities.

On the last day at the post, the last day with Wayapí people, I stayed with a young couple I'd known since they were children.

They had stayed for years on the post, the man in FUNAI service. Both spoke fairly good Portuguese and lived in a Brazilian frontier-style house. They had a gas cooking stove. They offered me packet soup, and coffee with milk. They wore Brazilian clothes. The woman mentioned the electric light that illuminated the post, and how she'd like to have that in her home, but they were only, in the Portuguese phrase, *gente pobre*, poor folk. For all the world, I seemed to have left the Wayapí far behind and to have already taken the step across the shadow line that was planned for the following day. But then came the impassioned torrent about Sora that I mentioned earlier, and a lengthy discussion about Anaconda. In a moment I was back at this mysterious turbulent centre of Wayapí concerns.

It's shamanism more than anything, more than the myths or the manners, that dislocates me and disturbs my complacent assumptions that understanding is all just a matter of time, just a matter of patience, just like learning the language. With the language, perseverance furthers, and you'll likely get there in the end. With shamanism I'm reminded that I can never be sure.

In the heady 1960s, before the rise of strident fundamentalism, when Christianity in particular was in soft-focus and appeared to be fading, Alasdair MacIntyre wrote an article called 'Is Understanding Religion Compatible with Believing?' It was a clever piece which dealt with nuances of the two words 'understanding' and 'believing', making the point that an effort of understanding has inevitably to be made from the outside. If you're already a 'believer' there's no 'understanding' effort required. It's *because* we don't believe that we have to make the interpretative effort.

A quarter of a century later the point was echoed in a moving phrase by Clifford Geertz who, discussing the interpretative efforts that anthropology finds itself struggling with, suggests that: 'We must learn to grasp what we cannot embrace.' It's a phrase that drifts in my memory, and keeps emerging as: 'We must learn to embrace what we cannot grasp'. Which way round? I think it's better put in Old Lafew's words: we must learn to submit ourselves to those unknown fears.

8

AIMA

I never really got to know Waiwai. He was Our Big One. As such he embodied an elemental political power and the responsibility distanced him. That was why the relationship between him and me remained protocolled and not available for intimacy – rather as shamanism remained for me a kind of understanding-from-without rather than a kind of believing-from-within.

It was important that our relationship should have been kept formal like that. In Waiwai's scheme of things my place was as someone from the outside, and in that he was being accurate and uncompromising. No time, no place for sentimental indulgence whereby I'd be 'accepted' in a let's-pretend way as one of them. I wasn't; and he knew that. What he had to work out was how useful I might be in the strategies he had to invent for dealing with the outside.

His consuming concern was with the survival of Wayapí people. True, he didn't have phrases like 'our culture, our way of life', or 'our heritage, our traditions' to justify what his vision was. But he didn't need words like that. For him, the question was whether his people were to get through or die. His struggle was a fierce vocation and nothing distracted him from it. I found that severe passion admirable.

Aima was the place where it began for Waiwai. He was a child there. It may well end at Aima too. When the Brazilian invasions get that far, the centre will be broken open, and the integrity of Wayapí lands lost. Perhaps the land will hold for many years yet, perhaps not. The outcome depends on distant political events, so I shouldn't make predictions that will look silly from a future perspective.

I hope the land will hold, whatever my doubts. Amazônia has now been mapped by photographic images taken from satellites in space. There are techniques whereby the very contents in the sub-soil and bedrock can be read off. Scientific experts can tell the business people where all the deposits of this, that, and the other are. These business people in the outside world know what the Wayapí are sitting on, and they want it badly, just as the European invaders wanted the gold five centuries ago. Today, the prospectors of the informal economy, the *garimpeiros*, are still after that same gold, while the big companies of North America and Europe and Japan want the cassiterite and the tantalite and the uranium and all the other stuff with names ending in -ite and -ium that I find difficult to remember. I wish Waiwai's fierceness could hold up all that and send them all packing, but I don't know if he'll be able to do so.

I've been presenting everything as if these times were a hinge of particular importance. They are indeed so. 'The Land, the Language, and the People.' If the land goes the seal of integrity is broken and there is no way back to reconstitute anything from the bits and pieces that remain. There's no point in saying that it was all a process anyway, right from the start; that cultures are always changing; that civilizations rise and fall; that nothing endures; that all is flux; that the old order changeth giving place to new. None of that will do.

Waiwai's lifetime was indeed a hinge of history. Something irrevocable happened then that the survivors a century on will look back at and try to make sense of. Waiwai knew that he was trying to save something vital and precious. He knew that he was to have inheritors. But the questions for them as for me are: what, exactly, was he trying to preserve? And what, exactly, will come through to later years?

If you took the whole kit and caboodle – manioc, hammocks, bows and arrows, house-building, relationship terms, myths, shamanism, *la couvade* and Anaconda – it would fit anywhere into the non-European Amazon all the way back to 1492 and beyond. Not that there is or ever was a uniformity. Patterns would vary without measure. But like shaking a kaleidoscope, those endless patterns of beautiful forms would appear through rearrangements of the same essentials – material conditions, ecological patterns, social arrangements, fundamental ideas and images. What's happening to Wayapí people, as has happened to culture after culture throughout Amazônia, is that the kaleidoscope is being broken as the trees are felled, and the fragments are being scattered.

Years later, generations later, a century on, it is precisely these fragments that will be collected, hoarded, and cherished. And in the exuberance of rediscovered ethnicity it is precisely these fragments that will be shored against the cultural ruins that remain.

The land, the language, the people. You could invent ways of representing the changes, charting them in various ways – statistics, graphs, diagrams, maps. You could itemize and quantify the processes. The first two, land and language, would be fairly easy to do. The maps of the area this century and next will show the encroachments of the Brazilian frontier, the routes of the roads, the areas of forest that are felled and cleared, the areas that are to be gradually removed from Wayapí people. The inheritors will see how the land went. To measure linguistic change a straight-forward census would do – how many can speak Portuguese in my times; and gradually, as the decades go on, how many don't use Wayapí as their first language or even won't be able to use it at all.

But the people? How do you measure the changes there? In the mid-1970s I had no idea what was going to happen to them. The road was threatening. Land invasions were looming. Government policy was inept and cynical. Time and time again over the centuries Amazonian peoples had come to this crux and failed to pull through. When I left Nipukú that time I thought I might never see any of them again. I thought the deluge was about to break on them. In their own myths they talked about the great fire and the great flood as it if was a single final cataclysm. When you think of how the forests are burned and the rivers dammed you'd think their myths were told by people with the second sight.

The deluge didn't break. The road was stopped in 1976 because of a collapse in the Brazilian economy, and the area remained relatively quiet. And quietly the processes of contact and change went on. When I went back for the first time after an eight-year gap I was overwhelmed with relief to find that nearly everyone was still alive, that one hundred new Wayapí people had come into existence, and that on first appearances little had changed.

Contact was well established, though. Every arm had its vaccination mark. Pots, pots, pots, everywhere – aluminium ones. There was a girlie magazine in Parahandy's house. That first morning at Mariry, a Sunday as it happened, there were no complacencies of the peignoir; no holy hush of ancient sacrifice. Nonato had got hold of a battery powered gramophone, and from his house across the clearing Elino Julião was belting out 'O primeiro beijo que eu dei em você' ('The first time I gave you a kiss'). Before the morning was out we'd had 'Carimbó e Sirimbó no embalo do Pinduca'. We'd had Jane e Herondy; and we'd finished up with Roberto Carlos – all the Brazilian pop stars of the day.

I looked around at the *things* that had come from the outside and thought of grading them in levels from useful to useless, trying to balance off how far each object was useful against how far it led to a need for a constant supply from the outside. I couldn't fit medicines, antibiotics, injections, on to the scale since these items brought in too many people, too many relationships, too much expertise and specialization beyond the material conditions of life. That apart I saw everything else fitting into six layers:

[I]   Axes, machetes, knives, files, fish-hooks, aluminium pots, metal sheets for making manioc scrapers.

Each of these brought enormous benefits in terms of convenience and security, and required only occasional replacement. Into this category went shotguns – a tricky matter this one. Well, they wanted them so much at the start. They certainly made hunting much easier. But I've since heard angry speeches from them about how they constantly needed powder and shot and cartridges; how the game had been shot out; how the young people couldn't use bows and arrows; how the old ways were better. I still don't know about shotguns. Bows and arrows, like dancing and language, always were a fundamental cultural marker, and I didn't like seeing them go.

[II]   Red cloth, and factory-made hammocks; tin plates and spoons.

They had their own cotton and their own dyes. They grew their own calabashes, *cuias* and *morotocos*. But tin plates and spoons brought in from the outside did last much longer. The cotton crop could get attacked by pests. It was an enormous amount of labour to make enough string for a hammock. And manufactured red cloth was much more comfortable to wear, and the colour much more pleasing. You'd have to be a terrible Spartan to say they shouldn't have had these things.

[III] Torches, razor blades, sandals, T-shirts.

Well, fine. But the items on this list wore out and needed replacing so quickly. Torch batteries particularly were expensive. Life could go on without these things.

[IV] Beads, mirrors, combs.

All very nice, and everyone wanted to look good and feel good. Nothing wrong with having them, but no one really needed them. (Their own combs were better than cheap plastic ones.) Combs and mirrors broke. Beads, by contrast, should maybe go into a category all on their own. They were the supreme aesthetic object. They *didn't* get lost. They were hoarded with great care. If only it had just been beads they got from the outside.

[V] Scissors, tweezers, needles.

These were practical equivalents of the aesthetic tools of [IV]. They were extras, and fine if available, but they were just gadgetry.

[VI] Radios and gramophones.

These were the end of the line as far as consumer throw-aways went. There was never a proper supply of batteries for them, and they went faulty in months or even weeks because cockroaches ate vital parts and because the machinery broke down in the humid conditions.

These things, together with speech and habits of dress, were the most striking indicators of their changing circumstances. The objects revealed a relationship with the outside that was economic, political, and social – in other words, it involved money, relationships of dependence, and the involvement of particular outsiders. They got the money by producing their own pieces of handicraft: featherwork, basketwork, articles of ceramic. When they first began to make pieces for sale they would whip up any old tat: a raggedy headdress or a basket with colours crudely painted on rather than woven with different coloured palm-strips. I appreciated that – a 'Who cares?' approach in making an object that was to be sold, contrasting with pride in craftsmanship that went with a fire-fan or a manioc squeezer for use in the village.

There were little that could be taken directly from the forest or the gardens for sale – not much to sell from harvesting vegetables or from hunting, although I saw an ocelot shot for its skin;

something that would never have been done in the old days by Wayapí themselves, and something that's not particularly reliable for the future since it's an illegal trade. The most dramatic turn of activity was to do with gold-panning work. Since the early 1970s Wayapí lands had been plagued by prospector invasions. At one point in the late 1980s they raided a prospectors' camp, drove the Brazilians out, kept the equipment, and held one of the invaders prisoner till he taught them how to get gold. Learning this particular skill of the Brazilian frontier was and is a useful short-term measure. I can't say how long it will last, whether it is a viable solution for the longer term, or what the results of entering the Brazilian frontier economy in this way will have on Wayapí people themselves. But it's a frightening direction to take. If they have to join in, it's hard to think of a more degenerate way to do it. Gold, of all things. I can't comfortably see how that business could forbode well. It's an enormous risk, but it's a risk that has been taken.

Gradually, then, the material conditions of their lives were drawing them in to the world of the Brazilians – that inexorable process towards . . . towards what? It's frightening to see what has happened already in so many other parts of Amazônia. When these waves of change threaten a particular group, all of us at the moment who are concerned look back and around at what has happened to other Indian peoples. There are few reassuring examples, apart from – and how can this be said? – apart from those that are never heard about.

The silences in Amazônia mostly cover untold tragedies, secret atrocities, and anonymous exterminations. But every now and again, usually when the good news is just ending, there emerge examples of how Indian peoples managed to keep going for long spans of time in promising conditions without their relationship with the Brazilian frontier degenerating into crisis. While a torrent of atrocity has been covered up, there's a trickle of hope that is also hidden from outside scrutiny.

I keep hoping that there still may be many unknown examples of that kind. It's an awkward and ambiguous hope since it depends on hearing nothing. To the extent that no one bothers with the headwaters of the Amaparí and the Nipukú and the Aima, then Waiwai and his people can keep what they had. But since their privacy is threatened by pictures from space, and since their land is not going to be left alone, what is going to become of them?

The changes they inevitably face are commonly described by a series of bland labels: acculturation, assimilation, integration; or by more awful words such as cultural disintegration and ethnocide. You can measure what's going on by acreages and census figures, and by the implications of objects. But it's harder to chart what the changes mean in terms of thought and feeling and sense of being. If they are to be 'integrated' what does that mean, and a hundred years on from now what will people mean when they say: 'I am Wayapí'?

Integrating

For years, the accepted view of the 'Indian problem' (as the various governments liked to refer to it) was that it presented a simplistic choice between integration into the national society, or the creation of a human zoo where indigenous peoples would be kept in artificial isolation within reservations. The distinction explicitly assumed that the human zoo option was romantic, ill-informed, and impractical. Here then was something called a problem which had two possible solutions, one of which was a non-starter. Just like the brave words 'Order and Progress' that flutter on the Brazilian flag, so 'integration' became an unquestioned axiom, inevitable and desirable for all concerned.

The phrase 'the Indian problem' is itself a preposterous inversion of values. It turns everything upside down: values of history and actuality, values of economics and politics, values of morals and ecology. The blazingly obvious problem in Amazônia is a constellation of destructive interests – the multinational corporation problem, the agri-business problem, the large-scale industrial construction problem (specifically, these days, dams), the logging industry problem, the land-lust problem, the lust-for-minerals problem, the military paranoia problem, the missionary problem. They are all one monstrous Brazilian problem, set to run alongside the incompetent government agency problem (in every aspect of public life), and the institutionalized corruption problem (in every aspect of public life). And the Indians? There never, ever, was such a thing as an 'Indian problem'. It has always and forever been the Indians who have had to face up to the Brazilian problem. 'Integration' is therefore a periphrastic way of saying: 'Welcome, Indians, to the Brazilian problem.'

The work of the Villas-Boas brothers, Orlando and Claudio, was an early example that challenged the slick assumptions of a choice between integration and human zoo. For decades, from the 1950s, they tried to protect the Indian peoples of the Upper Xingú River within a National Park. They fought hard against the galloping procedures of integration, but never entirely discarded the word as a description of what was bound to happen. They accepted that the process of integration was inevitable. Their argument was not that the process should be halted. It couldn't be halted, they said. But it had to be slowed up. It had to proceed under careful control, to avoid unnecessary destruction and suffering. Theirs was one way of dealing with the sadness.

At the end of the 1960s Darcy Ribeiro, a Brazilian anthropologist who had worked with the Indian Protection Service (SPI), the precursor of FUNAI, also wrote that the fate of indigenous cultures was inevitable. He devoted half his book *Os Índios e a Civilização* (Indians and Civilization) to a description of what he called the process of 'ethnic transfiguration', and thereby tried to make the word 'integration' more precise. 'Integration' for Darcy Ribeiro meant that the Indians would enter Brazilian society as Indians and would remain as such. They would not, however, be 'assimilated', in the sense of being converted into Brazilians and absorbed into the society:

They will remain Indians because their acculturation does not lead to assimilation, but to the establishment of a *modus vivendi* or a form of accommodation. This means that the gradient of ethnic transfiguration runs from tribal Indian to generic Indian and not from Indian to Brazilian.

What a striking term: 'generic Indian'. It means that people who were once Shavante or Tukano, Kayapó or Wayapí, and who might, once upon a time, have seen their own name and their names for others as referring to peoples irremediably different one from another, will all together gradually become *Índios* but will not go the further step of becoming *Brasileiros*. His conclusions were extraordinarily prescient:

It also means that ethnic groups are much more resilient than is generally supposed, because they need minimal conditions to keep themselves going, and because they survive [in ethnic terms] the total transformation of their tribal or cultural

218

inheritance. Further, it means that language, customs, beliefs, are external attributes of an ethnic entity. These attributes can undergo profound changes without the ethnic group going through mutation or collapse. Finally, it means that 'ethnic entities' refers to relational categories between human groups, composed primarily of mutual images and moral loyalties, rather than specific tribal or cultural traits.

For its day that is a statement uncanny in its accuracy. I wish I could hear a response to it from the 2090s.

There's an ambiguity in his category 'generic Indian' that's still active and obvious. Can you declare yourself *both* as Indian *and* as Wayapí? Of course you can. Today, in the United States and Canada the word 'Indian' has become suspect and people nowadays use terms such as Native Americans or First Nations. But in Brazil the word *Índio* has been defiantly hijacked by the Indians themselves and is now used as a powerful political slogan. It is also used with a bit more punch than just saying: 'We are Indians.' They add to that the particular strength of asserting their ethnic identity as well, declaring themselves Kayapó, Tukano, and so on. What they are doing is tapping in to a world-wide explosion where ethnicity (whatever that may mean in its thousand different forms) has become as potent a political force of my times as nationalism (whatever that meant in dozens of different contexts) was in the middle of the nineteenth century.

It's ironic, by the way, that a world-wide phenomenon should emerge to help Indians. Previously Indian peoples in the Amazon forest have always been at the mercy of materialistic world forces such as the price of rubber on international stock markets in the late 1800s, or the needs of the nuclear power industry for uranium and tantalite in the late 1900s; enormous material forces that guaranteed the destruction of their forest. Here is a world force (ideological this time rather than materialistic) emerging for once to their advantage.

Ethnicity

Commentators in the anthropology business (like me) have been trying to catch up with the Indians. We must have made a mistake, it is now said, when we talked of genuine ethnic identities being destroyed by the processes of integration. If ethnic identity is such a powerful force today, then it must always have been there. One of our errors in the past was to talk or write of the predicament of Indians in the Americas as peoples who have lived in a unique, timeless society, with no history; living for centuries in the forest with their bows and arrows, and gardens, and free estates in a kind of suspended animation; and who were suddenly overwhelmed by outside forces, culturally eviscerated, and left marginalized and washed up on the edges of the dominant society.

The intelligent move (or so the story now goes) is to appreciate that Indian peoples were not frozen in time until the invaders arrived; that they had a history before the European invasions; that they continue to have a history; and that they have always been adapting to the changes that came upon them. That primary mistake of earlier commentaries where Amerindians were presented as frozen in time, space, and culture was carried forward into what's happening today. The result was that anthropologists and other writers went about creating a false idea of ethnic identity when they described present-day Indians. The old-fashioned account would go something like this:

> To be an Indian meant fundamentally to belong to a residential indigenous community located in a marginal rural zone, to be preferably monolingual in a native language, to have a strong communal and ceremonial understanding of life, to show some rejection of the logic of the market economy, and to be satisfied with the repetitive and 'traditional' use of antiquated technology.

A picture like that is simply hopeless, says this up-to-date commentator, if we think of a Quechua from the Andes who works on a computer, a Shuar from the Ecuadorian Amazon with a PhD in education, a Tukano from Brazil with a pilot's licence, and so on. As I write, Parahandy is making films of Wayapí ceremonies with a VCR.

The big mistake, it's now said, was to assume that contact, modernization, and change would strip those people of their ethnicity. It was a mistake to say that their precarious cultural identity would vaporize as soon as they joined the modern world. When describing the process, old-fashioned anthropology would typically go into elegiac mode, lamenting the passing of these wonderful cultures. But, say these modern commentators, it has been seen again and again that once they have survived the biological disaster of first contact and invasion – let's be more precise: those who managed to survive it; so many didn't – they then become demographically stable, they become bilingual without loss of native languages, and in some cases their populations even begin to increase. Once native people become transnational, border-crossing, urban, professional, bi- and tri-lingual, then any talk of ethnic and cultural identity has left the traditional anthropological stereotype well behind.

Nowadays, all over the Americas, there are more and more examples of native peoples using their ethnic identity in astute, politically sophisticated, strategic ways: Quechua and Aymara organizations becoming politically effective in Bolivia; Ecuadorian Indian organizations capable of bringing the country to a halt; Mayans organizing in Guatemala in the face of the most appalling oppression.

I accept these up-to-date arguments, and I understand these descriptions of present-day Indians, but I don't think it's so easy to dismiss the previous picture. Of course Indians are Indians even when they drive Chevy pick-up trucks and watch soap operas on television. But it would be a disastrous loss to forget the most challenging and poignant examples of all – precisely those monolingual, isolated, vulnerable communities with their bows and arrows and other 'antiquated technology'. Yes they were there. Yes they are still there. That's precisely what the Wayapí were in the 1970s when they were contacted – monolingual, isolated, vulnerable, though managing quite well with their antiquated technology. And neither the discipline of anthropology nor any other aspect of our society has come anywhere near having had the final say on what that sort of existence meant to them, to Wayapí people themselves, and what that sort of existence means to us, as we look on as outsiders. Those of us who look at what's called 'primitive life' from an engaged point of view, whether we've been privileged enough to have been allowed to participate in communities like that, or whether we're looking back with the curiosity of survivors and inheritors, we need no convincing that this is where the heart of the mystery lies.

Those of us who got involved in that mystery are a dwindling number indeed, but we're still here too, and we do still speak and write with great sadness about what is being lost. When we see what's happening we cannot just jauntily say: 'Oh well; "Let the great world spin forever down the ringing grooves of change". Nothing to worry about. Their ethnicity will survive albeit in a different form.' That would be unforgivable – a terrible betrayal. Look at it like this. While future Wayapí may be capable of looking back and seeing themselves in Waiwai's people, could Waiwai looking a century ahead see himself so easily in them and their way of life?

Assertions of ethnicity come across in a language of essences. It's talked about as if it were an ingredient, peculiar and sempiternal. No matter that it has no precise outlines, that it is elusive, that it is described in the floppiest terms, it is firmly believed to be there; a grounding quality inhering within each person of the identified group, like a kind of human phlogiston. Mostly I'm not impressed by ethnic passions. I don't believe in these essences. Furthermore they make a mockery of the passion that inspired Waiwai. He lacked the abstract words to express what he was struggling to preserve, but his was the more precise passion. Yet, as the changes transform Wayapí life, I guess that even in his lifetime Waiwai too will have to learn the cloudy jargon of ethnicity. As the conditions of self-sufficiency dwindle away on the outside he too will have to hope that the essences will survive within.

Imagining

The Wayapí are moving out of the forest and are moving towards the world their inheritors will live in. As they leave the woods and as their material conditions are absorbed into those of the Brazilian frontier, so they begin a journey deeper into an interior world of imagination. A sense of being that was formerly just *there*, gets first of all brutally challenged by the assaults of an intense spell of contact, and then gradually, as the generations succeed, finds a kind of haven in a reserve of symbols and metaphors. That sense of being, when its material conditions are dismantled, will keep itself alive through its imaginative resources. It will transform into a present, conceived of as a symbolic past.

In a book called *Imagined Communities* Benedict Anderson considers the nature of nationalism – ethnicity on a grander scale. He questions a statement by another academic that nationalism '. . . invents nations where they do not exist'. Nations, in that way of putting it, were said to be false or factitious or fantasized communities. Fine, says Anderson, but that doesn't get you very far. The trouble is that if you want to think of nations as false and fabricated, you imply by contrast that there are other kinds of communities that are not made up in this way. You imply that there is such a thing as a *true*, real, genuine, authentic community. Anderson suggests that the contrast doesn't work. There's no point, he argues, of holding on to a distinction between fantasy communities on the one hand and real communities on the other: 'In fact, all communities larger than primordial villages of face-to-face contact (*and perhaps even these*) [my emphasis] are imagined'. It isn't just nations that are imagined. Regional identity; localities; cities; racial, religious, sexual, and professional sub-groups – whenever and wherever they are talked about as 'communities' to which we or others belong, they are all, everyone of them, *imagined*.

It's a challenging view. So many people find it impossible to adjust to, given how profoundly they believe in the essential ingredients of their identity category. And as if that wasn't challenging enough Anderson continues: 'Communities are to be distinguished not by their falsity/genuineness, but by the *style* in which they are imagined'. *Style*? That makes it sound like a fashion show. It would appear from his account that in this ethnic parade, points would be given, not for a quality called 'authenticity', but for 'creativity'. That's to say, if we think of our own ethnicity and our own cultural identity as a relationship with our past, the criterion is going to be how *creatively* we hang on to our past, how vigorously our imagination is working, rather than how genuinely we are connected with our past.

I'd want to hang on to Benedict Anderson's notion of imagining, while trying to make his notion of 'style' do a bit more work. Let's not give people fashion points for their style of imagining. Let's think of a crescendo and diminuendo of imagining; a process that goes as much for Waiwai as for me. It would concern the degree by which all of us are forced to become self-conscious of our collective identity, and the degree to which we are compelled to create our self-ascribed category.

I'll accept that our categories in the kind of lives we now lead are wholeheartedly imagined – all our identity categories; all our community categories. By contrast, the style of being of Wayapí people as they have been living up until Waiwai's time is as near as you'll get to Imagination Degree Zero. They were at such a degree because there were fundamental material conditions that allowed them an integrity of space and an integrity of culture. They were not forced by the intrusions of our world into gathering up their sense of identity, and fleeing with it for safe-keeping into the refuges of the mind, there to sit forever among the alien corn, remembering.

That's what has happened in North America to the indigenous peoples there, as well as in a more genial and fanciful way in the parts of Scotland I know. The imagination sets to work, finding stage props in the vanished culture which will stand for ethnic originality. But the ingredients and traits that are *later* imagined in this way as constituting an ethnic identity were not that at all in the beginning. They were not identity markers. They were the everyday details of practical culture. They were their way of getting on with life.

I try to think ahead to what will happen as Wayapí space and culture gradually erode. I try to guess along which lines the imagining will become more intense. Costumes, body paint, tools and artifacts, detached from the daily life that Waiwai knew and free-floating in a quite altered world, will, I suppose, be grasped in later times as emblems. There will be a general hardening of manners. Dances and rituals will be refined and formalized, ready for public parades in that altered world. Ideas and feelings that were diffuse and pervasive will be simplified into slogans and celebrated as distinctive traits of sensibility.

We could be severe. We could attack the 'ethnic movements' industry and say that these imaginings of the past are chicanery; the result of immature yearnings that get out of hand. We could say that they fulfil the same role as escapist fantasies and do no more than help people endure featureless areas of gloom and worlds of anomie. I'm sure they are, and I'm sure they do. But there's a more important point.

Yes I'm sceptical. Yes I'm aware of the imaginative quotient of these constructs. When I find myself operating in similar terms I do make allowances and try not to take myself seriously. (Will people ever outgrow the clichés of national and ethnic stereotypes?) But when I think of the kind of life that Waiwai was living when I first met him and the kind of adjustment he has had to make when he finds his world engulfed by the Brazilian frontier, I'd be on the side of any imaginative effort that served as a gesture of resistance against the onslaught.

What does it matter if there is an invented quality about these future imaginings? Let them all flourish. They are a defiant refusal to give up on what has gone. However faintly they echo the past, they are a defiant reaffirmation of ways that were precious. They keep alive the challenge that these former ways of life constantly present us with. It's a challenge that's both a warning, like the words on Ozymandias's pedestal, and an invitation, to change our ways of being and acting. They rescue these former ways of life 'from the enormous condescension of posterity'.

The last pastoral

In our attempts to understand our lives and the lives of others, in our attempts to appreciate alternatives and potentialities for human existence, the most challenging effort is the one that asks us to come to terms with those patterns of primitive life that are finally vanishing from the earth as this century I've been living in draws to its end. We all may be properly sceptical of Rousseau-esque idealizations of the Noble Savage, but when the survivors of these peoples look back and assert their connection with the kind of life I've seen, they are insisting that it will not be forgotten, that it cannot be ignored, and that those who glibly talk of civilization and progress cannot wave these lives aside as irrelevant.

The lessons have been presented to us in a gentler form over two thousand years through the literary convention of the Pastoral starting with the *Idylls* of Theocritus. There's always been a judgemental tendency that wants to dismiss the images of that tradition as soft idealism. Wordsworth was aware of the criticism and at times became defensive:

> Call ye these appearances –
> Which I beheld of shepherds in my youth,
> This sanctity of Nature given to man –
> A shadow, a delusion, ye who are fed
> By the dead letter, not the spirit of things . . .

Fighting back, he saw that the image of the pastoral is there for us to measure up to. It's there to challenge our assumptions about ourselves. A critic commenting on the image of the Forest of Arden in Shakespeare's *As You Like It* put it like this:

> The idea that sophisticated people, suddenly made part of a rustic life of which previously they had the most distant and imperfect knowledge, may discover truths obscured or undisclosed in the court is a very old one. Pastoral is a complex and enduring form, not because it is escapist, but because it is basically tough: it is a way of testing both the self and the assumptions of ordinary, urban society.

If that goes for literature, anthropology should be infinitely tougher, uncompromisingly so, especially when it comes across the kind of existence lived by Wayapí people during Waiwai's time.

Their life presents us with the most profound questions we could ask. Whence are we, and why are we? Of what scene the actors or spectators? Once that is addressed, a cascade of further questions queues up behind. How? Through what agonies? Through what failures and successes? Through what deaths and entrances?

The example of their life challenges and undermines the complacencies of all the -isms you could think of: religious ones, philosophical ones, those that have followed on from the ideas of the Enlightenment, especially the claims made in the name of science and reason; the social and economic ones like 'capitalism' and 'Marxism', as well as any of the sociologies that have appeared in the last couple of centuries. Also one of the most urgent lessons for my day challenges the way human beings regard their relationship with animals, birds, trees, water, and the earth.

The remote past is lost to us as a personal experience. What we know about it we get through the imagination and fantasies (in the best sense of the word) of those who are involved with archaeology. But I was lucky enough to glimpse a remote *present*; hence the sense of urgency in trying to grasp it before it vanishes. Archaeologists build up their pictures from potsherds and teeth. I build up mine on the basis of *convivência*, that lovely word.

'Fieldwork'

It's a tragedy that so little attention is given to primitive life in the world I know. Mostly it's regarded as a curiosity, perhaps a bit bizarre or shocking, but nothing more than that. Since these responses are so common I should have become accustomed to them by now, but I haven't. Given the questions, that indifference baffles me to this day. Perhaps an appreciation of the questions depends on a primary curiosity. Perhaps those who shrug their shoulders and pass by are simply not beset by that itch. Maybe you've either got it or you haven't.

Some years before going to the Brazilian forests I had travelled by canoe up the Rio de la Pasión in northern Guatemala, staying the nights in the houses of Kekchi-speaking people, and moving on the next day. There and then was the predicament of travel, mere travel. I'd come across an impenetrable language that covered an enigmatic way of life. Arriving at a house the spectacle of strangeness was wonderful. But leaving it the next day I'd look back restless and unsatisfied. How could I learn about that mystery? Why move on? Why not stay and plunge in? The same yearning was there again in the Peruvian Andes, seeing villages from the backs of trucks, or walking through remote hamlets to look for a camping spot beyond. That sense of curiosity has been irresistible, and it's been pushing and pulling me here and there until it became a formal venture backed up by university support: Anthropological Fieldwork.

When I eventually set out with a specific goal (formulated, applied for, and approved) I went off into the great woods with my head crammed full of those Great Questions that anthropology sets up so well. You have to give the discipline that. The questions are set up beautifully (however intractable they may prove to work with). Are there separate realities? Are there other logics? Are there alien minds? What is the basis of political power? What are the fundamentals of human morality? When we have identified an alien mode of thought and action, how do we respond to it? Can we understand something without believing it?

I take it for granted that learning about the unique lives of tropical forest peoples is one of the best ways of facing up to these enduring questions. I'm sure that in another century the puzzles will have been put into firmer perspective. The long juries will have returned with their verdicts and the long judgements will have been made. And incidentally, looking back from a distance at that short list of questions I'm sure people will see one gaping lacuna at a glance. If the great human questions as set by academic anthropology have mainly been of: truth, reality, logic and mind, rationality and mentality, reason and intention, interpretation and translation, thought-and-action, belief-and-thought, language-and-reality, language-and-thought; and if they're all explained by cracking codes of categories, orders, principles, structures, systems – if that's so, then we can see immediately that one or two simple words are sitting there on the sidelines like tragic outcasts: Affect, Emotion, Feeling, Love. The discipline set the questions very well indeed, but maybe they didn't get them all in.

I know, though, that when I went plunging off into the forest, the Great Questions were animated by a much more prosaic curiosity that had been there from the start; an ordinary question asking nothing more than: 'How on earth do these people do it, and can I learn the ways?' It was a simple curiosity about the sheer practicalities of daily life. I don't know if following the more elevated paths of enquiry can be realistically continued without that basis. If you're not interested in *that*, how can you be interested in anything else? On the other hand, if that does interest you, you are immediately faced with one of the most challenging questions of the Pastoral: what would be left of each one of us if the familiar veneers of technical and cultural sophistication were removed? This has nothing to do with escapist fantasies, and it's far more immediate and direct than the serious hypothetical challenges found in utopian and dystopian traditions from Plato's *Republic* to *Nineteen Eighty-Four*. It's a fearful question about what we are, here and now: 'Look unto the rock whence ye are hewn and to the hole of the pit whence ye are digged'.

Whatever the questions, whatever the goal, whatever the inspiration, all directions had to start with the the long process of getting familiar with the language. As that began to come, the general enigma began to focus on specific directions. The belief-thought-action question that emerged as particularly baffling to me was shamanism. That became the principal intellectual struggle when I got back to academia.

Returning to the forest for the second time after some years to renew the familiarity and to try to get more skilled in their ways, I hit a bad patch after a few weeks. I suppose I was particularly fed up with the conduct of the FUNAI people and the ragged cultural confusion they were creating. I wondered what I was doing there and if there was any point in carrying on.

Dejected, I looked back at all the work in the past, both in the woods and out of them. It looked as if I'd cracked the enigma of shamanistic beliefs, and the how and why of illness and death. What was said about the spirit-owners and the misfortunes they visit on us mortals was now normal everyday talk. I'd got it. This second time around I felt I'd broken through to that privileged level of understanding I'd been striving for. All the book-work had been worthwhile. I really had achieved something. But something had been lost too. Coming back that time was like returning to familiar countryside and enjoying a renewal of old acquaintance, but there wasn't the excitement of new places, surprising vistas, unknown corners. The difficult work was done. That kind of day was over.

Then, in camp, just as evening was coming on, Joaquim came to sit by the fire and he began to talk of Anaconda. He went on to describe a world turned upside down, where nothing was as it seemed, where apparent animals and fish were quite other in Anaconda's shamanistic vision. They formed a congeries of domestic things and pets for the snake. It was riveting stuff. I hadn't heard this before. I had difficulty getting off to sleep that night, my mind racing over and over. Earlier that day I had wondered what I was doing there. By that evening I felt I could stay forever.

I learned that night that the mysteries were forever unfathomable. I could certainly do years more on the language. I still don't think I could ever exhaust the myths or the nuances of cosmology. That sense of familiarity was only a provisional plateau. There was no end to the surprises.

Agitprop

If Waiwai could hear me saying these things I don't think he'd be particularly impressed. Far from being flattered, I can imagine him getting furious and laying it on the line that he and his people were not put on this earth either to be a source of intellectual enjoyment for academics or to be a moral lesson for civilized degenerates. What he wants from us all is some action, and he wants it now.

Just at the point when my zest for learning came alive again a letter arrived from the outside with news of FUNAI politics. The president of the organization had resigned having refused to sign the necessary documents that would remove the prohibition on mining operations in Indian lands throughout Brazil. A new FUNAI president had been appointed and he *had* signed. There were forty-three applications pending for schemes in the Wayapí area. The lands of the Yanomami, Atroari-Waimiri, Parakanan, Xikrín, and Kayapó peoples were also mentioned as being under threat.

It sounded like a disaster. Here they were in the front lines facing a colossal assault on their lives and their surroundings. Through the alarm and the anger, I felt that this kind of crisis put my priorities of involvement into better perspective. The book-work cracked the mysteries, and there was still mystery-work to do, but if there were politics and fighting coming up as well, the academic concerns had to take second place and shift for themselves on the by-line.

It's still difficult to see if publicizing these predicaments ever turns into effective agitation and propaganda. The forces stacked against the Indians are colossal. Not only that, these forces are brutally ignorant, such that it's hard to think of a way that words, in any form, are going to have any effect. Agitprop wouldn't dent these processes very much. That had to be accepted. But the story had to be told for its own sake so that it couldn't be forgotten.

I remembered an early conversation with A Certain Sertanista; a sertanista being the highest field-official, as opposed to a bureaucrat, in the FUNAI organization. Sertanistas were put in charge of contacts with isolated groups. They ran 'attraction fronts' and 'pacification fronts'. They ran important or sensitive *Postos Indígenas*. They were sent in as trouble-shooters in explosive situations. They were supposed to be experts both in the immediate and in the long-term interfacings with Indians. I had mentioned to A Certain Sertanista how obvious it was that sexual urges simply did not arise when living in Indian settlements. He considered my comment an indication of my lack of experience. 'Eventually everyone succumbs to the temptation', said he.

I knew immediately he was wrong and shrugged it off at the time as an irrelevant ignorance; a predictable ignorance. Years later I discovered what everyone else in the settlements had known all along – that he had indeed had sex with a Wayapí woman during one of their sprees. Some years later she had produced two hydrocephalic children. As far as Wayapí people were concerned her misfortune was the result of her sexual encounter with a *karai-ko*, a Brazilian. A subsequent sertanista, who presumably had no previous knowledge of his predecessor's peccadillo, had the woman removed to the hospital at the ICOMI manganese mine downriver to have her sterilized on account of her deformed progeny. Not the slightest effort was made to explain the point of the operation to the woman or to her immediate family.

What was done to that woman sexually by one sertanista is known to every single living Wayapí person. Presumably not a single Brazilian or FUNAI official, other than the perpetrator, knows of that. Contrariwise, neither she nor any other Wayapí person knows what was done to her by Brazilian doctors in the hospital at Serra do Navio as a result of another sertanista's intervention and as a result of the doctors' judgement on the nature of her children and her future fertility. Nobody in the outside world knows she was screwed by a Brazilian. Nobody in her own world knows she was sterilized by Brazilian doctors. What am I to do with both sides of this dismal story? Tell it, that's what.

Reportage

But there's telling and there's telling:

> Thus he was well placed for giving a true account of all he saw and heard. But in so doing he has tried to keep within the limits that seemed desirable. For instance, in a general way he has confined himself to describing only such things as he was enabled to see for himself, and refrained from attributing to his fellow-sufferers thoughts that, when all is said and done, they were not bound to have. And, as for documents, he has used only such as chance, or mischance, put in his way.
>
> Summoned to give evidence regarding what was a sort of crime, he has exercised the restraint that behoves a conscientious witness. All the same, following the dictates of his heart, he has deliberately taken the victims' side and tried to share with his fellow-citizens the only certitudes they had in common – love, exile, and suffering.

That's the ending of Albert Camus' *The Plague* where it turns out that Dr Rieux, one of the characters, was the narrator all along. It's a touching statement of faith in getting-it-right, being objective, and all the while retaining a human face. Get within smelling distance of the real thing, yes; state the facts, yes; but don't forget that you're part of it too. Give, sympathize, control; all at the same time. It's a fine credo for the fastidious and a fine formula for having it both ways.

Most people involved at the moment in telling what's happening in Amazônia would modestly agree that they strive for accuracy of vision, the better to convince sceptics, stir the socially slothful, and put an end to the violence of the villains. Nobody wants to exaggerate or lie. But that aside, they'd have little patience with fussing about how you tell the story. They wouldn't have the time for Dr Rieux's pernickety restraint. The stakes are too high. In Brazil today many decent journalists, lawyers, local officials and local organizers have found that taking any sort of stand against the agents of exploitation can put their lives in danger since the forces they are up against are at such a frenzied pitch. No one, least of all the victims, would be much concerned about the manner in which the chronicle of land invasions, betrayals, violence and brutality that Indian peoples are put through was presented. What matters is that the story be told again and again, through as many voices as possible, without restraint.

Agitprop of that kind depends on the external aspect of the relationship. We, on the outside here, want to do what we can to speak for them, in there. We want to do what we can to give expression to their fears and their desires and to let their voices be heard in a world that is ignorant of them and indifferent to them. When we get involved in doing that we speak as outsiders to other outsiders. When we are outwith that Indian world we speak *of* the Indians; not *with* them.

This effort is gradually coming of age. Speaking of them becomes speaking for them, which in turn becomes 'them speaking for themselves'. I've told something of their story and I've tried to convey something of Waiwai's voice. But nowadays, as he learns how effective he can be, he is speaking for himself, and as he does that more and more, I can stand aside. With his presence and his gift for oratory he will put a far better case than I can. Since I last saw him he has been taken to Brasília to confront politicians. He has been taken to visit other indigenous peoples. He has starred in documentary films where his 'hard talking' is translated in still subtitles. He has visited New York and Washington. And where he goes he commands attention.

All the agitprop is done for a purpose: to save their lands and their lives. But the plea is to preserve something more than mere existence. And this is where the anthropology comes into it. Curiously, that move from 'speaking of them' to 'them speaking for themselves' mirrors a shift of emphasis in anthropology this century. When Bronislaw Malinowski was writing his ethnographies in the 1920s he insisted again and again that what he was trying to do was to 'see things from the natives' point of view'. Since then, the study of anthropology has made more sophisticated claims about what it was up to: standing back from the people themselves and elaborating 'analytical concepts' that would reveal the fundamentals of 'social structure', for example. When the fashion of French 'structuralism' was taken up, comparative anthropology even claimed that it was revealing 'fundamental structures of the mind'. But whatever the heights of theoretical sophistication, the books, reports, and accounts that were written about particular peoples at particular times (that's to say the 'ethnographies' from which all the theories took their raw material) would usually follow Bronislaw Malinowski's aim – to present matters 'from the natives' point of view', in a sympathetic way of course. Indeed, with a few tweaks and adjustments Dr Rieux's statement of how he went about things could stand as a precise summary of what anthropology thought it was up to this century.

Fashions rise and fall, and along with the theoretical ebbing and flowing in the past decade there's been a growing awareness that it's possible to produce a style of ethnography which 'lets people speak for themselves', and in that way avoid the taints of imperialism, colonialism, paternalism, and all such forms of malign repression that mute the authentic voice. While a move like that is exactly right for agitprop, it doesn't quite work for ethnography. In an ethnographic context it's worthy but naïve.

Waiwai is fighting to preserve the land, the language, and the people. But what he's so proud of is a lot more than just the mere existence of the Wayapí. It's a lot more than just the land that can be measured out and the inhabitants that can be counted off. It's a lot more than just what can be seen and heard and described. At the centre of it all is that hidden reservoir of shared knowledge, shared memories, shared responses, shared associations, shared feelings, shared images – everything that is in that world of imagination towards which they are having to turn more and more.

Where imaginings meet

As Waiwai and all those Wayapí I know move into their realms of imagining, it's there I can meet them and talk with them. Going to meet them there I've had to step beyond the secure limits where we, as outsiders, can comfortably talk *of* them. I've had to go beyond the simple certainties of stating the facts, of being objective, of carrying reports. I've had to give up Dr Rieux's restraints and enter areas where there are few certitudes.

Just as you learn another language by being open to it and by being willing to enter it, so we learn the imaginings of others by making our own capacities open and available to be influenced and changed by theirs. When I translate from one language to another I let my language be fashioned by the strange one and fashion the strange one through mine. Similarly, whatever I understand of their imagined life is the result of its intermingling with mine. It's both creating and being created.

At the start of fieldwork there's no question of me fashioning and controlling what I see and what I understand. At the start it's very much a matter of not getting myself in the way and allowing a vision of things to emerge by itself. At the start, what's essential is that first enormous step of making oneself available, of giving oneself up to whatever happens. It's a mode of passive intensity where all sorts of images and experiences crowd in, pell-mell.

You might say that this is just where Dr Rieux's conscientious restraints come in to control and confine the senses; follow disciplined procedures, be methodical, the object being to distil 'the natives' point of view' from the confusion of what's registered. And that's right to an extent. But it's a limited view of what's going on.

No quality of vision nor degree of understanding is just there for the taking. Nor is it simply a matter of whittling away conscientiously at the mass of disparate experience until the appropriate kernel appears. It's too meagre to say that I report *of* them. It's naïve to say that I can reveal their point of view. It's simplistic to say that I should allow them to speak for themselves. These are the sombre and serious postures that the social sciences take up when they think in terms of objectivity and analysis, of facts and theory. The point is that there's so much more to do than that.

But habits of objectivity are ingrained. I heard a discussion in a Brazilian university amongst people involved with Indian rights and Indian politics. The conversation came round to the disappointing behaviour of certain Indian leaders who had become public figures and to some extent media celebrities. These leaders had on occasion revealed a blatant contempt for other Indian peoples who they considered 'primitive' (those who had been recently contacted, who spoke little Portuguese, and who were unfamiliar with town and city life). That disposition, the conversation went on, revealed the *true* picture of Indians. *Really*, Indians were the most ethnocentric people you could find, deeply tribal in their identity allegiance, and just as nasty in their judgements of other Indian peoples as any Brazilians could be. The behaviour of these leaders demonstrated how self-centred and mercenary Indians *really* were.

Conversely, the conversation went on, idealizing Indians and Indian life gave a *false* picture. The Noble Savage was a romantic fiction invented in the 1700s by Jean-Jacques Rousseau and made popular by notions of *liberté, égalité, fraternité* and the various forms of utopianism and communism that followed on. These are bundles of values that never had, nor will have, anything to do with Indian life as it *in fact* is or was.

Listening to such discussions it seemed that everyone wanted to own the Indians (in thought, if not politically). Everyone had their particular agenda for them. Everyone knew better than anyone else precisely what was out there and precisely what had to be done. Hence there was only room for the one correct view of what they *really* were.

There was so much wrong with these conversations. They reflected such a presumptuous posture; haughty, distant, and inert. One lesson from them was that side-swiping Rousseau like that didn't reveal anything about the Indians. It just revealed a shallow grasp of Rousseau – Rousseau as icon for a simple abstraction, rather than a detailed familiarity with the text of *The Social Contract*. A basic point about Romanticism, as with the idea of the pastoral, is not that it is escapist or misleading, but that it provides a vantage point to appreciate with clearer vision why our familiar forms of social life are so questionable. Demoting Indians from the ideal to the venal does not reflect a more accurate view of what's going on out there in the Amazon woods. All I see in that move is a failure to appreciate that it doesn't much matter what 'they' are or are not, except insofar as 'they' are seen in relation to 'us'. Our vision of them depends so much on what we think of ourselves – something that's notoriously difficult to get to grips with. And if we're so bad at doing that, we shouldn't be so quick to rush to judgement about them.

The better way is to see the process as one that moves from us to them and back again, shifting and changing like light and the weather. Instead of discarding one diagnosis of 'what they are' in favour of another, pasting it on to them like a label, all of us who get involved should take the responsibility for the accounts we give of them and accept that what we say to the outside world is a result of intermingling our experience with theirs.

A farewell gathering

It's a living engagement. It applies the resources of our creative imagination in an attempt which is as much to disclose something about ourselves as it is to disclose something about them. It's an engagement that tries to find a way of being open to them and a way of learning from them, and which, having tried once, will return and try again; renewing, renewing, renewing.

I'm so proud of them – proud of Waiwai and all the people who used to be at Nipukú; proud of 'Nazaré' (in her Brazilian name) and her family who have chosen to live close to the Brazilians; proud of 'Renato' (his Brazilian name) and his people who have decided to head off into the remotest parts he can find and keep himself as isolated as possible. I take heart when I remember how 'Joaquim' and 'Nonato' and 'Parahandy' expressed their defiance against the awful world that comes against them and that wants to 'integrate' them into its dismal ways. I long to hear that language again; Waimisí, with her extraordinary articulateness, explaining just what's what around the place, and Siro laying out the details of a myth with the patient and delicate skill of a craftsman.

Suppose their fate had been that of so many others: contacted by the brutal frontier, half-exterminated, corralled in, controlled, and left to find their own paths of moral disintegration. What kind of remains would have been left for their inheritors to pick through? A handful of dedicated Brazilians (including it has to be said some individuals attached to FUNAI) have struggled on, fighting to protect Wayapí land and welfare, and have achieved a great deal against all the odds – not just through agitprop but through persistent and effective organization and action. Theirs was a crucial intervention, and if Wayapí survivors a hundred years from now find a continuity of being that takes them back to Waiwai's days they will be able to appreciate what was done at that time by these individuals who stood up to the destructive threat of powerful institutional forces, and won.

I've been able to do next to nothing to help the Wayapí in their struggle for physical survival. I'm hoping that writing for the future will be one way of giving something to them in return for all they have given me. Waiwai is determined that his people will get through. He's determined that there will be survivors. I'm imagining that my work will be accessible to them.

If it is so, that will be the point where my effort will finally meet theirs in the future. When they look back over the wasted forests and try to understand the kind of life that was taking place within these woods a century before, they too will have to start taking interpretative risks. They'll have to bundle and go. They'll have to gather up all the creative procedures they can think of, and start imagining in a regenerative way. The forests will have gone. That way of life will have gone. But it will be up to them as survivors to invest the spaces around them with the imagined presence of Waiwai and his people.

> The trees inside are moving out into the forest,
> the forest that was empty all these days
> where no bird could sit
> no insect hide
> no sun bury its feet in shadow
> the forest that was empty all these nights
> will be full of trees by morning.

REFERENCES

1 Telling Names

p.4   'Suddenly Yellow Bird . . .'
James Mooney (1896) *The Ghost-Dance Religion and the Sioux Outbreak of 1890*, 14th Annual Report of the Bureau of Ethnology to the Secretary of the Smithsonian Institution 1892–93 Part 2: Washington 1896 (p. 869).

p.15 Bronislaw Malinowski:
(1922) *Argonauts of the Western Pacific*, G. Routledge and Sons; (1929) *The Sexual Life of Savages*, Routledge and Kegan Paul; (1935) *Coral Gardens and their Magic*, 2 Vols, Allen and Unwin; and on ignoring outside influences see:
(1967) *A Diary in the Strict Sense of the Term*, Routledge and Kegan Paul.

p.16 Raymond Williams (1973) *The Country and the City*, Chatto and Windus.

p.20 Marcel Mauss (1990) *The Gift*, translated by W.D. Halls, Routledge.

p.25 'Some years ago . . .'
Henry David Thoreau (1937) 'The Allegash and East Branch', 3rd Essay in 'The maine woods' in *Walden and Other Writings of Henry David Thoreau*. The Modern Library (p. 523).

2 At Long Hammock

p.29 'Thy glades forlorn . . .'
Oliver Goldsmith, 'The Deserted Village' (ll. 76, 78).

p.32 Heraclitus, 'All is flux . . .'
Bertrand Russell in his *History of Western Philosophy* (1946, p. 64) suggests that the famous saying, also translated as 'All things are flowing', is probably as apocryphal as Washington's 'Father, I cannot tell a lie' or Wellington's 'Up Guards, and at 'em'.

p.32 'The first man who . . .'
Jean-Jaques Rousseau (1988) 'Discourse on the Origin of Inequality', *Rousseau: Selections*, edited by Maurice Cranston,

REFERENCES

Scribner/Macmillan (p. 57).

p.37 'La Nature est un temple . . .'
Charles Baudelaire, 'Spleen et Idéal, IV, Correspondances'.

p.38 'Hills of sheep . . . and winds austere and pure.'
R.L. Stevenson, 'To S.R. Crockett. On Receiving a Dedication'.

Blows the wind today, and the sun and the rain are flying,
Blows the wind on the moors today and now,
Where about the graves of the martyrs the whaups are crying,
My heart remembers how.

p.39 'Red-faced, merely physical people . . .'
Hugh MacDiarmid, 'Island Funeral'.

p.47 'There must have been laughter . . .'
Arthur Koestler (1959) 'Fragment of the Diary of N. S. Rubashov'
in *Darkness at Noon*, translated by Daphne Hardy. Four Square
Books (p. 167), (orig. 1940, Jonathan Cape).

p.49 Zyklon-B at Auschwitz, see:
Martin Gilbert (1987) *The Holocaust: The Jewish Tragedy*,
Fontana/Collins (p. 239).

p.52 The fifteen varieties of manioc that Waimisí and Marikí mentioned
were: mani'o meko, mani'o tawa, mani'o ko, tapèsi, rapa-po'ang,
mywy-tawa, arary, ipotyrè, kumani-meware, meyo-ty-kwaka,
mani'o yiroro, mani'o ysimo, mani'o ka, tatorowai, kusiwar.

p.57 'The original affluent society', see:
Marshall Sahlins (1974) *Stone Age Economics* (Ch. 1), Tavistock.

3 Other Voices

p.60 'A Summer Institute of Linguistics worker . . .'
From commentary by Stephen Hugh-Jones in Brian Moser's film
War of the Gods in Granada Television's *Disappearing World* series.

p.65 'Here was perfect purity . . .'
'I have surely the right . . .'
Edmund Gosse (1907, 1986) *Father and Son*, Penguin Books (pp.
43, 248). The first passage refers to his mother and father.

p.69 Norman Lewis (1969) 'Genocide: from fire and sword to arsenic
and bullets – civilisation has sent six million Indians to extinction'
Sunday Times (Colour Magazine) 23 February, pp. 34–59.

4 Romance

p.89 'Ô le pauvre amoureux des pays chimériques!'
Charles Baudelaire, 'Le Voyage' II.

p.91 'You will ask, perhaps, . . .'
Mary Wollstonecraft (1989) 'Letters written in Sweden, Norway
and Denmark' edited by Janet Todd and Marilyn Butler *The Works
of Mary Wollstonecraft*, Pickering and Chatto Vol. 6, pp. 237–348:
'Letter XIV' (pp. 307–309).

p.95 ' "What," it will be questioned. . .'

240

REFERENCES

William Blake, 'A Vision of the Last Judgement', pp. 92–95.

p.98 'Penned up in petty souls. . .'
Carlo Levi (1982) *Christ stopped at Eboli*, Penguin Books (pp. 36 and 22).

p.99 'And hark, again! . . .'
Samuel Taylor Coleridge, 'Christabel' (Part 1).

p.117 *Gemeinschaft*:
Ferdinand Tönnies (1855–1936) developed the contrast between *Gemeinschaft*, the ties of intimate community, and *Gesellschaft*, the impersonal organizations we are used to in complex societies.

5   Four, Fire, and Giving

p.132 On DNA bases adenine, guanine, cytosine, and thymine see:
Steve Jones (1993) *The Language of the Genes*, HarperCollins Publishers, (passim).

p.134 On the Cuiva see:
Bernard Arcand (1977) 'The logic of kinship, an example from the Cuiva', *Actes du XLIIᵉ Congrès International des Américanistes* Vol. 2, (pp. 19–34);
Alan T. Campbell (1989) *To Square with Genesis*, Edinburgh University Press (pp. 153–163).

p.137 'Four Mighty Ones . . .'
William Blake, *Vala, or The Four Zoas* 'Night the First' (ll. 6 and 7).

p.139 *zoon politikon*:
'ανθρωπος φυσει πολιτικον ζῷον'; 'Man is by nature a political animal'. (Aristotle, *Politics* i, 2. 9. 1253a). Aristotle was fond of making pronouncements about the essential qualities of human beings.

p.139 'Men can be distinguished . . .'
p.140 '. . Life involves before everything else . . .'
Karl Marx and Frederick Engels (1976) *The German Ideology* Vol. 1, in *Kark Marx Frederick Engels Collected Works* Vol. 5, Lawrence and Wishart (pp. 31 and 41–42).

p.140 'And he tamed fire . . .'
p.141 '. . . tortured to his will. . .'
Percy Bysshe Shelley, *Prometheus Unbound*: II. iv: 66–67, 72–73, and 68–71.

p.143 'The whole of tribal life . . .'
Bronislaw Malinoski (1922) *Argonauts of the Western Pacific*, Routledge and Kegan Paul (p. 167).

p.143 Marcel Mauss (1990) *The Gift*, translated by W.D. Halls, Routledge.
'Constant, icy . . calculation' (p. 76). 'One might even say . . .' (p. 66). 'It is our western societies . . .' (p. 76).

p.143 'Ainsi, on peut et on doit . . .'
Marcel Mauss (1968) '*Essai sur le don*', in *Sociologie et Anthropologie*, Presses Universitaires de France pp. 145–279 (p. 263).

p.143 'Hence we should . . .'

241

Marcel Mauss (1969) *The Gift*, translated by Ian Cunnison, Routledge and Kegan Paul.

p.144 'We caught sight of men . . .'
Charles David Ley (ed.) (1947) *Portuguese Voyages*, II 'The Discovery of Brazil. 1500' pp. 39–59, J.M. Dent (p. 42).

p.145 For a description of a FUNAI contact see:
Adrian Cowell (1973) *The Tribe that Hides from Man*, The Bodley Head, especially Chs. 17, 18, and 19.

p.146 'The worst thing of all . . .'
John Hemming (1978) *Red Gold: The Conquest of the Brazilian Indians*, Macmillan (pp. 102–103).

p.150 'His little, nameless, unremembered, acts / Of kindness and of love.'
William Wordsworth, 'Lines composed a few miles above Tintern Abbey' (ll. 34–35).

p.150 Women as commodity for marriage exchanges, see:
Claude Lévi-Strauss (1968) *Structural Anthropology*, Allen Lane, The Penguin Press (pp. 61 and 83).

p.155 'To see a world . . .'
William Blake, *The Pickering Manuscript* 'Auguries of Innocence' (ll. 1–4).

p.156 'Who hath given man speech?'
Algernon Charles Swinburne, 'Atalanta in Calydon' (l. 1038), and see L. M. Findlay (1990) ' "Who hath given man speech": Swinburne, Myths of Origin, and Logocentricism' *University of Toronto Quarterly* Winter 1990/91 Vol. 60, No. 2, pp. 274–291.

6 Remembering

p.160 The story of Thoth and Ammon, see:
Plato *Phaedrus*, translated by Walter Hamilton, Penguin Books, pp. 95–97, (pp. 274–275).

p.160 Illiteracy and cognitive development, see:
J. Goody (ed.) (1968) *Literacy in Traditional Societies*, Cambridge University Press; and J. Goody (1977) *The Domestication of the Savage Mind*, Cambridge University Press. Most notoriously, on pre-operatory thought see: C.R. Hallpike (1979) *The Foundations of Primitive Thought*, Clarendon Press.

p.161 William Blake:
'Soon spreads the dismal shade . . .' *The Human Abstract* 13–17.
'With cold floods of abstraction . . .' *Visions of the Daughters of Albion*, Plate 5, 19–20.
'. . . his tygers roam . . .' *The Four Zoas* VII (a) 9–10.

p.162 Literacy as 'consciousness raising' see:
Paulo Freire (1972) *The Pedagogy of the Oppressed*, Penguin Books. Much of the argument in this section is presented in Brian V. Street (1984) *Literacy in Theory and Practice*, Cambridge University Press. Brian Street offers two competing 'models' of literacy: the 'autonomous model' and the 'ideological model'. I don't think it

can be reduced to two 'models', and I'm sure Brian Street doesn't think so either.

p.163 '. . . nineteenth century Canada.' The example is from:
Harvey J. Graff (1979) *The Literacy Myth: Literacy and Social Structure in the 19th Century City,* Academic Press. It is dealt with by Brian Street (1984) pp. 104 ff..

p.165 Claude Lévi-Strauss (1970) *The Raw and the Cooked,* Jonathan Cape.

p.168 Myth as the counterpart of ritual and ritual as the counterpart of myth, see:
Edmund Leach (1954) *Political Systems of Highland Burma,* G. Bell and Sons. 'Myth, in my terminology, is the counterpart of ritual; myth implies ritual, ritual implies myth, they are one and the same.
. . As I see it, myth regarded as a statement in words "says" the same thing as ritual regarded as a statement in action' (p. 13).

p.169 Winter's tales, see:
Hallett Smith (1974) 'The Winter's Tale' in *The Riverside Shakespeare,* Houghton Mifflin Company (pp. 1564–1568). 'Winter's tales were not supposed to have credibility, consistency, or conciseness. In the words of the Third Gentleman (V. ii. 61–63), *The Winter's Tale* is "like an old tale still, which will have matter to rehearse, though credit be asleep and not an ear open".' (p. 1568).

p.178 Linguistic relativism, see e.g.:
B.L. Whorf (1956) *Language, Thought, and Reality,* edited by J.B. Carroll, MIT Press.

p.179 'The grand Perhaps!'
Robert Browning, *Bishop Blougram's Apology* (l. 190).

p.180 Tupi migrations, see:
Alfred Métraux (1927) 'Les Migrations historiques des Tupí-Guaraní' *Journal de la Société des Américanistes de Paris,* n.s. Vol. 19, pp. 1–45.
Hélène Clastres (1975) *La Terre sans mal: Le Phrophétisme Tupí-Guaraní,* Editions du Seuil.
John Hemming (1978) *The Search for El Dorado,* Book Club Associates.

p.181 'Myth fulfils in primitive culture. . .'
Bronislaw Malinowski (1948) *Magic, Science, and Religion and other Essays,* Glencoe Illinois: The Free Press (p. 79).

p.182 Claude Lévi-Strauss (1964–1971) *Mythologiques* 4 vols., Plon; Vol. 1 (1970) *The Raw and the Cooked;* Vol. 2 (1973) *From Honey to Ashes;* Vol. 3 (1978) *The Origin of Table Manners;* Vol. 4 (1981) *The Naked Man;* translated by J. and D. Weightman, Jonathan Cape.

p.183 '. . . the admirable syntactical arrangement . . .' see Paul Ricoeur in:
Claude Lévi-Strauss (1963) 'Reponses à quelques questions', *Esprit* no. 322 vol. 31, pp. 628–653 (p. 653).

7 Submitting

p.186 Pelicans as half-brothers; 'it would be necessary . . .'
Godfrey Lienhardt (1954) 'Modes of Thought' in E.E. Evans-Pritchard et al. *The Institutions of Primitive Society* Basil Blackwell (pp. 95–107).

p.186 'There is a sense . . .'
M.I. Finley (1986) *The Use and Abuse of History*, The Hogarth Press (p. 111).

p.187 ' "In wretched and disintegrated conditions. . ." '
'One much-needed word . . .'
P. Anderson (1990) 'Witchcraft' *London Review of Books* Vol. 12, No. 21, 8 November 1990, pp. 6–11 (p. 11).

p.188 'Dreaming' etc. as modifications and disappointment, see:
Hans-Georg Gadamer (1975) *Truth and Method*, Sheed and Ward, (p. 75).

p.189 'They say miracles are past. . .'
Lafew in *All's Well that Ends Well* (II. iii. 1–6).

p.191 On Quine's best known example of *gavagai* as 'rabbit' see:
W. van O. Quine (1959) 'Meaning and Translation' in R.A. Brower (1960) (ed.) *On Translation*, Harvard University Press (pp. 148–172);
'Translation and Meaning', Ch 2 of *Word and Object*, MIT Press (pp. 26–79).
On Quine's notion of the 'entering wedge' see:
(1961) *From a Logical Point of View*, III, 5, Harvard University Press (pp. 60–64).

p.192 'Idols of the forum': one of Francis Bacon's four classes of errors to which the mind is prone. Errors in this class are due to the influence of words or phrases: the fluctuations of language. *Novum Organum*, i, 39.

p.192 For a cross-cultural survey of shamanism see:
Mircea Eliade (1964) *Shamanism: Archaic Techniques of Ecstasy*, New York.

p.202 *La Couvade*:
Sir John Lubbock (1882) *The Origin of Civilisation and the Primitive Condition of Man: Mental and Social Condition of Savages*, Longmans, Green, and Co. (pp. 15 ff.).

p.207 'Lesser breeds without the Law.'
George Orwell wrote:

> An interesting instance of the way in which quotations are parroted to and fro without any attempt to look up their context or discover their meaning is the line from 'Recessional,' 'Lesser breeds without the Law'. This line is always good for a snigger in pansy-left circles. It is assumed as a matter of course the the 'lesser breeds' are 'natives,' and a mental picture is called up of some *pukka sahib* in a pith helmet kicking a coolie. In its context the sense of the line is almost the exact opposite of this. The phrase

REFERENCES

'lesser breeds' refers almost certainly to the Germans, and especially the pan-German writers, who are 'without the Law' in the sense of being lawless, not in the sense of being powerless.

(1961) *Collected Essays* '1942 Rudyard Kipling', pp. 179–194, Secker and Warburg (p. 180). Christopher Fyfe, from the Centre of African Studies at Edinburgh University, tells me that Orwell's interpretation became a received view in his generation.

p.210 Alasdair MacIntyre (1964, 1970) 'Is understanding religion compatible with believing' in Bryan R. Wilson (ed.) *Rationality*, Basil Blackwell (pp. 62–77).

p.210 'We must learn to grasp . . .'
Clifford Geertz (1986) 'The uses of diversity' *Michigan Quarterly Review* Summer, pp. 105–122 (p. 122).

8 Aima

p.212 'The Land, the Language, and the People.'
'An Tir, an Canan, 'sna Daoine' was the motto of the Highland Land League on the Island of Skye at the end of the 19th century. It has been resurrected on the masthead of the *West Highland Free Press*.

p.218 'They will remain Indians . . .'
'It also means that ethnic groups . . .'
Darcy Ribeiro (1970) *Os Indios e a Civilização*, Editora Civilização Brasileira (p. 446).

p.219 On the subject of 'generic Indians' today see the account given in: Alcida Ramos (1988) 'Indian Voices: Contact Experienced and Expressed'. *Rethinking History and Myth: Indigenous South American Perspectives on the Past*, edited by Jonathan D. Hill, University of Illinois Press (pp. 214–234).

p.220 'To be an Indian meant fundamentally . . .'
Stefano Varese (1991) 'Think locally, act globally', *Report on the Americas* Vol. 25, No. 3: pp. 13–17 (p. 17).

p.223 'In fact, all communities . . .'
Benedict Anderson (1991) *Imagined Communities: Reflections on the Origin and Spread of Nationalism*, (revised edition) Verso (p. 6).

p.225 ' . . . from the enormous condescension of posterity.'
E. P. Thompson said that his objective in writing *The Making of the English Working Classes* (1963) was 'to rescue the poor stockinger, the Luddite cropper, the "obsolete" hand-loom weaver, the "utopian" artisan, and even the deluded follower of Joanna Southcott, from the enormous condescension of posterity' ('Preface' 1980, p. 12).

p.225 'Call ye these appearances . . .'
William Wordsworth *The Prelude* 1805–6, Book VIII, 429–432.

p.225 'The idea that sophisticated people . . .'
Anne Barton (1974) 'As You Like It' in *The Riverside Shakespeare* pp. 365–368, Houghton Mifflin Company (p. 366).

REFERENCES

p.228 'Look unto the rock . . .' Isaiah 51: 1.

p.231 'Thus he was well placed . . .'
Albert Camus (1960) *The Plague* translated Stuart Gilbert, Part 5, Ch. 5, Penguin Books (p. 246).

p.238 'The trees inside . . .'
Adrienne Rich 'The Trees' *Necessities of Life* 1966.

INDEX